"With the U.S. 40% (1900), 50% (1950) and shortly 80% urbanized, this topic and how we approach it is key. With little jargon, Jassen Callender did it— offering a high level yet gritty users guide that is not another checklist but deals with relationships and correlations to guide us into the future."

—**Pliny Fisk III,** *co-founder and co-director of the Center for Maximum Potential Building Systems, First Annual Sacred Tree Award—USGBC, Solar Pioneer Year 2000 American Solar Energy Society, Advisor MacArthur, Gates, and Enterprise Foundations, and Emeritus Professor Texas A&M University*

"Finally (at last!), a book that presents a strong, interconnected framework for both breadth- and depth-thinking about how cities need to be designed in order to be healthier, durable, and long-lasting places. *Building Cities to LAST* presents refreshing and thoughtful guidance asking us to consider Life Cycle Analysis from the start, rather than at the end of the design process."

—**Alison G. Kwok,** *PhD, FAIA, LEED AP, CPHC, University of Oregon, co-author of* The Green Studio Handbook *and* Passive House Details

Building Cities to LAST

Building Cities to LAST presents the myriad issues of sustainable urbanism in a clear and concise system, and supports holistic thinking about sustainable development in urban environments by providing four broad measures of urban sustainability that differ radically from other, less long-lived patterns: these are Lifecycle, Aesthetics, Scale, and Technology (LAST). This framework for understanding the relationship between these four measures and the essential types of infrastructure—grouped according to the basic human needs of Food, Shelter, Mobility, and Water—is laid out in a simple and easy-to-understand format. These broad measures and infrastructures address the city as a whole and as a recognizable pattern of human activity and, in turn, increase the ability of cities—and the human race—to LAST. This book will find wide readership particularly among students and young practitioners in architecture, urban planning, and landscape architecture.

Jassen Callender is concerned with broad relationships between seemingly diverse aspects of making and perceiving architecture and the relation of these to the success of cities. These concerns have prompted a unique path. In the '90s and early 2000s, Callender worked with several firms on award-winning projects in the American South. Still an occasional practitioner, he is a member of the Society of Architectural Historians and the US Green Building Council, and board member of the Mississippi chapter of the American Institute of Architects. His educational background underscores this range of interests, from undergraduate training in both architecture and philosophy, culminating in a Bachelor of Architecture, to graduate work in painting, sculpture, and art history leading to a Master of Fine Arts from the University of Minnesota. Former Director of Mississippi State University's

Jackson Community Design Center, today Callender is Associate Director of MSU's School of Architecture and directs the School's 5th Year Program in Jackson, Mississippi, where he teaches advanced design studios and advises thesis students. His first book, *Architecture History and Theory in Reverse*, was published by Routledge in 2017.

Building Cities to LAST

A Practical Guide to Sustainable Urbanism

JASSEN CALLENDER

Routledge
Taylor & Francis Group

NEW YORK AND LONDON

First published 2022
by Routledge
605 Third Avenue, New York, NY 10158

and by Routledge
4 Park Square, Milton Park, Abingdon, Oxon, OX14 4RN

Routledge is an imprint of the Taylor & Francis Group, an informa business

© 2022 Taylor & Francis

Library of Congress Cataloging-in-Publication Data
A catalog record for this title has been requested

ISBN: 9781032066066 (hbk)
ISBN: 9780367223786 (pbk)
ISBN: 9781003203049 (ebk)

DOI: 10.4324/9781003203049

Typeset in Dante and Avenir
by Apex CoVantage, LLC

Cover image: Michelle Spano

Contents

Illustrations

Contributors

Joan Blanton (mobility) holds a PhD in Urban and Regional Planning and is a member of American Institute of Certified Planners (AICP). She earned a master's degree in urban economics at the University of Maryland and a BS in economics from the University of Delaware. She spent nearly 20 years working as a professional planner in DeKalb County, Georgia, and in Knoxville, Tennessee. While completing her dissertation, she worked as a grants administrator for Jackson State University, where she began teaching research methods and statistics. Dr. Blanton currently serves as an adjunct professor in urban design at Jackson State and in the Architecture program of Mississippi State University. Dr. Blanton has always been fascinated by cities, frequently travelling the 25 minutes from "South Jersey" to Philadelphia by bus to be energized by the sights and sounds of city life. At 13, she took her first trip to New York City and fell in love with the city that she came to consider "the center of the universe."

Jassen Callender (author and editor) is concerned with broad relationships between seemingly diverse aspects of making and perceiving architecture and the relation of these to the success of cities. These concerns have prompted a unique path. In the '90s and early 2000s, Callender worked with several firms on award-winning projects in the American South. Still an occasional practitioner, he is a member of the Society of Architectural Historians, the US Green Building Council, and board member of the Mississippi chapter of the American Institute of Architects. His educational background underscores this range of interests, from undergraduate training in both architecture and philosophy, culminating in a bachelor of architecture, to graduate work in painting, sculpture, and art history leading to a master of fine arts from the University of Minnesota. Former Director of Mississippi State University's Jackson Community Design Center, today Callender is Associate Director of MSU's School of Architecture and directs the School's 5th Year Program in Jackson, Mississippi, where he teaches advanced design studios and advises thesis students. His first book, *Architecture History and Theory in Reverse*, was published by Routledge in 2017.

Caleb Crawford (shelter) is an architect and designer who struggles to reconcile environmental issues with his dedication to design and the visual arts. He holds a bachelor of architecture from the Pratt Institute and a master of architecture from SCI-Arc. Crawford is a principal of Chairs + Buildings Studio and has taught at Pratt, Penn State, Mississippi State, City College of New York, and the School of the Visual Arts. He is a registered architect, LEED AP BD+C, and Certified Passive House Designer.

C. Taze Fulford III (food) is an associate professor in the Department of Landscape Architecture at Mississippi State University. He received an undergraduate degree in landscape architecture from Mississippi State University and a master of architecture from the University of Idaho. Before arriving at Mississippi State University in 2006 to teach, he worked in the office of Maclay Architects and Planners in Waitsfield, Vermont, working on projects concerning living buildings, co-housing, net-zero, and LEED-certified buildings. He has delivered presentations and papers to multiple conferences concerning pedagogy and service learning in the design studio, both in the United States and Europe. His work in service learning has given rise to studio projects in collaboration with local governments and business partners that have developed concept designs for non-profit campus masterplans, playgrounds, and town markets and greens, one of which won a National Endowment for the Arts award in 2013. He continues to do research concerning pedagogy, student self-efficacy, and regenerative design.

Cory Gallo (water) is a licensed landscape architect and holds a bachelor of landscape architecture from Louisiana State University and a master of urban design from the University of Michigan. His professional resume includes work with SmithGroup JJR in Ann Arbor, Michigan and GreenWorks in Portland, Oregon. In practice, he contributed to several large-scale sustainable planning efforts, including the Lloyd Crossing Sustainable Urban Design Plan in Portland, Oregon and the Green Grand Rapids Master Plan in Grand Rapids, Michigan. Mr. Gallo has also been involved in the design of numerous green infrastructure projects, including Tanner Springs Park in Portland, Oregon and the Oktibbeha County Heritage Museum in Starkville, Mississippi, which was exhibited at the Cooper Hewitt, Smithsonian Design Museum. As a professor in landscape architecture for the last 12 years at Mississippi State University, Cory has taught courses on urban design, site hydrology, and watershed management. He has also researched and published on municipal green infrastructure and stormwater policy.

Introduction
A User's Guide

More than a decade of teaching an undergraduate architecture course on urban design and approaching two decades of teaching studio courses on the future of mid-size cities has taught me three valuable lessons that inspire this book. First, no one is sure what is meant by the term 'sustainable.' Second, very few are confident they know what urbanism entails. And third, the uncertainties latent in both terms are magnified when brought together to constitute a goal such as writing a practical guide to sustainable urbanism. It is not unlike being asked to solve $x+y=z$ with only vague and contradictory notions of the values of x and y. It is understandable that neither students nor practitioners know where to start.

The vagary extends even to names for the goal itself. Should we think in terms of sustainability or resilience? Environmentalism or ecological design? And what happened to "green"? Is our future one of cities or urban configurations? Metropolitan areas or megalopolitan regions? While there is some evidence that these terms circumscribe overlapping but subtly different concerns, debates about which to use are mostly evidence that we are so lost as to what we should be doing that we have digressed to another topic entirely. The solution, or at least its beginning, requires a restatement of the problem—the definition of z—in simple, direct language.

Sustainable urbanism or resilient cities or any other pairing of similar terms is shorthand for an implied, but often unanswered, three-part question: What are we trying to hold onto, for how long, and by what means? This question sets aside both the technical jargon and the popular

DOI: 10.4324/9781003203049-1

slogans as well as point-based systems and mandate-based approaches. It focuses us on the things that matter, the essentials. While the details change across time and from culture to culture, the essential aspects of *what are we trying to hold on to* are comprised of basic human needs and desires—(quality) food, (clean) water, (safe) shelter, and (freedom and connectivity through) mobility. The remaining two thirds of the question, *for how long* and *by what means*, must, in my experience, be answered across four planning and design metrics: Lifecycle, Aesthetics, Scale, and Technology—or LAST.

The LAST matrix (see Figure 0.1) presents the width and breadth of concerns that constitute an answer to the question: *What is sustainable urbanism?* The fundamental physiological needs of food, water,

Sustainability Measures *Types of Infrastructure*	**LIFECYCLE** Durability vs. energy & materials necessary for construction & maintenance	**AESTHETICS** Place making. The urge to live in & maintain cities for perceived value of (and to) identity	**SCALE** Building & human density, & green-grey- & brown-field land use for livable cities	**TECHNOLOGY** A balance of innovations to minimize carbonization & materialization
Food Production & Distribution Systems	**L F**	**A F**	**S F**	**T F**
Mobility Sidewalks, Buses, Light rail, Street Networks, etc	**L M**	**A M**	**S M**	**T M**
Shelter Housing, Retail, Civic, Industrial, and other buildings	**L S**	**A S**	**S S**	**T S**
Water Drinking Irrigation, Waste & Runoff	**L W**	**A W**	**S W**	**T W**

Figure 0.1 LAST Matrix.

Source: Jassen Callender

shelter, and mobility need no introduction as the terms are used here in their ordinary senses and the value of each to future humans is obvious. The ways in which food, water, shelter, and mobility differ in traditional and sustainable cities are explained in the appropriate passages in the body of the book. The terms running across the top of the matrix, however, are neither so ordinary in use nor obvious in value. Lifecycle, Aesthetics, Scale, and Technology demand brief introductions.

Lifecycle

It is probably a given that the average developer, on the one hand, and the typical proponent of recycling, on the other, interpret lifecycle differently. The former is likely to define the word from a common economic perspective, with emphasis on "upfront cost" and "exchange," and to have a deep affinity for a short, if not immediate, period of return. The latter is more likely to view the term "lifecycle" from a perspective of material preservation, believing the advance of civilization lies in reducing the amount of matter required to maintain cities in the long run. While it is fortunate that almost no one takes the developer's interpretation to be a sustainable model, it is unfortunate that so many accept that recycling/temporary construction proponents exemplify the best, or perhaps only, alternative.

Both developers and recycling advocates operate on the assumption that relatively short cycles of consumption are in our best interest and free us from the burden of material intensive investment. No doubt their motives are different. Predicated on five-year (and often shorter) returns, developer projects are often light on material usage in order to maximize profit; recycling proponents, on the other hand, build materially light structures to reduce resources extracted from the environment. Both strategies, however, tacitly assume the necessity of future renovation, if not complete demolition. Arguably, the only significant difference between the two approaches is the destination of the bulk of materials removed during renovation or demolition: the developer's waste destined for landfills, the recycler's intended for another building. Clearly the recycling model works to reduce the amount of matter embedded in the built environment, but it purchases this savings at the cost of increasing the amount of matter burnt as fuel for more frequent construction cycles, including transporting products, product refinishing, feeding and housing and transporting the laborers, etc.

There is a third way between recycled projects that are not intended to last and the quickly erected developments of real estate speculators that almost no one wants to last. The third way aims to slow the cycles of consumption through a more careful consideration of lifecycle. A meaningful approach to sustainability will certainly consider the initial investment of material and energy but only against the necessity for intervention in future decades, or centuries. Monuments like the Pantheon in Rome (Figure 0.2) and the Sydney Opera House (Figure 0.3) serve as two very well-known examples in a continuum of long-lived constructions that justify such belief. For the contributors to this book, building cities to LAST begins with building things capable of lasting.

Figure 0.2 Pantheon, Rome.

Source: Scott Penman

Figure 0.3   Sydney Opera House.

Source: Anne Graveur

Aesthetics

The statement that lifecycle is a critical component to cities and long-lived inhabitation is often challenged. One challenge inevitably made against proposals to build buildings to last for centuries goes something like this: "times change; needs change; and people like change; buildings will be renovated or torn down regardless of the durability of their construction; therefore, we should accept this and build infrastructure that is light, temporary, and recyclable." It is a reasonable argument. There can be little doubt that the First World thirst for novelty is at odds with investments in substantial infrastructure. And, with just as little doubt, it seems the most efficient means for appeasing such appetites while not giving up completely on hopes for a sustainable future compels us to accept the recycled/recycling model. It is worth asking, however, if such short-term efficiency serves communities, if it provokes its own upkeep, and, ultimately, if it is truly useful.

If the Sydney Opera House and the Pantheon are paragons of buildings that have continued to serve communities for decades, or millennia, it is reasonable to ask why these have not suffered the fate of demolition, of being scavenged for materials to the degree that so many buildings of the past were subjected to, or of being renovated beyond recognition. The problem with posing such a question is that the answer is both rather obvious and contradictory to many of the values we claim to aspire to in twenty-first-century construction.

The Pantheon and the Sydney Opera House look nothing alike. They exist in very different cultures. In fact, they have little in common except that both seem to inspire activity within and without and both inspire defense of their preservation. At root, this power to inspire is not an issue of style but one of shared aesthetic and culture values that ground community, evoking wonder at its most inspired and serving as a quiet backdrop at its most reserved. These monuments and others as well as great parks and river fronts inspire people to maintain their built environment and to gather in dense communities. Thin, immaterial, short-lived constructions seldom inspire such concern or ground such engagement. This is not to imply that a particular style (columns or pediments or billowing sail-shapes), or material (marble or brick or concrete), or any other trope of history is necessary. It is not an issue of style but of perception and even affection. The community that grows in an urban setting does not require the traditional imagery of New Urbanists nor the imitation of nature by Landscape Urbanists. Design can inspire community by challenging expectations, by evoking sensory engagement, and by triggering people's desire to be in public spaces. In this sense, though often given cursory attention in books of sustainability, aesthetics is central to sustainable urbanism and to making cities LAST.

Scale

Public space is one of the great draws of cities. Central Park in New York and Vondelpark in Amsterdam are exemplars in this regard. In order to trigger human desire to be in such spaces, however, open space must be limited. This might sound paradoxical, but, if stated the other way around, the meaning is clear: the greater the availability of open spaces, the less each will be utilized and valued. At the opposite extreme, if only a few, well-designed public spaces are created but at such remove from one another that the majority of citizens are not within walking distance of at least one such amenity, the greatest draw of city dwelling is lost. Aesthetics or place making only suffices at certain scales and, therefore, must take scale into account. Fortunately, the scales at which aesthetics or community might be argued to take root correlate with more familiar scales of sustainability.

Researchers approach sustainability in a multitude of ways, as suggested earlier. One point of near-universal agreement is the importance of resource management with an eye to protecting biodiversity. This shared ground is significant. Sustainability comes down to two interrelated economies of scale: maximizing the benefits of material usage and minimizing environmental footprints of where humans live, where they acquire resources, and the spread of the negative consequences of that resource use (pollution and environmental degradation). This rare agreement is the result of the widely held belief that population will increase, doubling or perhaps quadrupling by the end of the century. This increase means more land will be necessary for housing, for resource extraction, for manufacturing, for food production, and for recreation.

Recent debates regarding density and whether densification is really necessary are rendered moot if we take seriously evolutionary biologist E.O. Wilson's claim that an ecologically responsible approach to development entails limiting all of these activities to 50% of the earth's surface. When we build densely, we build smaller areas of roofing, exterior walls, and foundations and shorter runs of sidewalks, roads, telecommunication lines, water and waste pipes, etc. Energy usage per person to heat and cool the built environment is lower, on average, in cities than in rural and suburban developments. There is more room for agriculture and for species other than humans. As these words are written, the planet is still in the grip of the COVID-19 pandemic. Epidemiologists have made clear that this and future pandemics are and often will result from humans encroaching on other habitats, pressuring wildlife, and bringing them into contact with the frail species we are. Also, increasing levels of density has been shown to correspond to higher efficiencies in public transportation. As density increases, maximizing material benefits and minimizing environmental footprint, quality of life on the street—the aesthetic sense of place—improves too.

Technology

Cities are a conundrum. On the one hand, cities are the locus of enormous innovation. A cursory review of the history of technological research and development is synonymous with the history of the urban centers in which those technologies evolved. People come to cities with dreams and, from there, attempt to market those dreams to the world. On the other hand, the basic patterns of cities are low-tech. Except for dismay at our ubiquitous sprawl, a fifteenth-century cartographer would have little trouble understanding modern cities. And except for the extraordinary height and transparency of many buildings, ancient architects would immediately recognize photos of our streets as images of cities.

This conundrum is only apparent. What successful cities throughout history and across the globe share are rather significant investments in infrastructures with long lifecycles, that reinforce notions of place, and are built at reasonable or functional scales. The evident succession of technologies, on the contrary, appear as rather transitory experiments—one quickly giving way to another and another.

In this least permanent but no less important aspect of cities, the bulk of existing sustainability tools gain import. *USGBC's LEED, GBI's Green Globes, EPA's EnergyStar, EPA's Water Sense, Green House Gas Accounting, the Living Building Challenge, Net 0, etc.* are primarily measures of technologies and their effectiveness. Deployed in cities and on individual sites or buildings designed with significant lifecycles, inspiring aesthetics, and at ecologically responsible scales, the technologies of the sustainable/ecological/green movement can have extraordinary impact. Imagine the most beloved skyscraper in your region with solar panels, sun-tracking louvers, grey water and rainwater collection systems, etc. Now think of these same technologies (and perhaps many more) attached to a typical suburban office building. The former is sustainable. The latter, arguably, is not. That is to say, technologies come last in the factors that make a city LAST.

How the Book Works

The LAST matrix is a structure for visualizing the relationships between basic human needs and the four sustainable metrics of Lifecycle, Aesthetics, Scale, and Technology. The concluding chapter focuses on the matrix itself and how to use it to guide decision making.

Between Introduction and Conclusion, the book is divided into four parts. Part 1 addresses Lifecycle; Part 2, Aesthetics; Part 3, Scale; and Part 4, Technology. Each is divided into two chapters. The first chapter in each part covers the *Essentials*—a brief overview of considerations policy makers, planners, and designers should take into account in order to build cities that will LAST. Each *Essentials* chapter is thoroughly referenced to a corresponding chapter laying out the *Fine Print*. These four *Fine Print* chapters were prepared by expert contributors on issues of sustainability and food, water, shelter, or mobility. These detailed chapters provide concise explanations of major themes along with sources for additional information as well as photos, diagrams, and tables where appropriate.

This structure of paired chapters is intended to facilitate the ease of use that a practical guidebook should have. The brevity of the *Essentials* allows planners and designers with a wide range of expertise to survey quickly each of the four major sustainability metrics—Lifecycle, Aesthetics, Scale, and Technology. Some of the content is likely to be well known to readers and can be skimmed. Some content will be valuable merely to confirm assumptions or verify memory. Other passages, no doubt, will refer to material less well known to readers. Key words and phrases throughout the *Essentials* are followed by reference tags, for example **LF4.1**. The first letter stands for Lifecycle, Aesthetics, Scale, or Technology. The second letter refers to Food, Water, Shelter, or Mobility. The numbers indicate the specific location in the *Fine Print* to find additional information on that topic. Readers interested in the tag used now as an example, for instance, would turn to *Lifecycles: the Fine Print*, and find their selected entry under "Food" listed as item 4.1 (in this case, "ecological intensification").

Practical guidebooks, in order to be truly practical, must be selective. Given the breadth of concerns that play a role in making cities sustainable as well as the range of experience (from students to professionals) and disciplines of the readers that this book is intended to serve (architects, landscape architects, planners, and policy makers), many entries will seem to be mere introductions to some readers. Professional architects, for instance, are likely to know the information conveyed in the sections on shelter. Landscape architects will be well versed in the material on food and water. And urban planners are likely to be familiar with the possibilities regarding mobility. It is cross-disciplinary education, however, that is the central aim of this book. The non-expert will find extraordinary introductions to a range of topics in the pages that follow. And the expert will discover linkages previously unconsidered. Those, at least, are the ambitions.

LIFECYCLE **1**

Figure L1   L'église de la Madeleine, Paris.

Source: Heather Schmitt

DOI: 10.4324/9781003203049-2

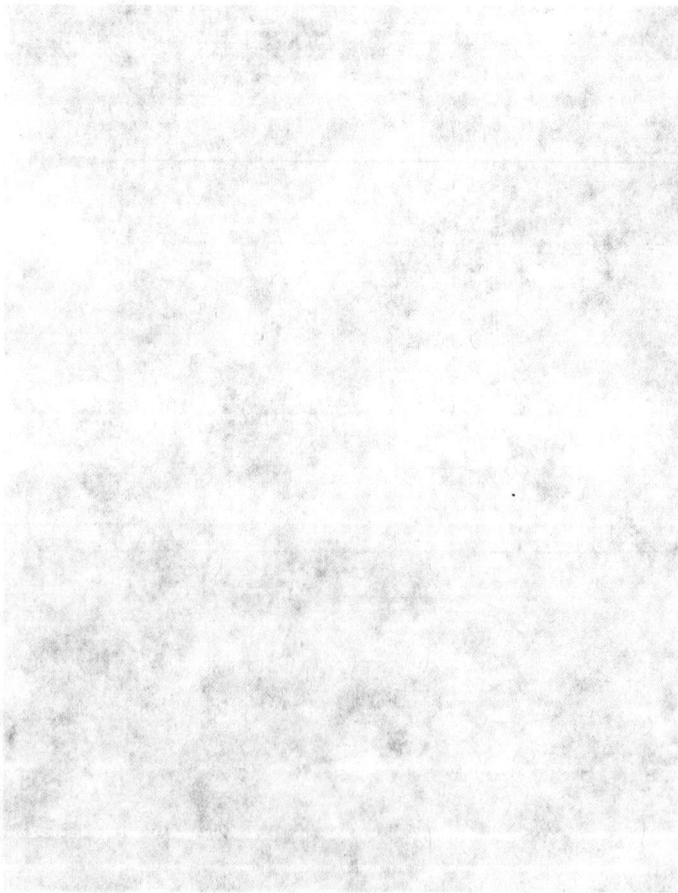

Lifecycle Essentials

Serious thought about the sustainability of cities begins at the end, or with ends in mind. Sustainability is future-oriented. What, we must ask, is here today or will we build or modify tomorrow that will be here in fifty years? A hundred years? Five hundred years? Then we have to consider how these things will change. If they will not function in their current capacities on timescales of millennia—and almost nothing humanity builds is so stable—how will they evolve: as useful resources long since upcycled or downcycled? or as detritus our descendants inherit and struggle to balance in their own pursuit of sustainability? There is no in-between.

It is fair to say that more of the decisions we make fall ultimately on the negative side of this divide. But this assessment doesn't mean it's easy to tease apart the future implications of our actions in the present. As architect Bill McDonough and chemist Michael Braungart so persuasively argued in *Cradle to Cradle* (2002), the things we make, and the methods employed in the making, often have consequences at least as damaging as those of the processes, materials, and artifacts we aim to avoid. This poses a stark conundrum. We have to build. As argued in the Introduction, cities will grow significantly during this century as both the world population and the percentage of that population living in cities increase. New infrastructure will emerge to serve that expanding population. Furthermore, existing infrastructure will need to be updated, made more efficient, and from time to time and place to place replaced. These urgent needs to plan smart yet build more, however, are at odds with the realities of construction, demolition, harvesting resources, and even recycling—processes

DOI: 10.4324/9781003203049-3

that produce, embody, or release carbon and other chemicals in climate- and life-threatening quantities.

Lifecycle issues, therefore, are as complicated as they are serious. The purpose of a practical guide is to focus actions on essential concerns without glossing over the complexities and complications. Acknowledging that lifecycles of the resources we utilize and of the infrastructures we plan come first in the dream of making cities last is not enough. Such a statement glosses the problem. We must ask, which resources and infrastructures matter most to the making of sustainable cities? One way to foster this sort of thinking is to turn the issue of resource and infrastructure lifecycle around and think it from the perspective of human necessity.

Lifecycle intersects with our base, or what Abraham Maslow would have termed "physiological," needs.[1] These are resources such as food, water, fresh air and non-contaminated soils, as well as infrastructure in the form of shelter. We need these things in stable supply in order to survive and hopefully thrive. As architects, landscape architects, planners, and others responsible for the design of the physical city, we should add mobility as essential to the pursuit of these base as well as higher needs.

These resources and their harnessing through various forms of infrastructure are interrelated and potentially mutually supporting in the design of sustainable cities. Feeding growing urban populations without increasing the already-exorbitant resource expenditures necessary to transport and store food supplies over vast distances will require that some water collection and food production be located within the urban environment. These needs will alter cities in numerous ways—including density and patterns of development **SS 1**, layout and forms of transportation **SM 1**, etc. First of all, however, it will necessitate coming to terms with the availability of water in the city.

Water is a finite resource. Water is vital **LW1.1**. To casual observers in some parts of the world, water appears limitless. In fact, the struggle in some regions seems to be managing its abundance—entire island nations disappearing beneath rising tides represent an extreme case. In other places, water is recognized as a precious commodity of which there is already too little, and less is expected in the future—the droughts and subsequent fires ravaging Australia serving as an increasingly common example. Neither view is wrong. Perceptions of water depend on context and value **LW1.2**. For designers of sustainable cities, it is important to recognize both extremes. Inevitably, the detriments of abundance and scarcity will impact cities of the twenty-first century and beyond. Learning to harness the former in preparation for the latter is critical.

The sustainable harvesting of water requires awareness of three distinct hydrologic cycles and the systems appropriate to each. The one that likely comes to mind first is the natural hydrologic cycle **LW2.1**. It is the cycle from which we drink and with which we cook. It is also the one most threatened by human pollution and waste production. While water is finite, the balance between cycles is susceptible to change. The natural or clean cycle increasingly gives way to the man-made cycle **LW2.2**. This water, too, has its uses. But its impact on sustainable cities lies more with mitigation and the systems necessary to return it to the environment productively and safely. Green infrastructure necessary to foster a regenerative man-made cycle **LW2.3** is crucial to the planning for the future.

Tracking and collection of sufficient quantities of water are paramount to feeding the world's growing population. But quantity alone is insufficient. High water quality **LF1.1** is prerequisite to meaningfully scaled urban farming of any type. With a quality water supply, hydroponics **LF1.2** and aquaponics **LF1.3** become feasible and active participants in the production of food for sustainable cities.

Water and soil are essential supports for urban farming. Whereas water is comprised of three different cycles, soil is a phase of nutrient cycling **LF2.1**. Soils in cities are often contaminated from previous or adjacent use. These urban brownfields **LF2.2** need to be reclaimed for food or other productive reuses given that sustainable urbanism demands an intensive use of land in order to preserve rural areas for natural flora and fauna (see also **SS 1**). For the purposes of food production, policy makers and designers need to implement incentives and strategies for soil replacement and composting **LF2.3**. Chief among the techniques for soil production and rehabilitation are vermiculture and mycelium **LF2.4**—that is, the development of habitats conducive to worms or fungi, respectively.

Air quality **LF3.1**, along with clean water and healthy soil, is the third major support for urban agriculture. Toxicity, while a problem anywhere, is common in cities due to the intensification of manufacturing and transportation-produced pollution **LM 2**. Air quality is not merely a metric of a necessary input to growing food. It is also a measurable product of thoughtful planning integrating organic materials into the built environment. Three solutions deserve policy-level mandate and, even in the absence of mandates, design-level implementation: vertical gardens **LF3.2**, green roofs **LF3.3**, and living walls **LF3.4**.

Finally, relative to lifecycle and food, it is important to consider what we should grow in cities. Which plants, what food, and why does selection matter? These decisions should not be limited to aesthetics, though aesthetics matter in the creation of sustainable cities **AF 1**, nor to the whims of a client or designer. Careful selection and siting of plant materials with an eye to their myriad interactions can foster ecological intensification **LF4.1** maximizing agricultural performance. Central to this intensification is a reduction in utilization of annuals and the abandonment of monoculture strategies that dominate both rural and urban agriculture in favor of perennial polycultures **LF4.2**. As noted in the Introduction, these are symbiotic systems. Plant selection plays an important role in attracting and fostering thriving communities of pollinators **LF4.3** and, in turn, these pollinators enable the reproduction of plants including ample opportunities for cross-pollination of urban fruit trees **LF4.4**. It is also important to consider heirloom **LF4.5** varieties for their genetic diversity and literal longevity across agriculture's history.

With agriculture, even the small-scale urban variety, comes the need for ready access to inexpensive and efficient mobility for the transportation of food to people and of people to food, in addition to all the other uses of mobility. Measures of expense and efficiency are, to a significant degree, issues of scale: reach of the transit system, density of population served, and the lengths and frequencies of commonly used routes (see **SM 5**). There are, however, three significant constraints that impact lifecycle—economic, environmental, and societal.

Economic **LM1.1** constraints are the financial realities that frustrate planners and city officials most. These realities impact every aspect of transportation planning—from the front-end investment needed to acquire right-of-ways, build infrastructure, and purchase equipment, to the day-to-day funds required to subsidize operations, to the long-term monies necessary to maintain, update, and occasionally replace infrastructure and equipment—and considered broadly, these issues often impinge transportation system development before it begins. Environmental **LM1.2** constraints are those moral and ethical concerns for the biosphere as a whole, and the difficulties of balancing the needs of humans with those of all other plant and animal life. Finally, societal **LM1.3** constraints are the limits and demands placed on transportation by human values and perceptions of specific modes of transit.

Detailed understanding of each individual constraint, not to mention their potential interactions, is well beyond the grasp of most designers of the built environment. For initial planning purposes, each type of constraint requires its own form of assessment and subsequently each assessment weighed against the others to make meaningful decisions about mobility. Societal constraints, for example, are best understood through analyses of societal lifecycle costs **LM2.1**. For the purposes of planning, environmental constraints can be filtered through an LEM, or Lifecycle Emissions Model **LM2.2**. And finally, economic constraints must be assessed within a framework connecting infrastructure and supply chain **LM2.3**.

These individual assessments determine the feasibility of sustainable transportation. Feasibility, however, is neither sufficient to justify the development of a transportation system nor, more importantly, to insure its long-term viability. The lifecycle of urban mobility systems ultimately rests on four pillars of effective transportation. These are: 1) effective governance of land use and transportation **LM3.1**; 2) fair, efficient, and stable funding **LM3.2**; 3) strategic infrastructure investments **LM3.3**; and 4) attention to neighborhood design **LM3.4**. This last pillar, neighborhood design, touches on many other aspects of sustainable urbanism—particularly issues of aesthetics and scale. But it also directly connects to issues of the lifecycle of buildings.

Shelter, along with food and water, is an essential physiological need. Shelter here is intended broadly—the housing of human activities including manufacturing, commerce, and entertainment in addition to dwelling. So pervasive are these needs and so great are the material impacts of accommodating population growth that durability is crucial to sustainability. Put most simply, lifecycle is about how long a shelter lasts/how easy it is to change, the environmental impacts of its making, and what happens when it can no longer be used. These things can be termed, respectively: durability, environmental costs, and circularity.

Durability is multi-faceted. Every decision regarding the durability of shelter first must take into account the relative permanence of the individual elements **LS1.1**, including site, structure, skin, systems, and space plan as well as the stuff that goes inside. Durability is also a function of the ease with which a building returns to use in the aftermath of some disruption. This is often referred to as resilience **LS1.2**. And given the wild fluctuations of weather patterns predicted with climate change, resilience will be an increasingly important factor in the livability of cities in the future. It is important to acknowledge the role that use or usefulness of a particular building plays in determining whether it should be built; and, if it should, where and to what level of durability. Some things need exist only for short periods of time. Impermanence **LS1.3** should be planned for where appropriate. Designers need to recognize that most urban buildings serve their originally intended function for remarkably brief periods of time. Industrial spaces become retail. Commercial spaces become residential. As important as use is to decisions of what should be built, adaptability **LS1.4** is arguably the greater determining factor in how long most buildings will be maintained without major renovation or replacement and therefore is incredibly significant to a shelter's effective lifecycle.

Lifecycle, however, is not simply a matter of a building serving a given function in the present or adapting to different needs in the future. The construction and durability of buildings must be balanced with environmental considerations in order to attain a comprehensive view of lifecycle. Two forms of costs are at play: economic and environmental. Each imposes its own type of lifecycle assessment (LCA). Economic costs are relatively straightforward. It is the sum total of significant periodic financial outlays and day-to-day expenses required to operate and maintain a building across its life. Where operating costs exceed value to the owner, the physical durability becomes irrelevant and the likelihood of a building being demolished or significantly renovated rises. Either alternative results in a substantial amount of embodied energy, in the form of building materials, being downcycled into the recycling cycle—or worse, entering a landfill. And either way, urban sustainability suffers. Environmental costs **LS 2** are more complex, less understood, and therefore of prime importance. These costs are composed of the total embodied carbon **LS2.1** in the physical artifact itself, the operational carbon **LS2.2** required to use it, the environmental disruption **LS2.3** caused by the making of the building, and the long-term consequences of dangerous materials, known as the red list **LS2.4**, on the health of the building's inhabitants.

The need for an expanded form of economy emerges with the realization that the existing construction/demolition/downcycling/waste model is predicated on the notion that some waste is inevitable and thus excusable. Ideas of circularity or the circular economy **LS 3**, however, discard linear economics and the notion of waste in favor of prolonged use and complete recovery of materials through upcycling—an idea made famous by McDonough and Braungart's *Cradle to Cradle* **LS3.1**. Key elements in their philosophy include design for repair **LS3.2**, design for disassembly **LS3.3**, and planning for the solid waste **LS3.4** generated by shelters. Such a conceptual shift is the ultimate goal in lifecycle thinking.

Note

1   Maslow, A. H. (1943). A theory of human motivation. *Psychological Review, 50*(4), 370–396.

Lifecycles
The Fine Print

Lifecycle & Food
C. Taze Fulford

LF1 Water

Water Quality. . .

"is a measure of suitability of water for a particular use based on selected physical, chemical, and biological characteristics" according to the (USGS) United States Geological Survey. Urban water quality can be affected in several ways such as overflow of sanitary or storm water sewers. Stormwater runoff can contain sediment, pesticides, litter, industrial waste, or oils from rooftops, streets, and parking lots, impacting both urban water bodies and water bodies further downstream. Sanitary sewers may overflow or leak into groundwater systems or streams, causing contamination from raw sewage. The United States Environmental Protection Agency's "How's My Waterway" website is a good tool for beginning to evaluate and analyze your watershed.

Data gathered can show impaired streams, condition of aquatic life, source and type of drinking water system, monitoring efforts, and any issues with water found in those data sets. American waterbody

DOI: 10.4324/9781003203049-4

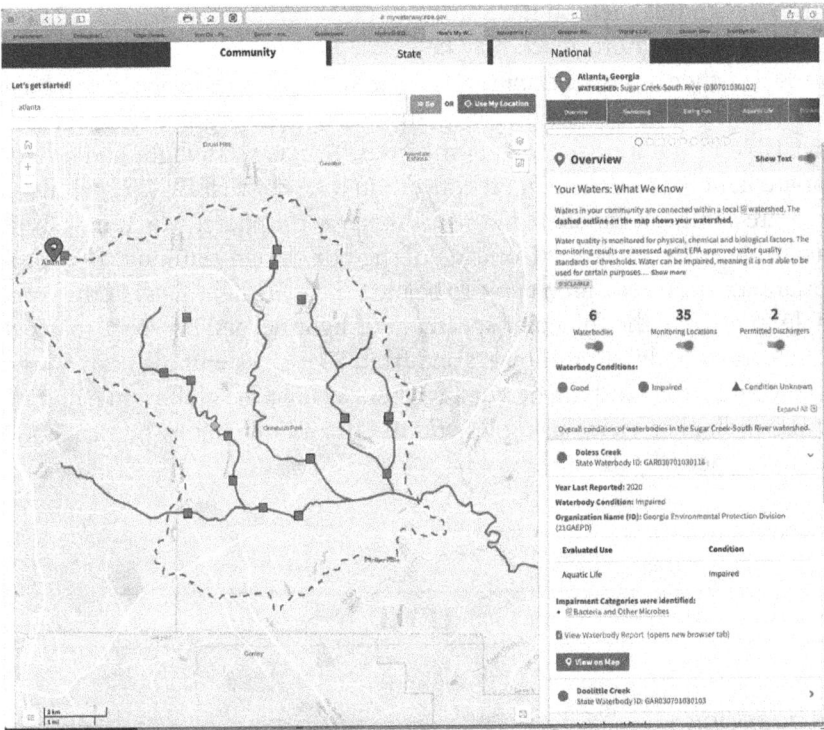

Figure L2 EPA's How's My Waterway website.

Source: EPA

restoration plans or pollution clean-up grants associated with the watershed can be found here. A similar resource is available in the European Union, run by the European Environment Agency (EEA) and titled WISE (Water Information System for Europe), and is an interactive web-based map that allows users to see which waterbodies contain pollutants.

LF1.2

Hydroponics. . .

is a method of cultivating plant materials, typically crops, with only water and needed nutrients dissolved in the water, creating a solution. Plants grown with this method need space to grow but can handle crowding if needed. While more space may be needed for horizontal-only-designed growing, there is also the ability for these systems to be designed and built vertically within a greenhouse or structure, adding growing space not available in traditional growing methods. Access to sunlight and appropriate light may be the biggest concern in the urban fabric. Grow houses require southern exposure in the northern hemisphere, which may limit available space or require outside-of-the-box design thinking. If appropriate sunlight levels aren't able to be met, there are lighting systems available to provide the full color spectrum of light needed for seeds to grow to maturity and put out flowers and fruit. These systems also extend the growing seasons and can be put anywhere around the globe while finding typically higher yields using less resources and helping to reduce "food deserts." See **SF1.3**.

LF1.3

Aquaponics. . .

is a system that utilizes aquaculture in growing fish, snails, crayfish, and similar species, with hydroponics in a symbiotic relationship. These fish and other species are utilized to consume waste from the hydroponically grown plant materials. Waste produced by these species in the system is then used for fertilizer or nutrients for the plant material, making a closed-loop system and mimicking natural systems or nutrient flow. This system opens up another income stream for the growers as protein in the form of fish can be sold to the local community from the tanks. These systems can easily be set up in urban areas as size required is similar to that used in hydroponics.

Further Reading and Resources LF1:

The Aquaponics Source. www.theaquaponicsource.com

www.eea.europa.eu

www.epa.gov/waterdata/hows-my-waterway

https://thehydroponicsplanet.com

in a reduced need for fossil fuel–derived fertilizers.

he past such that toxins, pollutants, or some hazardous substance may be released back into the environment if there is redevelopment or reuse of the property. Urban spaces may contain lead, asbestos, or petroleum products as typical pollutants that have remained in the environment after the original user has left. These properties must be properly assessed and remediated, and then may be safely redeveloped in some cases. Levels of exposure through ingestion, inhalation, or direct contact will vary from site to site but must be looked at in determining future use and safety and feasibility. Some sites may not be suitable for rehabilitation based on testing and planned land use. Residential areas located on brownfield sites will have longer exposure times as children will spend more time on the site. Gardeners will be in contact with soils and have a high probability of ingesting them. All urban gardens and agriculture should utilize Best Management Practices (BMPs) to limit exposure. These can include contaminated soil removal in extreme cases, to raised beds, wind breaks, mulching, and others.

LF2.3

Soil Replacement/Composting

In urban conditions, soils may be compacted from previous development. In this case, compacted soils can be removed and replaced by either taking the soil out and bringing new soils in or bringing new soil in to place on top of the compacted soils. Root depth will be limited by compaction and should be taken into consideration when preparing a site. Trees with larger root systems will require more depth. New soils for crops may be bermed or put in built-up planters to get required soil depths. Soils may also be tilled across the site and amended with compost material.

"Composting is the natural process of recycling organic matter, such as leaves and food scraps (not meat), into a valuable fertilizer that can enrich soil and plants" (Composting 101.org). Using composting will reduce waste on the site and the need for removal of organic material. The nutrient cycle will be reinforced by the use of local organic materials and will even aid in the reduction of erosion on the site with its ability to retain water.

Figure L3   Composting bins recycling organic matter.

Source: C. Taze Fulford III

LF2.4

Vermiculture and Mycelium

Vermiculture is the practice of keeping worms to turn waste into organic materials that can be used for fertilizer on crops. The process of composting is aided by the worms and simply requires both brown (ex. leaf litter) and green (ex. vegetable cuttings) materials in the compost that is then "turned" by the worms. As worms tunnel through the material, they aid in the aeration of the soil, allowing for a freer movement of both air and water. Worms will also leave excrement, which is a beneficial soil amendment.

Mycelia are also decomposers and can be added to the compost process to aid in the breakdown of organic materials. Fungi can break down not only leaves and green materials but coffee grounds, paper, cardboard, paints, glues, clothing, and other biodegradable materials. An added benefit is that you can have mushrooms growing and being harvested while they are decomposing materials.

Further Reading and Resources LF2:

www.chelseagreen.com/2020/mushroom-composting-and-recycling/

CLARINET (Contaminated, Land Rehabilitation Network for Environmental Technologies) readings funded by the European Commission. (2002). https://clu-in.org/wales/download/3CLARINET_brownfields_report.pdf

https://clf.jhsph.edu/sites/default/files/2019-02/soil-safety-guide-for-urban-gardeners.pdf

Ecological Landscape Alliance. www.ecolandscaping.org/01/developing-healthy-landscapes/soil/dealing-with-soil-compaction/

https://grocycle.com/urban-mushroom-farm/

https://happydiyhome.com/vermiculture/

National Resource Defense Council. www.nrdc.org/stories/composting-101

Pavlis, R. (2020). *Soil science for gardeners: Working with nature to build soil health*. Gabriola Island, BC: New Society Publishers.

www.soilquality.org/home.html

U.S. Environmental Protection Agency sources. (2011). www.epa.gov/brownfields/brownfields-and-land-revitalization-activities-near-you; www.epa.gov/brownfields/resources-about-brownfields-and-urban-agriculture; www.epa.gov/sites/production/files/2014-03/documents/urban_gardening_fina_fact_sheet.pdf; www.epa.gov/sites/production/files/2015-09/documents/bf_urban_ag.pdf

LF3   Air

LF3.1

Toxicity and Air Quality

Air quality in urban gardens or farms is a major concern as pollution from cars and industry is common. Urban gardens can become bio-monitors of the community, with research showing that crops can be utilized to show the prevalence of air pollutants such as heavy metals. While research has shown that some of these pollutants do get absorbed into crops, it has been under governmental-regulated thresholds. There is pollution, but with the design of green filter strips separating streets from gardens and designing crop areas to be set back away from the street, air toxicity can be reduced and keep any contaminants at a lower level.

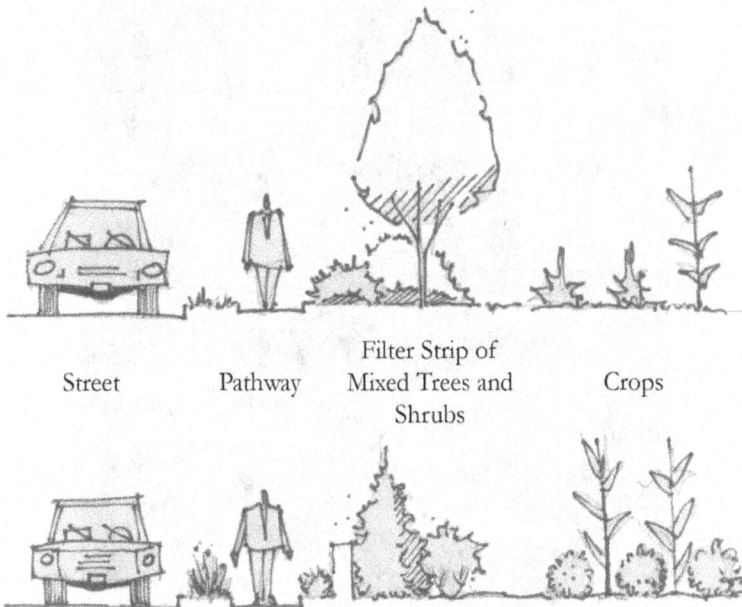

Figure L4   Planted filter strip.

Source: C. Taze Fulford III

LF3.2

Vertical Gardens. . .

can be multi-layer intercropping where crops/plants are grown on stacked shelving in bins with growing medium in structures such as trailers. These can be green walls utilized for air quality, cooling processes, environmental stress reducers or edible crops, or skyscraper farms in which entire buildings are used to grow crops while maximizing the footprint of the land in areas that typically have a higher cost per square foot to develop. See also **TF 4**.

Figure L5   Vertical farming in stacked shelving.

Source: Jeffrey Orkin

LF3.3

Green Roofs. . .

allow for access to light and space for growing crops or living materials on the roofs of structures. Green roofs add an insulation factor to buildings, aiding in reducing the cost of heating and cooling; they store or slow down stormwater runoff, reduce heat island effect, and can create green outdoor recreation or cultural spaces. In terms of growing food, urban rooftops allow for people, groups, or companies to produce local food, reducing the cost of transporting goods into the city. Food becomes part of the neighborhood again and can help eliminate food deserts and recycle food waste from local restaurants, helping to create a more closed-loop sustainable system. Green roofs can range in size from a small shed on an urban roof, to a future 150,000-square-foot (14,000 square meter) rooftop garden such as the world's largest urban green roof farm to be located in the suburbs of Paris.

Figure L6 Brooklyn Grange green roof farm.

Source: Jason Walker

LF3.4

Living Walls. . .

can be used in the interior or on the exterior of buildings. These systems, when used on the interior, are mainly for maintaining air quality and acoustics in the building for user comfort but may also contain edible plant materials. Exterior living walls can be used to protect the building envelope, are used for artistic value, and can have edible plant materials planted within a modular system that is made of trays with growing substrate and clip-on irrigation. As plants go out of season or die, the tray can be removed and replanted or interchanged with other seasonal plant materials. These structures bring nature into the interior of the building as well as into the urban fabric when used to break up hard urban materials with organic living structures. Typically, southern exposures are needed in the northern hemisphere and northern exposures in the southern hemisphere to receive adequate sunlight. Artificial light can be used indoors, or plants that can tolerate shade/lower light levels.

Further Reading and Resources LF3:

www.agritecture.com

www.brooklyngrangefarm.com

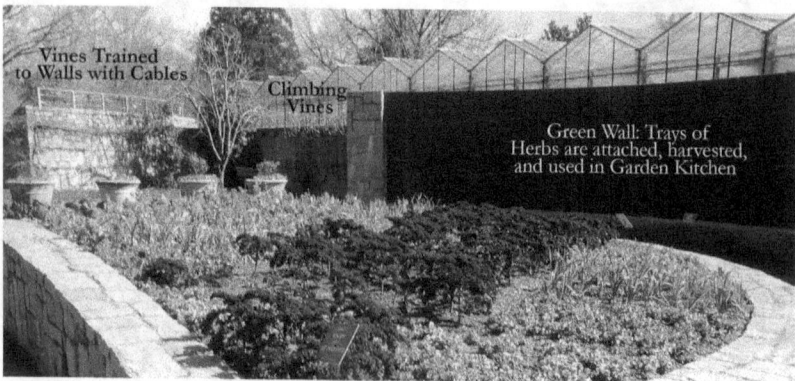

Figure L7   Edible living wall system.

Source: C. Taze Fulford III

Cities Need to "Green Up" to reduce the impact of air pollution, University of Surrey. (2017). https://phys.org/news/2017-05-cities-green-impact-air-pollution.html

Forbes. (2019). *World's largest urban farm to open—On a Paris rooftop.* www.forbes.com/sites/alexledsom/2019/08/29/worlds-largest-urban-farm-to-openon-a-paris-rooftop/?sh=16b55b239305

www.freightfarms.com/#new-lgm

https://greenroofs.org

https://gsky.com

https://livewall.com

http://rooftopgardens.ca

Vegetative Buffer Toolkit: Using Trees to improve Air Quality in Detroit. (2018). https://caphedetroit.sph.umich.edu/wp-content/uploads/2018/05/Reduced-Size-CAPHE-Buffer-Toolkit.pdf

https://verticalharvestfarms.com

LF4   Plant Materials

LF4.1

Ecological Intensification

The Food and Agriculture Organization of the United Nations describes ecological intensification as "using land, water, biodiversity, and nutrients efficiently and in ways that are regenerative, minimizing negative impacts." This process requires agriculture to move away from monocultures (single-crop agriculture) and linear process thinking (materials become waste) to multiple pathways (waste becomes food) to achieve a "closed loop" resilient system. Landscape management strategies are then used to maintain ecological services.

LIFECYCLE

LF4.2

Perennial Polycultures. . .

are systems consisting of more than one type of plant material and that last three or more growing seasons. These can have annual crops interspersed into the mix but typically are seeded to have plants that work together in "guilds" to mimic natural processes such as nutrient cycling in closed-loop systems designed to fit within the local climate. These systems can reduce water runoff and erosion, promote the use of beneficial insects in the garden to replace toxins from insecticides, and reduce the amounts of fossil fuel–derived fertilizers used, as cover crops are recycled and used for compost.

LF4.3

Pollinators. . .

are animals such as butterflies, bees, bats, beetles, birds, insects, and countless others that travel from plant to plant, carrying pollen to transport genetic material to the reproductive system of over 75% of all flowering plants. According to the Pollinator Partnership,

> pollinators provide pollination services to over 180,000 different plant species and more than 1200 crops. They add 217 billion US dollars (approximately 180 billion euros) to the global economy and are responsible for 1 out of every three bites of food you eat.

Pollinators have been reduced in numbers by insecticides or environmental contaminants, destruction of habitat, and invasive plant species. One major intervention that designers and planners can utilize to help pollinators recover is provide native plant materials for habitat and food. Landowners must be educated on the implications of maintaining large amounts of turf and non-native plant species as these reduce food and habitat for raising offspring. Some species, such as dragonfly and bee boxes, may require structures to help provide the needed space for breeding.

LF4.4

Urban Fruit Trees

Planting fruit and nut trees in public spaces creates opportunities to provide food in underserved communities or communities with food deserts (see **SF1.3**). These plant materials also offer opportunities to learn about nature, reduce heat island effects, reduce storm water runoff, purify the air we breathe, and volunteer with other community members. The largest drawback to fruit trees in urban areas has been litter and the resulting smells and associated insects. Groups of volunteers can come together to harvest fruit before it becomes a problem and then can disseminate the product to groups that feed the needy, volunteers, and local participants in growing and harvesting programs.

LF4.5

Heirlooms. . .

are seed varieties that have been collected and reseeded over many years after open pollination by pollinators or wind instead of hybridization. They will contain certain characteristics year after year that allow the plant material to be more productive, have larger fruit, be resistant to disease or drought, or possess a more robust flavor. These historically were collected by the farmer, and the stories associated with the plant and fruit are important to the family. Heirloom seeds now can also be obtained from seed companies but must not be genetically modified.

Further Reading and Resources LF4:

City Fruit. www.cityfruit.org

Falling Fruit: Map the Urban Harvest. https://fallingfruit.org

www.fp7liberation.eu/TheLIBERATIONproject

https://landinstitute.org/our-work/ecological-intensification/

Figure L8   Heirloom tomatoes, Bountiful Farms.

Source: Sam McLemore

https://landinstitute.org/wp-content/uploads/2014/11/PF_FAO14_ch24.pdf

Lyle, J. T. (1994). *Regenerative design for sustainable development.* New York, NY: John Wiley.

www.permaculturenews.org/2016/01/15/guidelines-for-perennial-polyculture-design/

Philadelphia Orchard Project. www.phillyorchards.org

Poizner, S. (2014). *Growing urban orchards.* Summertown, TN: Groundswell Books.

Pollinator Partnership. www.pollinator.org

The Prairie Homestead: Where to buy heirloom seeds. (2019). www.theprairiehomestead.com/2018/01/buy-heirloom-seeds.html

LIFECYCLE

USDA Natural Resources Conservation Service. www.nrcs. usda.gov/wps/portal/nrcs/main/national/plantsanimals/ pollinate/

U.S. Fish and Wildlife Service. www.fws.gov/pollinators/

U.S. Forest Service. www.fs.fed.us/wildflowers/pollinators/

Lifecycle & Mobility

Joan Blanton

LM1 Constraints

The costs of building, maintaining, and replacing transportation infrastructure fall primarily on public government entities. These costs are constrained by three main influences: economic, environmental, and societal.

LM1.1

Economic

Budgeting for transportation is a function of how much tax and other revenues can be generated for that purpose, and thus restricts the extent of what can be built. Once built, costs are also incurred for maintenance. When the economy declines, the sources of funds follow suit, and new projects are delayed, while maintenance is often abandoned.

LM1.2

Environmental

If environmental concerns are to be given their due, transportation planning must take into consideration the fragility of a given region and possible effects on the ecosystem of expanding transportation systems that increase the use of petroleum products and other toxic materials.

LM1.3

Societal

The existing culture of a society determines the demand for transportation and what type is preferred. If, for instance, the demand is for extensive systems of roadways, governmental representatives will be elected to fulfill that demand. Prevailing sentiment will determine how much attention is given to solving both the Economic and Environmental constraints.

LM2 Assessment

LM2.1

Societal Lifecycle Costs

As Chester and Horvath point out, "to appropriately mitigate environmental impacts from transportation, it is necessary for decision makers to consider the lifecycle energy use and emissions." Social Life Cycle Assessment (SLCA) approaches attempt to measure the environmental impact of the production and use of transportation systems and are useful in making decisions about how to decrease emissions. They do so by creating inventories of comprehensive lifecycle energy, greenhouse gas emissions, and selected criteria air pollutant emissions. The results of SLCA approaches (Chester and Horvath) show energy consumption and greenhouse gas emissions for a variety of modes of transportation. In their study, automobiles, pickup trucks, and off-peak diesel buses are the biggest offenders, not taking into consideration airplanes and trains. In Figure L9, the varying levels of CO_2 for autos in the countries of the European Union can be seen. Only Luxembourg's vehicles emit more than the average American vehicle's 4.6 metric tons.

The average car in the EU emits 1.8 t of CO_2 per year, from 720 litres of fuel

(bar chart — countries listed from top to bottom: Luxembourg, Ireland, Slovenia, Finland, Denmark, Croatia, Belgium, Austria, Latvia, Sweden, Germany, Spain, Netherlands, Estonia, France, United Kingdom, Czech Republic, EU, Bulgaria, Portugal, Hungary, Italy, Slovakia, Lithuania, Romania, Greece, Poland; x-axis from 0 to 5.5)

Tonnes of CO2 equivalent emissions per car

Source: Transport & Environment from Member States' reporting to the UNFCCC (emissions data) and Eurostat (population and motorisation rate)

Note: EU-26 average weighted on population and motorisation rate (EU-28 without Malta & Cyprus, as data not available)

TRANSPORT &   @transenv   @transenv
ENVIRONMENT   transportenvironment.org

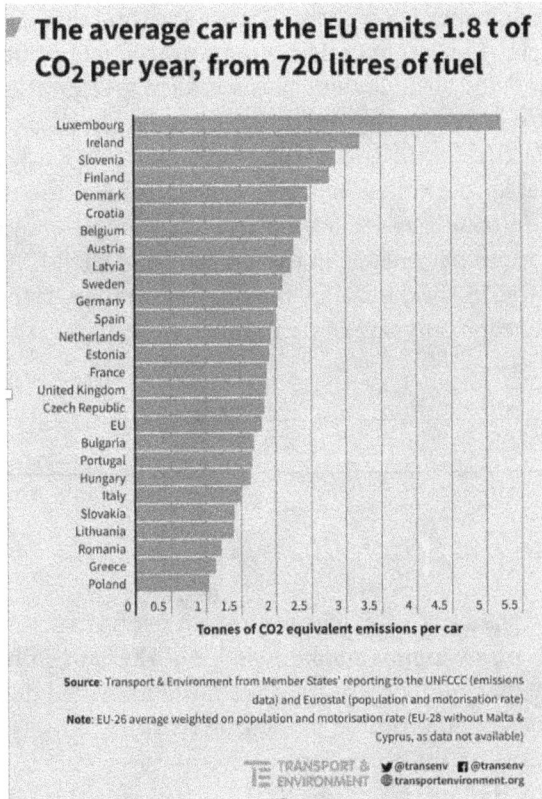

Figure L9   Average annual emissions from cars in the EU in 2015.

Source: Courtesy of Transport & Environment

The US Government's Environmental Protection Agency found that greenhouse gas (GHG) emissions from the transportation sector account for about 28% of total US greenhouse gas emissions. In their assessment of GHG globally, the transportation sector is accountable for only 14% of the emissions.

LM2.2

Lifecycle Emissions Model (LEM) . . .

is available for thirty countries and estimates energy use, criteria pollutant emissions, and CO2-equivalent greenhouse gas emissions from a variety of transportation and energy lifecycles. For transport modes, it represents the lifecycle of fuels, vehicles, materials, and infrastructure. It includes energy use and all regulated air pollutants plus so-called greenhouse gases. It also includes input data for up to twenty countries, for the years 1970 to 2050, and is fully specified for the US. Starting in the late 1990s, it was extensively revised to be able to estimate lifecycle emissions from the use of energy and materials in countries other than the US. Data sets were created for the most important parameters in the model. Now, the LEM can estimate lifecycle emissions from the use of transportation fuels, transport modes, electricity, and heat in any one of up to thirty countries.

LM2.3

Infrastructure and Supply Chain

Designers' and planners' roles in transportation infrastructure choices are limited. However, awareness and knowledge of the issues, both budgetary and environmental, allow them to make more informed decisions about the design choices and products in their own projects.

The definition of infrastructure is the physical structures and facilities needed for the operation of a transportation system. This includes roads, railways, trams, subways, and power supplies. A supply chain is "the sequence of processes involved in the production and distribution of a commodity." It is argued that the appraisal of the environmental effects of passenger transportation, which is responsible for 28% of US energy use, should be taken into consideration when making choices about infrastructure and supply chains.

Lifecycle assessment (LCA) is a methodology for assessing environmental impacts associated with all the stages of the lifecycle of a commercial product, process, or service. For instance, in the case of a manufactured product, environmental impacts are assessed from raw material extraction and processing, through the product's manufacture, distribution, and use, to the recycling or final disposal of the materials composing it. See also **LS 3**.

Further Reading and Resources LM2:

Chester, M. V., & Horvath, A. (2008). *Environmental life-cycle assessment of passenger transportation: A detailed methodology for energy, greenhouse gas and criteria pollutant inventories of automobiles, buses, light rail, heavy rail and air v.2.* Berkeley, CA: Arpad Department of Civil and Environmental Engineering, University of California.

Chester, M. V., & Horvath, A. (2009). Environmental assessment of passenger transportation should include infrastructure and supply chains. *Environmental Research Letters, 4,* 024008.

Contribution of Working Group III to the Fifth Assessment Report of the Intergovernmental Panel on Climate Change. (2014). https://www.ipcc.ch/report/ar5/wg3/

Delucchi, M. A. (2002). *Overview of the lifecycle emissions model (LEM).* Berkeley, CA: Institute of Transportation Studies, University of California.

Delucchi, M. A. (2005). *A multi-country analysis of lifecycle emissions from transportation fuels and motor vehicles.* Berkeley, CA: Institute of Transportation Studies, University of California.

www.epa.gov/transportation-air-pollution-and-climate-change/carbon-pollution-transportation

Jørgensen, A., Le Bocq, A., Nazarkina, L., & Hauschild, M. (2008). Methodologies for social life cycle assessment. *The International Journal of Life Cycle Assessment, 13*(2), 96–103.

Wachsmuth, D. (2016). Infrastructure alliances: Supply-chain expansion and multi-city growth coalitions. *Economic Geography, 93,* 44–65.

LM3 4 Pillars of Effective Transportation

In considering the 4 Pillars—which cover Governance, Financing, Infrastructure, and Neighborhoods—the most accessible for architects, designers, and planners, and where they might have the most influence, are Governance and Neighborhoods. Governance for transportation includes local, regional, statewide, and national levels and offers opportunities for input especially from these professionals. Neighborhoods are the quintessential opening for influencing transit-oriented design and educating people on the issues of sustainable transportation design.

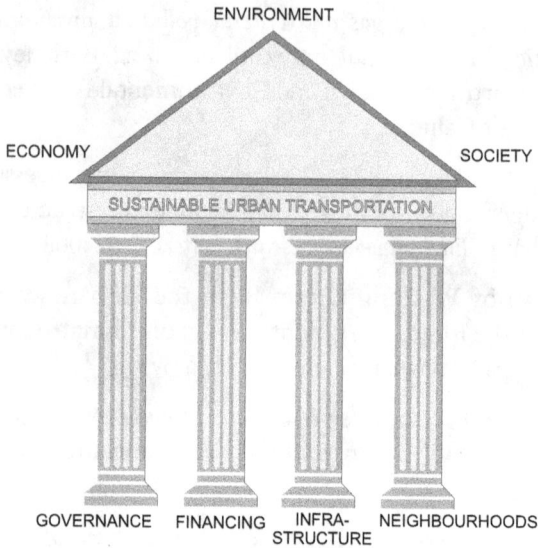

Figure L10 The four "pillars" of sustainable urban development.

Source: Christopher Kennedy, Eric Miller, Amer Shalaby, Heather Maclean and Jesse Coleman (2005), "The Four Pillars of Sustainable Urban Transportation," Transport Reviews, Vol. 25, No. 4, 393–414, July 2005

LM3.1

Pillar 1—Effective Governance of Land Use and Transportation

Research has shown that as residential areas move further from the center of the city, the number of miles travelled, vehicle emissions, and total travel costs by car increase and that this pattern of expansion and travel is not sustainable over the long run. Effective governance of both land use and transportation could help resolve this situation. Unfortunately, in most locations, the authority for these two functions is split between planning and transportation agencies. Examples of where this conflict has been overcome include Curitiba, Brazil; Zurich, Switzerland; and many cities in the Netherlands (World Bank, 2002).

Curitiba is a particularly good example of this pillar. Although changes resulting from governmental movements take a very long time, in a succession of Master Plans, planners used zoning regulations to establish residential and industrial growth along the transport arteries radiating out from the city center. In the 1970s, Mayor Jaime Lerner established a bus rapid transit system (see **SM3.1**) along those arteries. He integrated dedicated bus lanes along the city's main arteries, with stations placed on medians along the routes: cylindrical, clear-walled tube stations with turnstiles, steps, and wheelchair lifts. Passengers pay fares as they enter the stations and wait for buses on raised platforms.

LM3.2

Pillar 2—Fair, Efficient, Stable Funding

The current predominant means of funding transportation systems is through sales taxes and fuel taxes. In the United States and other countries, public transit systems are also funded through farebox revenues—although the US derives much less than other countries from fares. Canada recovers 50% of the cost of public transit through fares, and Australia and parts of Asia earn up to 100%.

Modest vehicle license fees are also common, but some cities have raised these fees to substantial levels, such as Hong Kong and London. This has both generated revenues and substantially reduced auto-ridership. Other sources of revenue are listed in Figure L11 next:

	Non-vehicle related	Vehicle-related
Non-location-related	General tax base Local transportation levy	Fuel taxes Vehicle license fees New vehicle or vehicle parts sales taxes Vehicle use fees Emissions fees
Location-related	Development fees Transit impact fees Right of way fees Leverage real-estate assets	Road tolls Congestion pricing Parking fees Transit user fees

Figure L11 Potential sources of funding for urban transportation systems.

Source: Christopher Kennedy, Eric Miller, Amer Shalaby, Heather Maclean and Jesse Coleman (2005), "The Four Pillars of Sustainable Urban Transportation," Transport Reviews, Vol. 25, No. 4, 393–414, July 2005

The World Bank (p. 402, 2002) notes that there are three significant issues that often thwart effective financing of transit:

- Infrastructure responsibility is separate from service responsibility.
- Various modes of transport are not centrally managed.
- Infrastructure financing and service pricing are not coordinated.

LM3.3

Pillar 3—Strategic Infrastructure Investments

If the first two pillars can be put in place, then cities and other jurisdictions would be able to invest in expanding needed transportation infrastructure. Unless technology can create more efficient automobiles, it is suggested that available financing be applied to equalizing resources between automobile transit and rapid transit. Where to spend available resources becomes the question. Which of the available transit modes will yield the best, i.e., most efficient and sustainable, results?

LM3.4

Pillar 4—Attention to Neighborhood Design

The ability of the first three pillars to "hold up the roof" depends on passengers being able to access the transportation system easily from their neighborhoods, i.e., shopping and business areas must be conveniently located or connected to residential areas. The foundation of this fourth pillar requires local land use and transportation policies that lead to mixed-use land planning, increased density, and car-restraint measures. Land uses that support these goals can be found in Form-Based Codes. A manual for these type of zoning codes can be found in smartcodes such as those published by the Center for Applied Transect Studies. See **SM 5**. An example of such measures being used can be seen in London, where they implemented a congestion-pricing program and land use policies to create automobile-free squares. This has reduced car traffic into the inner city.

Further Reading and Resources LM3:

www.theguardian.com/cities/2015/may/26/curitiba-brazil-brt-transport-revolution-history-cities-50-buildings

Kennedy, C., Miller, E., Shalaby, A., Maclean, H., & Coleman, J. (2005). The four pillars of sustainable urban transportation. *Transport Reviews, 25*(4), 393–414.

www.reimaginerpe.org/curitiba-bus-system

https://transect.org/codes.html

World Bank. (2002) *Cities on the move: A World Bank urban transport strategy review*. Washington, DC. https://openknowledge.worldbank.org/handle/10986/15232 License: CC BY 3.0 IGO.

Lifecycle & Shelter

Caleb Crawford

LS 1.0   Durability

A key strategy in lifecycle is to extend serviceable life. A longer service life means, potentially, a lower environmental cost. Durability is how a material or assembly can resist wear or decay. No material lasts forever, even with maintenance. Stone steps wear down under thousands of footsteps, UV light degrades organic materials, water can cause materials to corrode or crack when it freezes. But some things wear out and require replacement far more frequently than others. Current lifecycle assessments assume a sixty-year building life. We need to think about our shelters in terms of centuries.

LS 1.1

Elements

In considering lifecycle in relation to shelter, we must consider both the parts and the whole. Generally, different systems have different lifecycles.

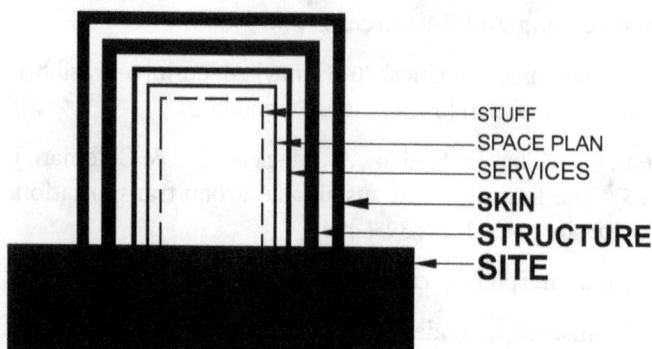

Figure L12   Frank Duffy's shearing layers of change: building in order of permanence.
Source: Caleb Crawford

We can order these from the most permanent to the least (see figure L12). This permanence also relates to adaptability **LS 1.4**.

LS 1.1.1 Site is the most permanent element and the least likely to change.

LS 1.1.2 Structure accounts for approximately 80% of the embodied carbon in a shelter (see **LS 2.1**) and is the building component least prone to change over time.

LS 1.1.3 Skin refers to the exterior envelope: walls, windows, doors, roof, etc. These exterior components are slow to change and are designed to endure the environment in which the shelter is located.

LS 1.1.4 Systems includes the plumbing, heating, cooling, ventilation, electrical, fire protection, data and communications, and the myriad other equipment of contemporary shelters. Components with moving parts—pumps, fans, etc.—have relatively short lives as moving parts wear out and technology advances, providing efficiencies and better performance. Changes to skin and reorganization of space plan often force systems to change.

LS 1.1.5 Space plan is the interior arrangement, including but not limited to interior partitions, ceilings, and stairs. For a building to be adaptable, these are typically low-mass and readily removed and replaced without damage to the structure or exterior skin.

LS 1.1.6 Stuff is the final layer, the furniture, goods, appliances, personal effects of the occupants, and other equipment.

For durability, the qualities of materials and assemblies must be assessed: impact resistance, surface wear, corrosion resistance, ease of maintenance, ease of repair. The qualities of assemblies must be assessed: resistance to static and dynamic loading to assure the longevity of structure; hygroscopic and thermal analysis—where, for example, is the dew point in the assembly? Ease of repair or replacement of components permits continuity.

LS 1.2

Resilience. . .

is the capacity to recover quickly from difficulties—i.e., toughness. Contemporary urban environments are highly centralized, especially for power. Any disruption to central supply causes individual shelters to fail. Storms, floods, fires, and earthquakes can be disruptive to services. Events like monsoon flooding in Bangladesh, wildfires in Australia, or the 9/11 attack in New York City disrupt the lives of millions for weeks or months, even into years. Resilient urban systems are based on interconnected and distributed networks, each shelter being semi-autonomous. They feature diversity and potential redundancy; excessive reliance on a common solution is a problem when the conditions that support that solution may be disrupted. Resilient systems are capable of self-organization, learning, and adaptation. Fortunately, a shelter designed for energy efficiency is also often correspondingly resilient. Such a shelter will be able to maintain internal temperatures for days with low- to no energy input, and the energy input is generated by the shelter itself from renewable sources. Resilience therefore has a link to the four priorities of building safety: preservation of life, preservation of structure, preservation of contents, and continuity of operations; it is the last, continuity, that becomes incredibly important in crisis situations.

It is important to site shelters in locations at low risk for damage or disruption from floods, storms, wildfires, earthquakes, etc.—or if shelter must be built in such areas, to design and build in such a way as to minimize the effects. It is curious to note, however, that resilience measures may not be the most efficient. Resiliency measures such as redundancy and oversizing run counter to many recommendations for right-sizing **TS1.3**.

LS 1.3

Impermanence

As a culture, we do require temporary shelter. These can be for unfortunate things like relief for natural disasters or human conflict. These can serve happy occurrences like street fairs, festivals, stage sets, and temporary follies. Such shelters should be treated in no different a manner, except that the duty cycle is shorter.

LS 1.4

Adaptability

Buildings designed with a "loose fit" have a greater opportunity for being repurposed should the original use of the shelter no longer be required. Conversely, a shelter designed with a high degree of specificity in the spatial arrangement and structural organization—a "close or tight fit"—is difficult to adapt to other uses than that for which it was designed. The immediate use for a shelter must be considered when designing, but while satisfying that use, the ease of transformation must be addressed. This is critical when considering the most permanent elements of a shelter: the structural system and the exterior envelope. The use of simple structural and spatial organizations is ideal, with the longest beam spans practicable for the building type. This allows for a great deal of flexibility for future uses. Based on the size of the structure, ceiling heights and live loads could permit easy conversion from commercial to residential, light manufacturing, or back again. Envelope upgrades without displacing residents is an important consideration, especially for residential shelters. Can exterior-finish materials, windows, weather-resistant barriers, and insulation be replaced entirely from the exterior? Can systems be upgraded without major disruption? Risers and branches that are easily accessed from public spaces for plumbing, fire protection, and electrical are recommended. Consider the longevity of a distribution system and the ability to reconfigure or adapt that system for new space plan arrangements and upgraded technology.

Further Reading and Resources LS1:

Brand, S. (1994). *How buildings learn: What happens after they're built.* New York, NY: Viking.

Hall, E. T. (1969). *The hidden dimension: An anthropologist examines man's use of space in public and in private* (Ed. L. Printing). New York, NY: Anchor Paperback.

LS 2   Environmental Costs

Shelters are composed of thousands of distinct materials, and each has an environmental and human cost associated with it. Shelters must be assessed in relation to the demands they put on the environment for their construction and upkeep through a lifecycle assessment (LCA). LCA is still an emerging study, since even seemingly small differences in component composition can have large effects on environmental impact. Concrete, for instance, can vary widely based on the manufacture of its cement, the additives, and the sources of aggregates in terms of embodied energy and environmental disruption. We can assess the lifecycle of individual materials, assemblies, or a whole building.

An LCA asks questions: What is it made of? From where do the materials/components come? How is it made? What are the environmental impacts? How does it affect worker health and safety? How does it get to the factory and then the construction site? What processes are involved in the installation? How much waste is produced during construction? Where does it go when it is no longer of use?

There are two basic types of LCA: economic cost and environmental cost. Economic cost is a relatively straightforward calculation of the financial cost of a material or assembly over the life of a shelter, which includes maintenance and replacement. The problem with the strict financial assessment is that it does not include many "externalities," such as environmental degradation and public health. Environmental LCA is a lot more complex. It involves an accounting of the materials, energy, and environmental disruption required to make something relative to its service life, maintenance inputs (e.g., energy to run) and issues during its service life (repair or replacement), and the possibility of the materials or assembly re-entering a new product after its service life. The quantity of each component material in any product is separately assessed from resource extraction, processing, forming, packaging, and transportation to the site of the shelter; the length of the duty cycle (how long it lasts); and what happens to that material at the end of its service life. Environmental Product Declarations (EPDs) are an emerging method of data input for LCAs. In both economic and environmental LCA, a relatively precise accounting can permit a review of materials to judge the overall impact of design choices over time.

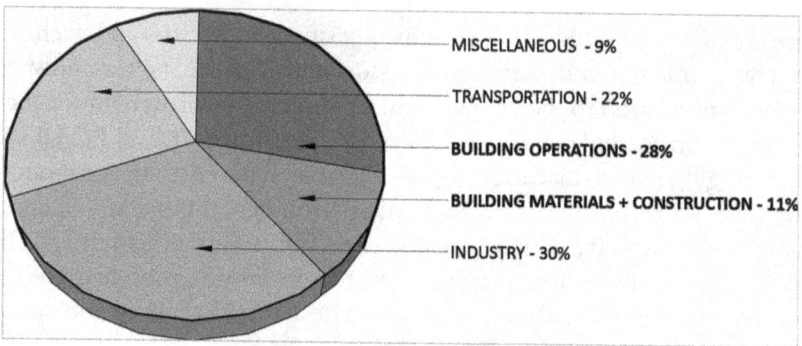

MISCELLANEOUS - 9%

TRANSPORTATION - 22%

BUILDING OPERATIONS - 28%

BUILDING MATERIALS + CONSTRUCTION - 11%

INDUSTRY - 30%

Figure L13 Global CO_2 emissions by sector.

Source: Diagram by Caleb Crawford based on data from EIA Energy Outlook 2017; UN Environment Global Status Report 2017

Figure L14 UL Certified Environmental Product Declaration (EPD) label.

Source: Underwriter's Laboratory

LS 2.1

Embodied Carbon. . .

refers to the amount of greenhouse gases (GHG) released during the production of a given material and has recently become the preferred accounting method (previously we spoke of embodied energy). Fossil fuels are still the dominant energy source in the world economy. It is estimated that 11% of global carbon emissions are from the manufacture of building materials and construction. Some materials require far more energy to extract, refine, process, form, and fabricate than others. For example, approximately 8% of total world GHG emissions are attributed to concrete. Even if a product can be made entirely with renewable energy, it is also important to limit embodied energy—all energy production has an environmental cost.

Structure accounts for about 80% of the embodied carbon of a shelter and is the place that the design team can make the greatest reductions in embodied carbon (further illustrating the divide between environmental and economic costs, structure only accounts for 10–20% of the economic cost of a shelter). Techniques for reducing embodied carbon include:

- Right-sizing: design for the loads and the use you anticipate for the shelter; proper heat gain/loss modeling will give an indication of the optimal amount of insulation—why use 10" of insulation when 8" will be sufficient?
- Evaluate the embodied carbon of a material: understand the material and compare with alternates.
- Evaluate the service life of a material or assembly. Vinyl composite tile has a low first cost and low embodied carbon relative to a durable material like terrazzo, but its service life is shorter and carries other environmental costs. Over the lifespan of a building, the vinyl tile may be a poor choice.

LS 2.2

Operational Carbon

Until recently, the design professions were primarily concerned with the energy shelters used during operations. Most of that energy is currently derived from the burning of fossil fuels, thus the term operational carbon. Reducing that consumption is essential. We use the term "efficiency" to describe a building that uses less carbon in operation than similar buildings. Efficiency continues to be important even with an electrical grid run on renewables, since less consumption translates to less equipment for generation and transmission (see **SS 3**).

LS 2.3

Environmental Disruption

All construction creates a great deal of damage. Construction materials are extracted from the earth, whether by mining, quarrying, or cutting. This immediately impacts the ecology of the location where these activities occur. The processing of these materials further impacts the environment surrounding factories, especially those that rely on the processing of petrochemicals. Understanding the kinds and amounts of environmental damage helps designers make decisions.

Environmental LCAs evaluate a range of issues, with embodied carbon perhaps the most significant. Environmental LCAs address economic negative "externalities," an injury to others who did not choose to incur that injury and were perhaps unaware of the risks. These are things such as worker health, occupant exposure to pollutants, and environmental damage (ground-level ozone, eutrophication, ocean acidification, etc.) due to extraction, manufacture, operation, and disposal of parts or the whole of a shelter. An LCA can help inform the designers of shelter in their selections of materials by making comparative studies of options. There are many software tools, countless studies, and a growing wealth of manufacturer Environmental Product Disclosures (EPDs) with standardized measures that can assist designers. The analysis is often highly complex, and even small component material variations in an individual product can have significant impacts. Building information modeling (BIM) programs have features that can assist LCAs. Accurate quantities of materials can be generated, allowing for the assessment of alternate selections.

LS 2.4

Red List. . .

is a list of products developed by the International Living Future Institute. These are the "worst in class materials prevalent in the building industry." Many of our materials, furnishings, and finishes contain toxins that have a detrimental effect on human health: Volatile organic compounds (VOCs); formaldehyde; heavy metals such as lead, mercury, and chromium; asbestos; pesticides; fungicides; and flame retardants are common additives to materials. Materials on the Red List are known to cause health problems to people or ecosystems through manufacture, the product itself, or disposal: carcinogens, endocrine disruptors, neurotoxins, and particulates are among the issues. The list includes over one thousand chemicals, heavy metals and minerals, two thousand more of priority concern, and over three thousand on a watch list.

Further Reading and Resources LS2:

Athena Sustainable Materials Institute. (1997). www.athenasmi.org/

Building Transparency. (n.d.). www.buildingtransparency.org/en/

International Living Future Institute. (2019). *The red list.* https://living-future.org/declare/declare-about/red-list/

International Living Future Institute. (n.d.). *Living-future.org.* https://living-future.org/

Miflin, C., Spertus, J., Miller, B., & Grace, C. (2017). *Zero waste design guidelines.* www.zerowastedesign.org/

Mindful Materials. (n.d.). www.mindfulmaterials.com/

One Click LCA. www.oneclicklca.com/

Open LCA. www.openlca.org/

LS 3   Circularity/Circular Economy

Nothing lasts forever. Any discussion of lifecycle must include consideration of the end of life for components or even an entire shelter. According to WRAP (Waste and Resources Action Programme),

> [a] circular economy is an alternative to a traditional linear economy (make, use, dispose) in which we keep resources in use for as long as possible, extract the maximum value from them whilst in use, then recover and regenerate products and materials at the end of each service life.

LS 3.1

Cradle to Cradle. . .

is the concept where all materials, at the end of their duty cycle, become the feedstock for new materials. There are two major types of materials, which are classified based on their ability to re-enter a material stream: natural and technical. Natural materials are derived from living things or the earth with minimal processing: wood, cotton, wool, and stone are examples. At the end of their service life, they can be left to decompose in a natural cycle, becoming food for other organisms. Technical materials are man-made from extractive industries: metals, glass, ceramics, and the myriad plastics are examples. These materials have the potential to feed back into industrial processes and be reconstituted into new products.

Care must be taken to allow for easy separation of natural and technical materials or for separation of different types of technical materials. Mixed natural and technical materials must be avoided as they are difficult or impossible to separate. Layered boards of paper, plastics, metals, molded fiberglass with polyester resins, laminates of stone, aluminum, plastic, and textiles of cotton and polyester are examples of materials difficult or impossible to separate and can only become waste at the end of a duty cycle rather than re-entering a material cycle.

LS 3.2

Design for Repair

Most shelters are capable of repair—buildings can be repainted, broken windows, worn-out pumps or other equipment replaced. Repair becomes particularly important for mechanical equipment. Too often, entire assemblies are discarded because one element ceases to function long before the technology becomes outmoded.

LS 3.3

Design for Disassembly

Shelters are assemblies and collections of hundreds of thousands of individual pieces. Most assemblies aren't designed for disassembly; thus, the entire assembly must be discarded, and the natural and technical nutrients contained in them are lost from the cycle. Assemblies need to be able to be taken apart and reduced to their base materials, and those materials must either be reused or used as raw material for future products. There is a growing movement of design for disassembly, where structural components are fabricated with the end in mind, so that beams and columns can be repurposed at the end of the duty cycle.

LS 3.4

Solid Waste

Shelters are for human activities. These activities are supported by a range of goods: food, appliances, office supplies, clothing, furniture, tools, ad infinitum. All these have a duty cycle, with food being the shortest. Shelter needs to consider the storage and organization of these materials prior to their transport back to their respective nutrient cycles.

Further Reading and Resources LS3:

The Cradle to Cradle Products Innovation Institute. (2010). *Cradle to cradle.* www.c2ccertified.org/

McDonough, W., & Braungart, M. (2002). *Cradle to cradle: Remaking the way we make things.* New York, NY: North Point Press.

Zero Waste Design Guidelines. www.zerowastedesign.org/

Lifecycle & Water

Cory Gallo

LW1   The Life of Water

LW1.1

Water Is Vital. . .

for life on Earth. Without a doubt, water is essential for our existence. Humans are 70% water. Most of the fruits and vegetables we eat are over 90% water. Water drives the process of photosynthesis that makes oxygen. The surface of the earth is 71% water. Water's unique qualities (density, high specific heat, cohesion, adhesion, universal solvent) make our world habitable. Without it, we simply would not be here.

It's also finite. This is a critical concept in understanding how water is unique as a resource. Unlike renewable resources, the amount of water on Earth is fixed. The water that is on Earth today is the same water that was here when the Earth formed billions of years ago. So, we can think of Earth like a contained system that constantly recycles the same water. Because of this constant recycling, the Earth is perfectly capable of cleaning water by itself under natural conditions. The problem is that we pollute water faster than the Earth is capable of cleaning it. More-over, the Earth isn't capable of easily removing many of our modern waste streams. For instance, plastics can remain in our waterways and

Figure L15   End of the Mississippi River Watershed at Port Eades, Louisiana.

Source: Cory Gallo

oceans for millennia, permanently impacting life on Earth. It's estimated that over 10 million tons of plastics enter the ocean each year, which kill millions of seabirds and thousands of marine mammals and are ingested into aquatic species as micro pieces of plastics.

LW1.2

Context and Value. . .

are critical when considering water as a resource. The two concepts are intrinsically linked. The value of water is proportional to its availability, and its availability is primarily driven by location or context. Water's value, both monetarily and to the environment, depends on location. Unlike currency, which has a similar value everywhere, the value of water drastically changes based on circumstance. This is in large part because water is so difficult to move both to where it's needed and away from where it's not wanted. In areas of water scarcity, where about 10% of all humans (700 million people) live, water is extremely valuable. In areas of great abundance, it can be almost worthless. Water's value also depends on time. When a stream is dry, water is quite valuable to create base flow and

Figure L16   The aftermath of Hurricane Katrina illustrates the power and destruction of water.

Source: Cory Gallo

keep aquatic life thriving. However, the more water a stream receives, the less value to the environment it has. Related to human settlements, this is even more obvious. Oceanfront homes can be extremely valuable for their proximity to water. Oceanfront homes are less valuable as they're threatened by storm surge.

This duality in value impacts the ways in which we think about water. On one hand, we celebrate it, and on the other, we vilify it. Rain that falls to water crops, creates lakes to swim in, and refreshes our bodies is good, but rain that destroys our homes is bad. We celebrate the life-giving qualities of water, but we also fear its life-taking qualities. As we think about designing cities to work with water, we must first understand how water is valued and what it is valued for, because these realities often drive codes and ordinances that govern water management.

Further Reading and Resources LW1:

Fishman, C. (2012). *The big thirst: The secret life and turbulent future of water.* New York: Simon and Schuster.

Lynden-Bell, R. M., Morris, S. C., Barrow, J. D., Finney, J. L., & Harper, C. (Eds.). (2010). *Water and life: The unique properties of H2O*. Boca Raton, FL: CRC Press.

Wynveen, B. J. (2011). Water: The epic struggle for wealth, power, and civilization. *Journal of Rural Social Sciences, 26*(3), 231.

LW2   The Hydrologic Cycle

LW2.1

The Natural Hydrologic Cycle. . .

can be described in its simplest form in three steps:

1. Water falls from the sky as rain or precipitation,
2. it evaporates back to the sky where. . .
3. it condenses, and then falls back to earth.

While this is technically accurate, it's also extremely simple, and explains a process that might be completed in a day. In reality, the journey of water through the natural environment can take many twists and turns and is much less linear. A more complex explanation might look like this:

- Water falls from the sky as precipitation.
- It will either move across the land as surface runoff or infiltrate into the ground and become groundwater.

  o Groundwater can:

    - percolate deep into the ground to fill aquifers OR
    - be absorbed as uptake into plants to be transpired and evaporate back to the sky and thereby drive the process of photosynthesis OR
    - flow laterally through the ground to slowly feed wetlands, lakes, streams, and rivers, where it might be consumed by wildlife or

      - eventually reach the ocean OR
      - evaporate to the sky.

o Surface runoff can:

- Be evaporated close to where it fell and move back to the sky OR
- Flow into wetlands, lakes, streams, and rivers, where it might be consumed by wildlife or
  - eventually reach the ocean OR
  - evaporated to the sky.

• Once it is evaporated, it condenses and forms clouds, which then precipitate back to earth.

This begins to describe a very complex process that might take days but also might take thousands of years. Water that reaches the ocean might take three thousand years or more before it's evaporated again. Even this fairly detailed description, however, leaves out one crucial component: HUMANS. More specifically, because one could argue that we're covered under "wildlife" that simply consume water, it leaves out things humans build. As we consider how to design cities that work with water, we must acknowledge that cities impact every aspect of the hydrologic cycle. We cannot change the rules of the hydrologic cycle, but we can change the outcomes. How we change the outcomes are most often not for the better.

LW2.2

The Man-Made Cycle. . .

refers to how humans modify the hydrologic cycle through industry, transportation, agriculture, and urban development. This narrative focuses primarily on the latter. The face of the Earth looks the way it does, in large part, because of how much water falls on it, and how much of that water moves over it. Every location on Earth has evolved over millennia based on its unique relationship with the hydrologic cycle. Every stream, river, lake, etc. was formed because of how much water it receives. The amount of water it receives is based two variables: first, simply how much water falls on the watershed above it, and second, how much of that water becomes surface runoff. Climate change aside, the first part is fairly constant. The second, related to runoff, is where human development comes in.

Anything we change on the ground changes the way water interacts with the Earth. If we were to create 1 square foot or meter of concrete in the middle of a pristine forest, we would change the way water moves through that forest. It would be a miniscule amount, but a little less water would infiltrate into the ground, a little more water would run off, a little more water would evaporate, and a little less water would transpire. One raindrop that is diverted from its natural course doesn't make much of a difference, but enough raindrops falling on pavement, roofs, and other impervious surfaces can dramatically change how surface water leaves a watershed.

As we increase impervious area in cities, we change runoff in a few key ways. Understanding these changes allows us to better understand how to mitigate their negative impacts.

- First, we increase runoff. The less water that can be infiltrated or absorbed by plants, the more water leaves a watershed. This increased runoff reduces water that infiltrates to feed aquifers, supports healthy baseflow for streams, and is available for plants to uptake to generate photosynthesis.
- Second, we increase the rate or intensity at which water leaves a watershed. This one relates to friction and the idea of the smoother the surface, the easier it is for water to move over it. This also relates to the energy or force water has as it moves. This force can be devastating to streams and rivers as it scours and down-cuts natural streams, turning them into deep and lifeless ditches.
- Third, we decrease the time it takes for water to move through a watershed. Related to intensity, this reduced time dramatically increases the amount of water that reaches the bottom of a watershed. This concept can be thought of as a race where millions of little raindrops reach the bottom within a much smaller window of time creating a bottleneck or, more specifically, flooding.
- Fourth, and lastly, water itself changes along the way. It picks up things that we put on the ground and carries them with it into streams and rivers. It becomes more polluted. Water that flows over urban areas has an increased temperature from hot surfaces, picks up sediment from construction sites, mixes with pesticides and fertilizers to ultimately make an unhealthy cocktail of pollutants that run into our streams and rivers.

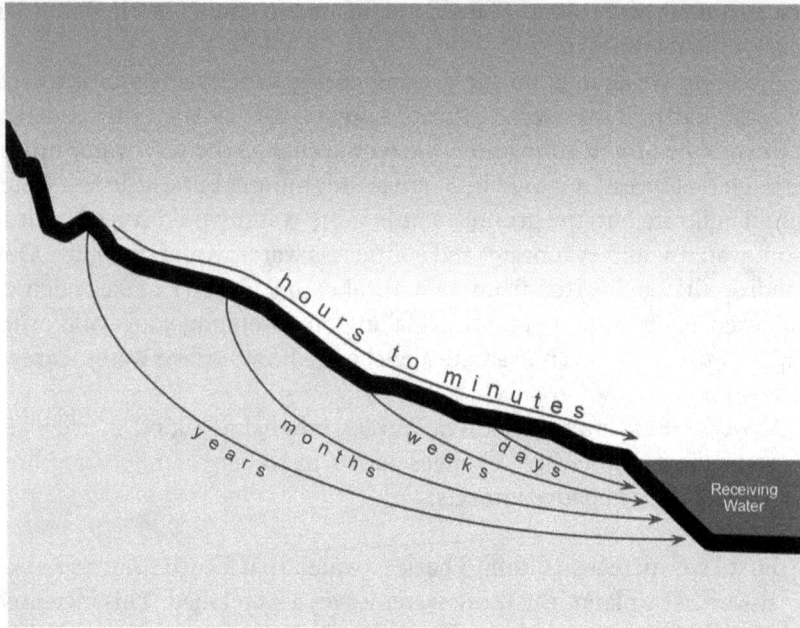

Figure L17 Impervious surfaces and the hydrologic cycle.

Source: Photo by Cory Gallo

In addition to these direct impacts of runoff is an indirect process that is equally as devastating related to the way cities were built prior to the 1960s. Before we cared about cleaning wastewater, cities literally dumped raw sewage directly into streams and rivers. Today we have two separate pipe systems, wastewater and stormwater, but many older cities still have just one pipe that leads to a sewage treatment plant. When it rains, these plants often overflow, creating a Combined Sewer Overflow event or CSO event, dumping raw sewage directly into streams and rivers. Without completely rebuilding cities, the best way to combat these events is to simply reduce runoff and keep it from getting to sewers.

Rainwater is not the only water that cities use. Much of the water used in cities comes from aquifers, rivers, and lakes that might be miles away. It is then cleaned if needed and distributed to homes and businesses. This underappreciated modern marvel allows us to have access to safe drinking water at the touch of a button or turn of a knob—something that would have been unheard of just 150 years ago. As we use water from these sources, how we clean and send it back into the environment also impacts the hydrologic cycle. While most cities were built around waterways for transportation, many newer cities were built around the automobile. These cities have a precarious relationship with water and have taught us in recent years that access to clean, drinkable water cannot be taken for granted. Las Vegas, situated in the high desert, actually uses less water per capita than any other city in the US because it has had to adapt. However, the elevation of Lake Meade, Las Vegas' primary water source, continues to drop to precariously low levels.

LW2.3

A Regenerative Man-Made Cycle. . .

is one that attempts to allow water to be used by humans as a resource but move back into the natural environment in a better condition than when it was extracted for human use. William McDonough uses the analogy of attempting to create buildings like trees: where a building absorbs and cleans rainfall, uses it to create oxygen, and even uses it to sustain itself. The idea is simple but very powerful. It means that a building should be a part of nature rather than separate from it. If we extrapolate this idea, we can think of a city like a forest.

The goal of regenerative or green infrastructure is to build cities that interact with water and the hydrologic cycle the way a forest would. Cities should absorb and infiltrate rainwater to recharge aquifers, feed the base flow of streams, and be available for plants to uptake to drive the creation of Oxygen. Cities should use water that falls on them to live on and grow. Cities should slow down and clean water that moves through them to support aquatic life and healthy watersheds downstream. While this goal is lofty, the application of green infrastructure is built on the principle that every new impervious surface increases runoff and the management of that additional runoff should occur as close to where it's created as possible.

Further Reading and Resources LW2:

Debo, T. N., & Reese, A. (2002). *Municipal stormwater management*. Boca Raton, FL: CRC Press.

Lyle, J. T. (1996). *Regenerative design for sustainable development*. New York: John Wiley & Sons.

Figure L18   A naturalized urban stream corridor designed to mimic natural, open water movement.

Source: Cory Gallo

McDonough, W. (2004). Principles, practices and sustainable design: Toward a new context for building codes. *Perspecta, 35*.

Tibbetts, J. (2005). Combined sewer systems: Down, dirty, and out of date. *Environmental Health Perspectives, 113*(7), A464–A467.

AESTHETICS **2**

Figure A1   Canals of Venice.

Source: Anne Graveur

DOI: 10.4324/9781003203049-5

Aesthetic Essentials

We live in a time of pragmatic, end-oriented, the-future-is-dangerous seriousness. Cities are crowded and growing, stretching infrastructures and resources to capacity and beyond. Climate change threatens coastlines, food and water supplies, and building stocks predicated on both the continuous burning of fossil fuels and predictable weather patterns. COVID-19 and fears of future pandemics have prompted many commentators to question the wisdom of living in dense traditional cities at all and to speculate that the future might be best served in eco-friendly towns, suburbs, and villages.

It is not a surprise that those tasked with addressing such challenges in the design of buildings, landscapes, and cities have little time for seemingly quaint pursuits that do not aim at solving big objective problems. The more serious the conversation and venue, the greater the likelihood that comments about 'beauty' or 'image' or 'aesthetics' will elicit eye-rolls or guffaws, or both. The belief that population growth, climate change, and pandemics are deadly serious issues is correct. Any response that ignores aesthetics, however, is wrong—dangerously so.

No doubt there are architects, engineers, and naturalists for whom high-end environmental performance offsets concern for traditional notions of beauty or place making. Many of the other seven billion people on the planet, however, feel differently. Look back to the momentum behind the ecological or environmental design movements of the late 1960s and '70s—from the products of the *Whole Earth Catalog*, to passive solar buildings with quirky windows and tilting walls,

DOI: 10.4324/9781003203049-6

to the evolution of Earthships. Notice the absence of those buildings in significant numbers in today's landscape. Put those two observations together, and it becomes clear why aesthetics matter. The majority of those proudly anti-aesthetic, strictly performance-based buildings were razed or remodeled to the point of diminished sustainability, and very few people have been inspired to emulate the model. More unfortunately, the counter-culture aesthetic of those early movements became associated with sustainable design, arguably leading those less committed to issues of climate change to dismiss a future of sustainable living. The takeaway for non-designers was something like: "If being sustainable means I have to live in something like THAT, I'll stick with my suburban developer house."

As designers and planners of sustainable cities, we have to do better. Aesthetics matter. Aesthetics here does not imply adherence to formulaic styles or proportional rules of some earlier time. It means concern for sensory, emotional, and sociocultural pleasures in the design of the built environment. These are not luxuries or frills but are essential human needs. Once we secure our base physiological needs described in the preceding chapter along with such things as safety, meaningful relationships, and love, we aspire to larger cultural and creative ambitions. Abraham Maslow termed these drives the realm of "self-actualization," the pinnacle of human needs.[1] This realm matters because real sustainability necessitates a change in prevailing patterns of living. Sustainability requires gathering people in dense communities where they choose to live over long periods of time without desiring to see the city's buildings, streets, parks, etc. endlessly remodeled. Thus, buildings, streets, and parks need not only be built with lifecycle in mind. They need to be objects and places of beauty.

Shelter, a city's total building stock, is particularly expensive—environmentally and economically—and therefore should be built to be both physically and aesthetically durable. Physical durability is a relatively straightforward concept (even if difficult to achieve). Aesthetic durability, on the other hand, is less straightforward. Perhaps it is helpful to think of aesthetic durability as another way of calling for a timeless quality in the design of buildings. No attempt, however, is made here to define timelessness, as thousands of books and essays have been written across centuries to that end. Instead, and in keeping with the ambitions of a practical guidebook, aesthetic durability is addressed here through three broad forms of engagement between people and buildings—namely, sensory, emotional, and cultural design considerations.

Sensory considerations are, by definition, subjective. The experience of shelter and the built environment in general is an individual affair, and highly personal. Nevertheless, there are objective, physiological mechanisms and psychological principles that underlie these experiences that, if understood, can be used to frame perception. Comfort, arguably, is the most tangible aspect of aesthetics. It can be understood as a phenomenon emerging from a constellation of increasingly studied, and relatively straightforward, perceptions of physical conditions.

Thermal comfort **AS1.1** is a product of design involving ambient temperature, the movement of air, and exposure to light which impacts bodies through the skin. It is not enough, however, that air moves. Air quality **AS1.2** must not simply support the long-term health of inhabitants but should be sufficiently high to enhance experience in the moment, or at least not detract from it. Light, beyond its thermal value, delights the senses. It is central to defining the visual environment **AS1.3**. Whether interior or exterior, the colors, contrasts, and quantities of light reflecting off surfaces are well within the control of designers of cities. The same can be said of sound. Though seldom well defined in city design guidelines, the auditory environment **AS1.4** is increasingly a metric by which inhabitants rate their experiences and, by extension, the city. Finally, it is important to note that if basic levels of sanitation **AS1.5** are not provided, no amount of attention to the preceding sensory concerns will foster positive aesthetic experiences.

Emotional considerations in design that promote well-being contribute to aesthetic durability. In short, happy and healthy inhabitants have a vested interest in maintaining their shelters. Designers and planners have two obligations in this regard. First, buildings should promote physical activity **AS2.1** in their internal layout as well as siting. Second, buildings should promote mental health **AS2.2**. This can be facilitated through physical access to nature, views to nature, and use of natural materials.

Even designs providing seemingly universal sensory (thermal, tactile, visual, auditory, and olfactory) and emotional (physical and mental health) conditions exist in, and have to respond to, the particular locales in which they are placed. Designers and planners, therefore, must address the unique cultural context of each place and its inhabitants to secure cities that are aesthetically durable. The easiest method to anchor a building in its locale is to acknowledge and pay homage to attitudes about craft and authenticity **AS3.1**. Craft, however, is not enough. Sustainable cities must incorporate a wide range of uses, scales, materials, forms, and, more importantly, people. Diversity **AS3.2** is the cultural corollary

AESTHETICS

of what contrast is in the realm of the senses. People, as Freud said, "are so made that we can derive intense enjoyment only from a contrast and very little from a state of things," which he takes as a more certain version of Goethe's "nothing is harder to bear than a succession of fair days."[2] People seek one-of-a-kind encounters. It is difficult, however, to imagine cities composed entirely of unique buildings; it is unlikely that such can be mandated by policy; and it is probably good that such places do not exist. In lieu of absolute and constant novelty, which would be disconcerting, it is useful to understand the roles of both innovation and tradition **AS3.3**. This extends beyond issues of style or form and the top-down imposition of one or another by an architect or planner. The relationship between diversity, innovation and tradition demand involvement of the community or communities themselves in the design and review process.

Sociocultural aspects of aesthetic appreciation extend beyond shelter to the other human needs, even mobility. As with shelter, some elements of the design and planning of mobility systems intended to foster perceptions of beauty need to focus less on traditional formulas and instead seek first to remove obstacles to enjoyment. Foremost among these is cost. Affordability **AM1.1** contributes to aesthetic pleasure indirectly by allowing the other joys of travel to be experienced without financial distraction and, somewhat more directly, by encouraging greater participation and thus providing the joys of people watching and being part of the crowd. Relatedly, creating social equity **AM1.2** in terms of access to transportation removes stigmas attached to some modes of transportation while enlarging the sense of rights to the city. There is a degree of joy engendered by the vibrancy of the city. People attract people. And accessibility **AM1.3** is key to ensuring that everyone can participate in the sustainable city.

Mobility offers other pleasures that are far more direct. Simply taking a stroll is a human pastime. Quality design can intensify enjoyment. Sidewalks **AM2.1**, for example, can be more than utilitarian pathways for pedestrians. Similarly, urban bike trails **AM2.2** should be designed with more than function in mind. Landscaping and sculpting of such paths can be enriching even to those who never straddle a bike or take leisurely walks. The question to every promise of beauty is, of course, 'in whose eyes?' And it is important that designers approach the design of sidewalks, bike trails, and rails with more than their own preferences in mind. Context-Sensitive Solutions (CSS) **AM2.3** is a particularly effective methodology for weighing the needs and desires of broad groups of stakeholders relative to transportation design.

Understanding those needs and desires and the relation of these to the city's larger material and energy flows is key to the sustainability of all systems of mobility. Mobility is key to appreciating the city insofar as it is difficult to appreciate what you are unable to go out and experience for yourself. Reciprocally, appreciation for the city is key to encouraging engagement. Special attention, therefore, should be paid to organizational systems **AM3.1**. These should not be laid over the city top-down, Robert Moses style. As noted earlier in regard to shelter, organization needs to take into account the world as it exists. Over the years, a host of tools have been developed to assist planners and designers in understanding the interactions of the complex web of natural, technological, and cultural pressures. These tools, all forms of multi-criteria analysis **AM3.2**, reveal potential synergies that subtly open the city to all.

Once there, food is fundamental to our conception of place. This importance stems from its dual constitution: food is nature **AF1.1**, and food is culture **AF1.2**. Part of the pleasure we take in perusing farmers markets **AF1.3** derives no doubt from the degree to which these two constitutions merge in such venues to reinforce the particularities of place. The underlying desire for connection to place is responsible for a rise in the number of people who are committed locavores **AF1.4**, participants in the slow food movement **AF1.5**, and frequenters of farm-to-table **AF1.6** eateries. This move toward locally sourced food should be encouraged by planners and designers alike by maximizing the experience of place.

Food is, of course, an experience in itself. Food is an essential need around which humans have bonded for millennia. This innate need intersects the world of physical design and policy in several ways. Community-Supported Agriculture (CSA) **AF2.1**, for instance, is a modern-day instantiation of the traditions of sharing food in a closely knit community of friends and family, and it requires space in the city to thrive. The city can implement programs to strengthen these connections in childhood, forging a citizenry that understands and values food in a richer way. Various programs, for example, now exist to teach kids about nourishment and stewardship in a community setting, such as the Edible Schoolyard project **AF2.2** and the Garden to Cafeteria program **AF2.3**. To some extent, these initiatives are extensions of the Victory Gardens **AF2.4** that emerged around the globe, particularly as a response to the shortages caused by the World Wars, and remain a symbol of resilience and community today.

AESTHETICS

Beaches, waterfalls, and rivers—the allure of water in nature is well known. In itself, water has no shape **AW1.1**. But, in the course of history, cities and empires have grasped the beauty of water management. It is through its collection, conveyance, and storage that water has meaning **AW1.2**. One of the great charms of Rome is the system of aqueducts and fountains that once served both political and very practical ends. Water, both controlled and in its natural state, has sculpted our landscapes and defined the form of cities **AW1.3**. It is essential in every sense.

Less commonly considered but arguably essential in the creation of cites that might LAST is the aesthetic of sustainable water management **AW2.1**. This is comprised of three systems of infrastructure. Conveyance **AW2.2** systems run the gamut from gutters and downspouts to curbs, channels, and canals. Management **AW2.3** systems are concerned with slowing and providing cleaner runoff by implementing urban forests, constructed wetlands, green roofs, and other technologies. Storage AW2.4 systems collect water for myriad practical uses while also providing character to the visual environment. Exposing these forms of infrastructure allows for aesthetic appreciation and learning about the importance of water conservation, and it puts the water closer to where it can serve the public and contribute to the future of the city.

Notes

1   Maslow, A. H. (1943). A theory of human motivation. *Psychological Review, 50*(4), 370–396.

2   Freud, S. (2005). *Civilization and its discontents* (75th Anniversary edition). New York, NY: W.W. Norton (Original work published 1930), p. 53.

Aesthetics
The Fine Print

Aesthetics & Food

C. Taze Fulford

AF1 Place and Food

AF1.1

Food Is Nature

We have reduced food to monocultures, megafarms, and big box stores. We hunt and gather in grocery stores, not fields and forests as our ancestors did. As we reduce the diversity of what we eat, we use more land for a smaller variety of staples. Big agriculture clears forests, contributes to soil loss through wind and water erosion, and pollutes waterbodies with animal wastes and chemicals. Most humans are no longer tied to the land that grows their food or understand how to grow food. Most humans lack access to organic fresh foods and have unhealthy relationships to food. Food, however, is derived from an understanding of natural processes, a care of the land and for nature, and attention to our place in the world. Whether humans like it or not, we are tied to the land for sustenance. We are tied to nature and the food it provides for nurture.

DOI: 10.4324/9781003203049-7

AF1.2

Food Is Culture

The making of food—from preparing the fields, planting the seeds, nurturing, harvesting, and preparing for the table—is a conscious cultural act. It has been shaped by "climate, geography, the pursuit of pleasure, and the desire for health." Food has shaped cultures around the world with the invention of the kitchen to bring foods in from the fields to prepare in different methods such as roasting, broiling, or frying, which became new words in our languages and then were written in instructions and passed down for others to understand the making process. Meals have given clues to class structure, religious affiliations, or political leanings, and immigrants have taken cooking methods with them to new countries as an expression of cultural identity.

AF1.3

Farmers Markets. . .

were first seen along the Nile five thousand years ago as Egyptians brought their crops to sell to the people in the cities. In the United States, the first farmers market appeared in Boston in 1634. These are locally supported venues which, once established, are re-occurring and allow growers and artisans to market and sell goods directly to the consumer. Each market defines "local" and may also determine if goods must be considered organic to be sold at the venue. Fresher foods are provided to the consumer, and more food dollars stay in the local economy through farmers markets.

A culture of community is developed from meeting the people that grow your food or other community members. As cities expanded and farms were located farther and farther from the city center, there needed to be a space for farmers to bring their goods closer to the consumer, and in larger cities, plazas and squares were ideal spaces for commerce. In 2019, the United States had 8,600 local farmer markets. While this number has increased greatly from the two thousand that were around

Figure A2   Istanbul fruit market.

Source: C. Taze Fulford III

in 1994, a shortage of local farmers is beginning to emerge as well as too few consumers buying produce at these markets.

AF1.4

Locavores. . .

are people who only consume locally produced foods, usually outside the streams of traditional big box marketing and large-scale production. According to Jessica Prentice, one of the founders of the locavore movement, "The prefix 'loca', has to do with place—as in location and locus . . . The ending 'vore' has to do with eating and is the same root as the word 'devour'." To her, the word "locavore" means "a person who eats the place" or "one who eats with a sense of place." Farm to Fork events are promoted by local Main Street organizations in the United States to allow for citizens to partake in food grown locally and prepared by local chefs.

European communities have set up locavore tourism so that visitors can participate in the everyday working of the farm and food-making experience. These build a bond between local agriculture and the citizenry, which can lead to better support for the local system.

AF1.5

Slow Food Movement. . .

started "in the 1980's with the aim to defend regional traditions, good food, gastronomic pleasure and a slow pace of life" (slowfoodnations. com). The movement recognizes the "strong connections between plate, planet, people, politics, and culture" (slowfood.com). Access to whole foods—that is, foods that are of quality and healthy, produced in a way that doesn't harm the natural environment, and provides farmers fair wages and consumers fair prices—is the overall philosophy of the group. Planners, designers, and officials may take an active role in promoting this movement through promoting local farmers markets (see **AF1.3** Farmers Markets) and events for citizens to be educated and participate in events that promote the lifestyle. Policies that allow citizens to grow and share food from their own properties along with allowed urban gardens can build a consensus that not only produces good foods but gives rise to connectivity of people, farms, and local restaurants.

AF1.6

Farm to Table. . .

also known as Farm to Fork, is a concept that develops a supply chain for restaurants and hotels to purchase produce, meat, poultry, fish, and honey along with other goods locally. Farmers are directly supported, keeping money in the local economy. This model also helps to safeguard the quality and freshness of goods by forming working relationships between businesses and producers. While the farmer must strive to provide the freshest and best-quality goods, it also means that the restaurant must consider how animals are raised, slaughtered, and processed, that certain produce may not be available at all times of the year, and that costs will be higher for the consumer than at restaurants using the traditional supply chain. Policy makers and local organizations can easily provide the places and events that give space in the urban environment to both grow foods and then showcase the goods to the public. Green roofs can be used for growing honey and produce, vacant lots can become gardens, and parks and urban spaces can be allowed to host events to showcase the goods and the work of local chefs. Policy makers must make room for agriculture through policy that advocates for urban farmers to operate.

Further Reading and Resources AF1:

Farmer's Market Coalition. https://farmersmarketcoalition. org/education/qanda/

Language Log. (November 13, 2007). http://itre.cis.upenn. edu/~myl/languagelog/archives/005109.html

Montanari, M. (2006). *Food is culture.* New York: Columbia University Press.

NPR: Why are so many farmer's markets failing? Because the market is PBS. www.pbs.org/show/farm-table/

Public Broadcasting System: Now—10 steps to becoming a locavore. www.pbs.org/now/shows/344/locavore.html

Robinson, J., & Hartenfeld, J. A. (2007). *The farmers market book.* Bloomington, IN: Indiana University Press.

Saturated. (March 17, 2019). www.npr.org/sections/thesalt/ 2019/03/17/700715793/why-are-so-many-farmers-markets-failing-because-the-market-is-saturated

Slow Food. www.slowfood.com

Slow Food Nation. https://slowfoodnations.org/participant/ carlo-petrini/

Slow Food USA. https://slowfoodusa.org

Thrillest: What it really means when a restaurant is "farm-to-table" by Emma Diab. (2016). www.thrillist.com/eat/nation/ what-it-really-means-when-a-restaurant-is-farm-to-table

Webstaurant Store Blog. www.webstaurantstore.com/blog/ postdetails.cfm?post=1532

World Wildlife Fund for Nature. (2018). https://wwf.panda. org/?336730/Food-for-thought-91-per-cent-of-people-dont-realize-our-food-system-is-the-greatest-threat-to-nature

AF2 Food as Experience

AF2.1

Community-Supported Agriculture (CSA) . . .

is a way for farmers, and potentially consumers and non-profits, to bring produce and goods directly to the community. Shares are sold to the public before each growing season and then are delivered on an agreed schedule to the shareholder during the course of the season. The concept is to give farmers a stable income through the shares and to give a connection to local food back to the public. The farmers and shareholders share in the benefits and the risks of the production of food.

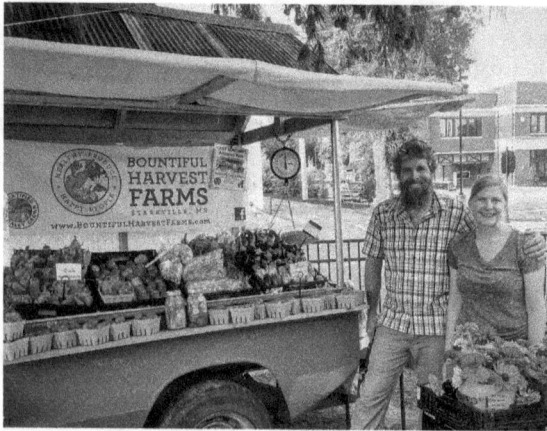

Figure A3   Community-Supported Agriculture produce delivery.

Source: Sam McLemore

AF2.2

The Edible Schoolyard. . .

is a gardening and cooking program that builds a curriculum for school children to learn how to grow and prepare food on school grounds. This concept was originated by Alice Waters in 1995 in Berkeley, California.

The principle used to develop the program was "children deserve to be nurtured in body and mind, treated with dignity, and shown that they are valued."

Students are taught how to work the soil, plant the garden, harvest, perform food preparation and cooking techniques—such as how to mince, create salad dressings, approximate recipes, etc.—and then reflect about how the process went. The project is also about changing children's lives for the better through teaching them about foods, nature, themselves, and the relation of each to the other. A connection to food, place, and health is the mission for the education of children for a sustainable future.

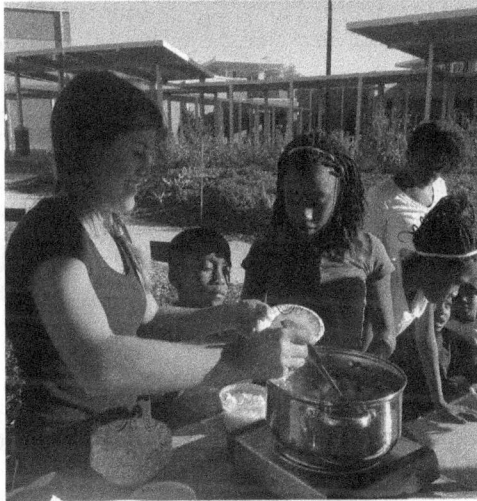

Figure A4   Teacher and students cooking from the garden.

Source: Karen Schauwecker

Figure A5   Elementary school teaching garden.

Source: Karen Schauwecker

AF2.3

Garden to Cafeteria. . .

may or may not be a part of the school property. This can simply be a connection with local farmers or producers providing produce for the school system. The aim of the collaboration is to help districts and parents know where the food is coming from and if it has been treated with chemicals in any way or is genetically modified. This also results in healthier, more sustainable foods being provided to the children, faculty, and staff with less inputs from fossil fuel–driven transportation costs, fertilizers, and pesticides. The added benefit of the garden is on-site exercise, connection with place, and transfer of knowledge for children.

AF2.4

Victory Gardens. . .

also known as 'Gardens for Defense,' are a concept that first started in the United States during World War I, in which the people began to grow a portion of the food they needed to survive. People planted on their own property, public parks, or any vacant land to take stress off of the national food supply so that food could be sent to allies in Europe. These gardens were used again during World War II, after 9/11, and in 2008 during the great financial crisis, and have shown up during COVID-19 as 'recovery gardens.' A new twist to the concept is called 'Victory Gardens 2007+,' which states that victory is "independence from the corporate food system, community involvement and getting people closer to the natural environment."

Further Reading and Resources AF2:

Biodynamic Association. www.biodynamics.com/content/community-supported-agriculture

Future Farmers. www.futurefarmers.com/victorygardens/history.html

Figure A6 The Fruits of Victory.

Source: Public Domain

Gowdy-Wygant, C. (2013). *Cultivating victory: The women's land army and the victory garden movement*. Pittsburgh, PA: University of Pittsburgh Press.

Lawson, L. (2005). *City bountiful: A century of community gardening in America*. Oakland, CA: University of California Press.

Michigan farm to school: Garden to cafeteria. (2014). www.canr.msu.edu/foodsystems/uploads/files/garden_to_cafeteria_guide.pdf

New York Historical Society Museum & Library: "Recovery gardens" are the new victory gardens. (2020). http://womenatthecenter.nyhistory.org/recovery-gardens-are-the-new-victory-gardens/

Slow Food USA. https://slowfoodusa.org/school-gardens/

USDA National Agricultural Library. (2019). www.nal.usda.gov/afsic/community-supported-agriculture

Waters, A. (2008). *Edible Schoolyard*. https://edibleschoolyard.org/curriculum

Aesthetics & Mobility

Joan Blanton

AM1   Sociocultural Impacts

AM1.1

Affordability. . .

in regard to users' costs, must be taken into account if transportation systems are to be efficient and sustainable. Transportation affordability is also important because of its correlation with housing affordability. The degree of the correlation varies by location. The US Department of Housing and Urban Development (HUD) has constructed a Location Affordability Index (LAI) that provides estimates at the neighborhood level for the US and Europe of the relationship between transportation and housing costs.

Transportation systems that people cannot afford to use are not only inefficient but will negatively impact the sustainability of the city. Research shows that housing costs generally decrease as the distance from the center city increases but that the resulting transportation costs increase due to the dependence on automobiles and the increased distances travelled, especially if there is a lack of public transit. Research has also shown that affordable housing rarely exists in areas that are accessible to public transit.

AM1.2

Social Equity

By definition, social equity in transportation would result in transit and transportation systems that were equal in quality and accessibility for all sectors of society. It also denotes an equitable distribution of the benefits, advantages, and costs of the system.

AM1.3

Accessibility

Affordability and Social Equity would be inadequate if people still could not get to the places they need to go, i.e., if they were not accessible. Accessibility refers to people's ability to reach goods, services, and activities, which is the ultimate goal of most transport activity. Many factors affect accessibility, including:

- mobility (physical movement),
- quality and affordability of transport options,
- transport system connectivity,
- mobility substitutes, and
- land use patterns.

Resulting accessibility can be evaluated from various perspectives, including the needs of a group, mode of transport used, location, or activity. A group may be an ethnic division or age group; mode would be pedestrian, biking, buses, light rail, etc.; location is the relationship of distances between particular amenities, such as the distance between grocery stores, for a particular group; and activity would be the availability of amenities such as parks, playgrounds, cultural attractions, work sites, or retail establishments.

Further Reading and Resources AM1:

HUD Exchange. www.hudexchange.info

Litman, T. (2012). *Evaluating accessibility for transportation planning: Measuring people's ability to reach desired goods and activities*. Victoria Transport Policy Institute. http://vtpi. org/access.pdf

Manaugh, K., Badami, M. G., El-Geneidy, A. M. (2015). Integrating social equity into urban transportation planning: A critical evaluation of equity objectives and measures in transportation in North America. *Transport Policy, 37*, 167–176.

Saberia, M., Wua, H., Amoh-Gyimaha, R., Smithb, J., & Arunachalamb, D. (2017). Measuring housing and transportation affordability: A case study of Melbourne, Australia. *Journal of Transport Geography, 65*, 134–146.

AM2   Beautification/Landscaping

AM2.1

Sidewalks. . .

are the basic infrastructure that can support walking and its benefits, including improved health, access to other forms of transportation, recreation, and improvement of the environment. Sidewalks are used by people who want mobility and space for stationary activities for leisure and work.

The Global Designing Cites Initiative's *Global Street Design Guidebook* recommends that designers consider local culture, identify the uses and functions needed, shape streets to improve the quality of life, and engage local communities when designing sidewalks. And, where possible, sidewalks should include four zones: frontage, clear path, street furniture, and buffer (see Figure A7).

Well-designed sidewalks can greatly enhance the experience of a city's walkability, which is an assessment or measure of how well the built environment supports and encourages its residents and visitors to walk. Most definitions consider some or all of the following in their appraisal: number and quality of footpaths and sidewalks, traffic and road conditions, land use patterns, building, safety, and accessibility to retail, transit, and attractions, among others. Sidewalk design will vary according to intended use (see Figures A8, A9, and A10).

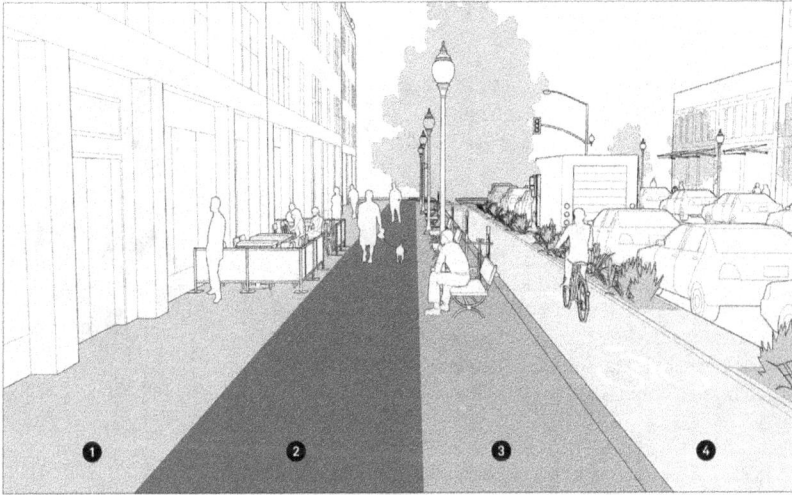

Figure A7   The four sidewalk zones.

Source: Global Street Design Guide, by NACTO. Copyright © 2016 National Association of City Transportation Officials. Reproduced by permission of Island Press, Washington, DC.

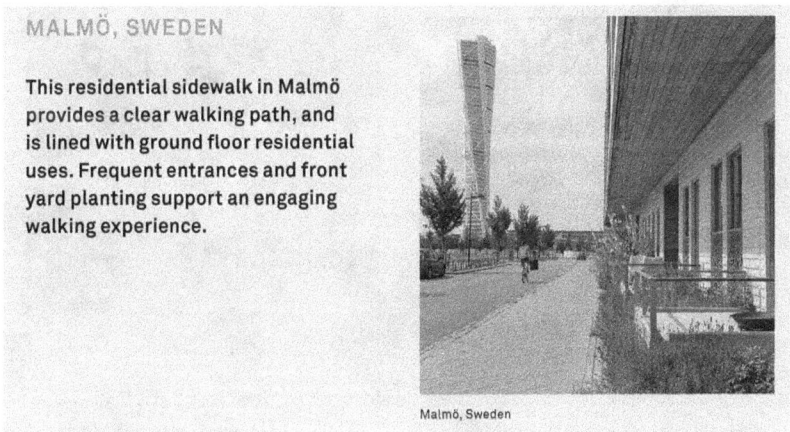

MALMÖ, SWEDEN

This residential sidewalk in Malmö provides a clear walking path, and is lined with ground floor residential uses. Frequent entrances and front yard planting support an engaging walking experience.

Malmö, Sweden

Figure A8   A sample residential sidewalk in Malmo, Sweden.

Source: Global Street Design Guide, by NACTO. Copyright © 2016 National Association of City Transportation Officials. Reproduced by permission of Island Press, Washington, DC.

FORTALEZA, BRAZIL

Avenida Monsenhor Tabosa was redesigned in 2014, costing 5,9 million reais, or US $1.65 million. Improved sidewalks with wide clear paths replaced 200 m of parking and service lanes along the 700-m length of the project, and new shade structures, lighting, bus stop areas, and seating opportunities improved the pedestrian experience and accessibility. Raised crossings and intersections were also included to induce speed reduction.

Av. Monsenhor Tabosa; Fortaleza, Brazil

Figure A9   A sample of a redesigned sidewalk in Fortaleza, Brazil.

Source: Global Street Design Guide, by NACTO. Copyright © 2016 National Association of City Transportation Officials. Reproduced by permission of Island Press, Washington, DC.

NEW YORK CITY, USA

Broadway is one of the main commercial corridors in New York City, running 21 km down the length of Manhattan. The wide sidewalks are typically between 6–8 m wide, catering to heavy pedestrian volumes and allowing space for large street trees, bus stops, street furniture, and for commercial activities to spill out. Recent sidewalk widening expanded the width to 14 m in areas of midtown.

Broadway; New York City, USA

Figure A10   A sample of a main commercial sidewalk in New York City, USA.

Source: Global Street Design Guide, by NACTO. Copyright © 2016 National Association of City Transportation Officials. Reproduced by permission of Island Press, Washington, DC.

AM2.2

Urban Bike Trails. . .

offer an opportunity to increase the connectivity of a city's transport system as well as to create park-like spaces for the enjoyment of all city dwellers. The Netherlands has been offering top-notch bike paths and trails for decades. They have even turned paths into electricity producers, e.g., their Solaroad, which is constructed with pavement that converts sunlight into electricity. There are, however, many global cities that have embraced biking as a form of transportation and created enviable bike trails. They include:

- Copenhagen, Denmark: www.visitcopenhagen.com/biking
- Malmö, Sweden: https://theculturetrip.com/europe/sweden/articles/the-most-spectacular-places-to-cycle-in-malmo-sweden/
- Lyon, France: https://en.lyon-france.com/Discover-Lyon/Eco-friendly/bike-tourists-welcome-to-lyon
- Singapore: The Park Connector Network: www.nparks.gov.sg/gardens-parks-and-nature/park-connector-network; https://honeykidsasia.com/singapore-park-connector-network/
- Melbourne, Australia: www.bicyclenetwork.com.au/tips-resources/maps-and-rides/melbournes-top-family-friendly-bike-trails/

The US is developing a nationwide Bike Route System that has fourteen thousand miles of bikeway as of 2020. Its stated purpose is to create ways for anyone to bicycle for travel, transportation, or recreation. Also, the Rails-to-Trails Conservancy (RTC) is a non-profit organization active in many parts of the United States and dedicated to creating a nationwide network of trails from former rail lines.

Sidewalks, bikeways, and streets are all contributors to the plans called for by a group called GREEN PATHS, which represents a new way of planning cities by focusing on urban issues through social research and architectural intervention. Their primary objective is to develop a sustainable rating system for the design and construction of shared-use paths to promote environmental, social, and economic benefits through the development process.

AM2.3

Context-Sensitive Solutions (CSS) . . .

consider the total context of a transportation improvement project and include all stakeholders in the project: technical professionals, local community interest groups, landowners, facility users, and the general public. This collaborative, interdisciplinary approach builds a commitment to community that matches the context or setting and preserves historical and environmental resources while maintaining safety and mobility.

The benefits of CSS are that it stays active throughout the project, preserves scenic/aesthetic/historic/environmental resources, maintains safety and mobility, and continues after the project is completed.

Further Reading and Resources AM2:

Adventure Cycling Association. www.adventurecycling.org/routes-and-maps/us-bicycle-route-system/

Business Strategy and the Environment Bus. Strat. Env. 14, 300–314 (2005) Published online in Wiley InterScience (www.interscience.wiley.com). DOI: 10.1002/bse.490

Curbed. (2018). https://archive.curbed.com/2018/2/7/16980682/city-sidewalk-repair-future-walking-neighborhood

de Cerreño, A. L. C., & Pierson, I. (2004). *Context sensitive solutions in large central cities.* New York, NY: NYU Robert F. Wagner Graduate School of Public Service.

The Green Paths. (2021). https://open.spotify.com/show/2GtIWhcPNzlcC0Tyk09Oar

Mateo-Babiano, I., & Ieda, H. (2005). *Theoretical discourse on sustainable space design: Towards creating and sustaining effective sidewalks.* Bunkyo City, Tokyo: Civil Engineering Department, University of Tokyo, Japan.

Rails to Trails. www.railstotrails.org/

Speck, J. (2012). *Walkable City: How downtown can save America, one step at a time.* New York, NY: Farrar, Straus and Giroux.

AM3   Urban Metabolism

Urban metabolism may be defined as "the sum-total of the technical and socio-economic processes that occur in cities, resulting in growth, production of energy, and elimination of waste" (Kennedy et al., 2007). The concept, conceived by Wolman (1965), is fundamental to developing sustainable cities and communities. It is loosely based on biological lifecycles of organisms and ecosystems. Urban metabolism includes the myriad transformations that support and maintain urban life from the biological necessities of water and food to the technologies of air conditioning and computers. It also describes the way these things are infinitely connected in both physical and social processes.

This approach to cities lends a different perspective when analyzing a city's entire transportation system and all its modes of transport. The most successful organisms and ecosystems are the ones that are efficient and evolve for sustainability. If roads, parking lots, railways, and other paths are taking up a majority of the space and resources, can that "organism" or city LAST?

AESTHETICS

AM3.1

Organizational Systems

Researchers, planners, and designers have begun to acknowledge that sustainability and environmental concerns must be addressed in our transportation systems. Organizational systems are being developed to speak to this challenge.

One such approach is Transportation Asset Management Systems, which are geared to making decisions in sectors that have a substantial asset base for their operations. An asset management decision-making framework needs to be guided by performance goals, cover an extended time horizon, draw from economics as well as engineering, and consider a broad range of assets. More recently this type of system has been used to incorporate climate-induced change into state and local transportation decision making.

AM3.2

Multi-Criteria Analysis (MCA) . . .

is a type of analysis for the development of policy and management tools that simultaneously consider different criteria (economic, environmental, social) in decision making. MCAs produce indexes for their results which make comparisons between options easier. These technical research methods would not normally be employed by designers or planners. If such analyses are needed, a seasoned statistician or researcher would need to be consulted.

Further Reading and Resources AM3:

Deng, H. (2015). Multicriteria analysis for benchmarking sustainability development. *Benchmarking: An International Journal, 22*(5), 791–807.

Giampietro, M., Mayumi, K., & Giuseppe, M. (2006). Integrated assessment and energy analysis: Quality assurance in multi-criteria analysis of sustainability. *Energy, 31*(1), 59–86.

Heynen, N., Kaika, M., & Swyngedouw, E. (2005). Urban political ecology: Politicizing the production of urban natures. In Nik Heynen, Maria Kaika and Erik Swyngedouw (eds.), *In the nature of cities*. New York: Taylor & Francis.

Kennedy, C., Pincetl, S., & Bunje, P. (2007). *The study of urban metabolism and its applications to urban planning and design.* Toronto, ON, Canada: Department of Civil Engineering, University of Toronto.

Oltean-Dumbrava, C., Miah, A., & Watts, G. (2015). Towards a more sustainable surface transport infrastructure: A case study of applying multi criteria analysis techniques to assess transport noise reducing devices. *International Journal of Cleaner Production, 112*(4), 2922–2934.

Transportation Asset Management Systems. https://trid.trb.org/view/910705

US Federal Highway Administration Asset Management. (2017). www.fhwa.dot.gov/asset/if08008/amo_02.cfm

Aesthetics & Shelter

Caleb Crawford

Aesthetics relates to the interaction between an individual and an object, environment, or event. The individual's response in turn is shaped by culture. Nothing is inherently aesthetic. Instead, we as cultures define as aesthetic those qualities we appreciate in things, then attempt to imbue our environments with those qualities.

Aesthetics is a topic addressed by so many great thinkers that to even opine on the topic is intimidating. We must recognize the history of philosophy but stake out a new reading when examining the aesthetics of shelter in relation to sustainability. Three concepts in aesthetic philosophy provide parallels for an aesthetics of sustainability: physicality, emotion, and culture. In relation to shelter, these translate to comfort, wellness, and cultural bias.

Comfort is composed of and requires an analysis of sensory inputs—visual, auditory, tactile, olfactory, and gustatory. We evaluate the quality of our experiences related to these inputs.

A work of art may elicit an emotional response in the participant: joy, awe, dread. Wellness is a result of a positive emotional response to our environment, and an environment that specifically considers the happiness and well-being of the users.

How we make and experience shelter is a result of our cultural biases. We need to question our positions and entertain those of others. Aesthetic judgment is rarely divorced from social, cultural, and political points of view. A Walmart shopper might feel profoundly uncomfortable going into Brooks Brothers. How one regards a work of art or design has less to do with the work itself, and mostly to do with social status, level of education, cultural background, political affiliation, and the expectations these engender.

AS1   Sensory Considerations

Whether it is a meal, a painting, a concert, or a city, we use language prompted by these stimuli to describe our experience. Many of the terms we use for aesthetics pertain to comfort. Unlike in philosophical variants of aesthetics, however, there are metrics of comfort. Comfort, defined as "a condition or feeling of pleasurable physical ease or relief from pain or stress," is quantifiable. Research has identified specific measurable conditions or ranges regarding temperature, humidity, air movement, air quality, quality and quantity of light, and the levels of sound at which most people are comfortable. Restated in terms appropriate to shelter, human comfort can be quantified by thermal comfort, air quality, visual environment, auditory environment, and sanitation.

AS1.1

Thermal Comfort

Despite similarities across cultures determined by human physiology, comfort is relative to context and upbringing. Someone from Sweden will have different acceptable thermal comfort ranges than someone from Libya or Indonesia, and someone sitting at a desk will experience variations in temperature differently than someone doing physical work. Thermal comfort is controlled by the interrelated environmental conditions of temperature, humidity, air movement, and radiant temperature, and personal factors of clothing, metabolism, and activity. These sensory conditions affect people's enjoyment of and willingness to be in a space. The conditions of thermal comfort in the interior of a shelter can be controlled by the technology of the shelter through control of the boundary between the interior and the exterior **TS2.1** and heating and cooling equipment **TS2.2**.

AS1.2

Air Quality

Smells, borne in the air, can either please or repel. Smells trigger memory. Even absent overt odors, air quality affects us. Fresh air promotes a sense of well-being; a lack of fresh air causes fatigue, an inability to concentrate, headaches, and worse, depending on the pollutant. Indoors, there are three strategies for indoor air quality: eliminate the sources of pollutants, provide ventilation, and actively improve air quality. Many of our materials contain toxins that can have a detrimental effect on air quality **LS2.4**. Many of our building processes can introduce pollutants, like printing, cooking, or smoking—even just people breathing. The outdoor environment can introduce toxins through polluted air. Balanced ventilation **TS2.2** can alleviate this by providing filtered outdoor air.

AS1.3

Visual Environment

Approximately half of the human brain is devoted to processing visual signals. It is no wonder that the visual environment, defined by the quantity and quality of light, dominates experience. Architecture and interior design devote a great deal of attention both to the interaction of form and material to light, but also to the quality of light in relation to human comfort, and the use of light as a means of expressing the narrative of a space. Light allows us to see color and texture, and light can be used to accentuate the qualities of materials and spaces.

Daylight holds enormous aesthetic importance to shelter, a sense of beauty, and feelings of contentment and comfort. Electric light is no less important; it extends the times, places, and qualities of our activities. The three aspects of natural and artificial light that contribute most to comfort are color, contrast, and quantity.

AS1.3.1 Color. Light is energy. Visible light is a very small band of the electro-magnetic spectrum. Different wavelengths produce different colors. Color affects the way things look. We perceive color because materials reflect the color we see and absorb the rest of the spectrum. Thus, materials influence the color of a space through reflection. Poorly designed electric lighting can distort color and create discomfort. Light color can affect our circadian rhythms. Contemporary LED lighting has high color fidelity and can support circadian rhythms by adjusting the color temperature over the course of the day, allowing for better sleep after work, and healthier and more productive employees. "Cool" light—light with a lot of blue—is similar to what is experienced in daylight, where a great deal of light is reflected from the sky. "Warm" light is the tone of fire, typically what is experienced at night.

AS1.3.2 Contrast. The difference in the brightness of objects within the field of view creates contrast. The Italian Renaissance concept of chiaroscuro, light and dark, has been an aesthetic concern for at least three thousand years, well before the Renaissance. It can provide incredible drama to space, but it can also make it uncomfortable when it reaches levels of glare. Glare can be influenced by materials as well as the direction of light. Glossy surfaces reflect light directly. Matte surfaces diffuse light. Highly textured surfaces can be accentuated by light across them. Contrast varies depending on the use but is generally needed for clear visual tasks and the definition of space. It can, however, be exploited for artistic effect.

AS1.3.3 Quantity. The amount of light needs to be aligned with the goal of the space. Sufficient light needs to be provided for a task with levels varied according to the activity. More light is needed in a kitchen than a dining room. Higher light levels are appropriate to a fast-food restaurant than a fine dining establishment. Minimum light for egress is 1 foot-candle (fc) (11 lux). Ambient light for stairs and corridors is 5 fc (54 lux). Average task lighting (offices, classrooms) is 40 fc (430 lux). Highly intricate tasks can demand 200 fc (2150 lux). Daylight can reach 10,000 fc (107,600 lux).

AS1.4

Auditory Environment

Essential to the design of performance venues, acoustic character has become more central to the thinking of everyday spaces, including offices, restaurants, and residences. Noise is unwanted sound. Spaces should be designed to limit noise from the outside, from adjacent spaces, and within spaces. There are symmetries here with energy-efficient technologies: in particular air sealing, mass, vibration isolation, and insulation reduce sound transmission between spaces. Surfaces that diffuse or absorb sound such as textured surfaces and textiles can help limit the propagation of noise within a space. The logarithmic scale of the decibel (dB) is used to measure sound intensity. Zero dB is the threshold of hearing; human speech ranges from 10 dB for a whisper to 80 dB for a shout, with normal speech at 55 to 65 dB. Chain saws and diesel trucks can exceed 100 dB. A jet plane taking off exceeds 150 dB at 25 meters, which is capable of rupturing eardrums. Codes require separation of tenant spaces with partitions rated with a Sound Transmission Class of 65, meaning it can stop sound at 65 dB—the upper range of human speech.

AS1.5

Sanitation

Shelter must be free of dirt and vermin and allow for the proper disposal of waste. Materials and finishes must be easy to clean and maintain, and not harbor dirt. Consideration should be given to the sorting, storage, and removal of waste, with consideration for diversion of waste back into useful materials. See also **LW 2** and **TW 2**.

Further Reading and Resources AS1:

Alexander, C. (1977). *A pattern language*. Oxford: Oxford University Press.

Grondzik, W. T., & Kwok, A. G. (2019). *Mechanical and electrical equipment for buildings* (13th ed.). Hoboken, NJ: John Wiley and Sons, Inc.

Illuminating Engineering Society (IES). Illuminating engineering society—The lighting authority. www.ies.org

International Living Future Institute. The living building challenge. (2021). https://living-future.org/

Lechner, N. (1991). *Heating, cooling, lighting*. New York: Wiley-Interscience. Especially chapters 4, 5, 12, 13, 14.

USGBC. The LEED standard. https://new.usgbc.org/

AS2 Emotional Considerations

Wellness is "the quality or state of being healthy in body and mind, especially as the result of deliberate effort." Wellness incorporates the conditions of human comfort, and adds in physical activity, physical health, mental health, and community and civic engagement.

AS2.1

Physical Activity

Shelter should be designed to promote physical activity. Site selection determines how easy walking, bicycling, and access to public transit are (see **AM 2** and **SM 5**). Interior design should make use of stairs easier and more inviting by privileging their access over elevators as well as by making the stair design more appealing—larger dimensions, daylight, views, and sculptural quality. Provide exercise facilities and spaces for exercise, and facilities such as showers and changing rooms in commercial buildings to support exercise and human-powered commuting. Provide easily accessed and secure bicycle storage to promote transportation alternatives.

AS2.2

Mental Health

The physical spaces of shelter can significantly affect mental health. Stress, anxiety, depression, substance abuse, and a host of other diseases can be ameliorated or exacerbated through the design of shelter. Spaces for or in support of physical activity (see earlier) contribute to mental well-being. In addition to physical activity, access to nature is shown to significantly improve mental well-being.

AS2.2.1 Nature. Biophilia, the term coined by E.O. Wilson, is the innate emotional affiliation of human beings to other living organisms. We recognize the utilitarian environmental services provided by biological systems, but they also provide incredible emotional and intellectual services. And they are beautiful. The health benefits of even brief exposure to nature have been well studied and affirmed. Environmental services include reduced air pollution and associated diseases such as asthma, reduced heat island effect, reduced stormwater runoff, etc. (see **LF 3 LW 2 TW 1**). Emotional services include stress reduction, faster illness recovery, greater focus on tasks, enhanced productivity, intellectual development, stronger social ties, and improved quality of life.

Practices yielding environmental and emotional services are green roofs, roof gardens, green walls, garden terraces, green atria, daylit interiors, natural ventilation, urban trees, and green streets (see **LF 3 LF 4** and **TF 4**). At the very least, we can surround ourselves with house plants. Domestic animal life can be included—fish, reptiles, birds, and rodents—with minimal space and maintenance requirements.

AS2.2.2 Views . . . are found to be performance-enhancing. Contemporary office spaces have open floor plans which put staff at the perimeter, and place private offices and conference rooms at the interior, the inverse of the mid-century hierarchy with private offices on the perimeter. This gives everyone access to daylight and views. Daylight is important to reducing energy use, but it has been found to be critical to happiness.

AS2.2.3 Natural Materials. Many materials with amazing properties have been made possible by modern science; unfortunately, many of them are toxic to humans and other life, and their manufacture and disposal degrade the environment (see **LS 2** and **LS 3**). Natural materials have beneficial effects. Wood, stone, and old masonry have qualities of never-ending uniqueness. They have the added benefit of being better for human and environmental health.

Further Reading and Resources AS2:

The Active Design Guidelines. https://centerforactivedesign.org/

The Well Standard, The International Well Building Institute. www.wellcertified.com/

Zero Waste Design Guidelines. (2017). www.zerowastedesign.org/

AS3 Cultural Considerations

Culture influences the making, use, and understanding of shelter. A shelter is an embodiment of cultural, social, and political influences and an instigation of cultural readings. Aesthetics are not independent of culture. Much like language, it is unique to groups of people, joining some and excluding others. This isn't to say that a shelter of one culture cannot be appreciated by another, just that aspects may be read in different ways, and some individuals and groups may be excluded from participation. While recognizing cultural bias, we have to recognize the amazing aesthetic value that the presence of divergent cultural heritages and attitudes have on the urban environment, and how that influence creates conditions worth sustaining. The cultural considerations most important for the design of sustainable cities are craft, diversity, and familiarity.

AS3.1

Craft and Authenticity

We are drawn to spaces, surfaces, and details that are well made, express the qualities of the nature or culture from which it is drawn, or the skill of the craftsperson who made it. Anonymous spaces, poorly crafted, with indifferent and inexpensive materials may repulse us. Think lumpy drywall, vinyl composition tile (VCT), fluorescent lights in an inexpensive acoustic tile ceiling. The value of craft is longevity—we care for and respect things that are well made as we do for things that seem authentic.

AS3.2

Diversity. . .

is essential to species and ecosystems. Monocultures, common in industrial farming practices, do not occur naturally and are more subject to pests and disease, which require inputs of pesticides and other toxins to combat. Diverse ecosystems rely on diffusion and symbiotic relationships. Fewer similar species means less likelihood for an entire area to be affected by a particular blight or pest. There are synergies between species where an exchange of nutrients is mutually beneficial (see **SF 3** and **TF 2**). Analogously, diversity is related to traditional criteria for evaluating art: contrast, color, pattern. Diversity in shelter in the urban environment is related to use, scale, materiality, and form.

Patterns of use, scale, materiality, and form are driven by culture. Shelter must accommodate myriad needs: housing, workplaces, cultural institutions, commerce, etc. Each varies in size and takes on a different shape to accommodate the use. Mixed-use structures allow for proximity and density while supporting tremendous diversity, with residences supporting commercial spaces, and commercial spaces providing jobs. Diversity of scale tends to evolve over time, with smaller shelters standing adjacent to and displaced by large ones. Variety in form and material makes for contrast, relieving monotony. This is the diversity our built eco-system demands.

Perhaps more important than use, the diversity of users must be considered: race, religion, ethnicity, national origin, gender, age, ability, and all the wonderful divergences that make up humanity. At stake is our species. With diversity goes equity and inclusion. Health and a clean environment should not go only to those who can afford them. Shelter must be built where there is access to employment, quality food, health services, clean air and water, clean power, and clean transportation. Shelter must be free of toxins of any kind, comfortable, and affordable. Developers of low-income housing are finding that developments built to the Passive House standard have lower turnover and lower maintenance costs, because the residents like living there. They see the quality, they take better care of the apartments, and there is far less vandalism in the public areas. Decisions regarding patterns of use, scale, materiality, and form should not be made independent of the people who will use the spaces. Ask what they want and listen to their answers. Treat people with respect, and they will give respect.

Depending on the scale of the interaction and the culture, there are diverse effects on behavior and social interaction. Proxemics is the study of how people perceive and organize the spaces and distances they main-tain between each other in culturally specific situations. The field identi-fies the following scales: intimate (<0.5 m); personal (0.5–1.25 m); social (1.25–3.75 m); and public (>3.75 m). The size of spaces varies accordingly from the restaurant booth, the conference table, and the sports arena.

AS3.3

Innovation and Tradition. . .

are two contrasting approaches to the design of shelter. Architectural form and materials are aspects of a language. They are signifiers giving users clues to a building's identity and user behavior. There is comfort in the expected, while we often struggle with unfamiliar terms. The big door in the middle signifies main entry, symmetry denotes stability, representational elements (faces, plants, landscapes) are immediately recognizable, and expensive materials such as polished stone and wood paneling indicate an elevated class aspiration, whereas vinyl composite tile and plastic laminate denote humility and utility. Yet, the history of design is one of innovation and change. We must be open to new forms and new typologies. We must remember that much of what we now consider to be traditional, such as land use zoning creating suburban sprawl, is actually a recent innovation. We are drawn to the new, and it often changes the way we look at things.

The designer must always question and engage the community for their feedback. What are the needs and desires of the users and the

Figure A11   St. John's Place Passive House Condos.

Source: ZH Architects

community? How does a shelter relate to its physical and cultural context? Is adherence to a tradition or departure from innovation justified? Why take one approach versus the other? What is the nature of the shelter? What is the evidence that leads to a particular solution? The designer must ask these questions to create shelter that will LAST.

Further Reading and Resources AS3:

Hall, E. (1990). *The hidden dimension* (Anchor Books a Doubleday Anchor Book, First Paperback, ed.). New York: Anchor.

Venturi, R. (1977). *Complexity and contradiction in architecture* (2nd ed.). New York, NY: The Museum of Modern Art.

Aesthetics & Water

Cory Gallo

AW1   Form and Meaning

AW1.1

Water Has No Shape. . .

rather, it conforms to the shape of its container. As an aesthetic, the physical structures that move, manage, or hold water are the objects which we most often associate with how water looks in an urban context. This holds true for almost any form of water in a city. As the container gets larger, however, the surface of water becomes more dominant and forms our perception. A small water feature is seen as a structure that holds water, whereas the ocean is seen as a vast expanse of water because we can no longer perceive the container.

Water in motion is also viewed differently than water that is static. This movement changes our perception and therefore appreciation of water. The Ira Keller Fountain, by Lawrence Halprin, is one of the greatest examples of urban water features of Modern Design. When the fountain is turned off, the pool of water is calm, reflective, quiet, still. When

Figure A12   Lawrence Halprin's Freeway Park Fountain is an abstract mountain stream.
Source: Cory Gallo

the fountain is on, however, the movement of water is exciting, thrilling, noisy, energizing. Similarly, perceptions of the ocean change depending on the size or frequency of waves crashing on the shore.

AW1.2

Water Has Meaning. . .

that has been interpreted by civilizations for millennia. It is perceived differently based on climate, its availability, and its role in the landscape. These contextual differences play into psychological connections. Water that is driven by a storm creates fear or danger. Water in abundance can be overwhelming and vast. Water that exists in isolation can be precious and cleansing. It's these various states that make water so dynamic as an aesthetic.

Cultures that have a more direct connection to water, either though abundance or scarcity, have a more profound cultural connection to it. In traditional Japanese Zen Gardens, water can be imagined and symbolized through gravel, which represents void, emptiness, and meditation. Here the use of water is representative of a mountainous island nation that intimately views the ocean as large expanse of water from above. In cultures where water is less abundant, it's often celebrated for its value, scarcity, and purity, which can represent a spiritual or heavenly connection. It also can reflect a pragmatic need to cool and humidify dry, arid climates. The Alhambra's many gardens have examples of the ways Islamic culture venerates water and celebrates its heavenly properties. Water's life-giving qualities are represented in the traditional Paradise Garden, which is central to most Islamic landscapes.

During the Renaissance, first in Italian Villas and later in French Palaces like Versailles, water was directed and even pumped to create formal

Figure A13   The Alhambra's gardens represent a spiritual connection with water.

Source: Cory Gallo

landscapes where control and mastery of water create sound, movement, and reflection. It's this heritage that has influenced most western cities' aesthetic values with water. From the Trevi Fountain in Rome to the Washington Mall, water is ordered, formalized, and structured to illustrate wealth, technology, and control. Here, that which is essential to life and has no shape of its own is put on grand display, manipulated to create order, and used solely to create an aesthetic.

AW1.3

The Form of Cities. . .

is influenced by their relationship to water. Water, along with geologic processes, shape landforms, and cities have no choice but to respond to the resulting topography. Beyond water's life-giving qualities, throughout most of human history, rivers and oceans have been essential for transportation, trade, and commerce. Even with modern transportation, 40% of the world's population still lives in coastal communities. In communities that are located on rivers and oceans, water's influence on urban form is sometimes practical, other times necessary.

A city that is directly influenced by a river or water's edge shifts, rotates, and adapts to the curves and stretches of the water. New Orleans, situated along the Mississippi River, is one such city. Here, the changes in the river's course resulted in an adaptive grid where two separate orders came together, creating dynamic variations in the road network. New York's grid, while less obvious, is also directly influenced by the water around it. The narrow north-south and long east-west block pattern was intentional to allow commerce to move efficiently across the island.

In cities built at the water's edge, the influence on form and aesthetic can be dramatic. Cities like Venice and Amsterdam illustrate cities where water is so extensive that it creates the negative or inverse form of the city. Instead of water being an object within a city framework, the city is the positive form within the framework of water. Functionally, these canals and waterways allow water to move through and around the city, but aesthetically they define the character and image of these cities.

Figure A14   Amsterdam is a city shaped by and formed by water.

Source: Cory Gallo

All cities that lie along the ocean are under new threats as sea level rise has created an existential challenge. With sea level models predicting as much as 1 meter of rise in this decade, communities like New Orleans and Venice will need to confront a world where they might not be able to exist without major adaptation. Many cities are actively engaged in mitigation or resilience planning to create opportunities for open space and recreational amenities that allow for staged sea level rise and an ever-changing future.

Further Reading and Resources AW1:

Bacon, E. N. (1974). *Design of cities*. London: Thames and Hudson.

Kostof, S. (1991). *The city shaped: Urban patterns and meanings through history*. London: Thames and Hudson.

Lane, M. (2020). *Royal gardens of the world: 21 celebrated gardens from the Alhambra to Highgrove and beyond*. London: Hachette UK.

Walker, S. (2017). *The Japanese Garden*. New York: Phaidon Press.

AW2   Water in Sustainable Urban Design

AW 2.1

The Aesthetic of Sustainable Water Management. . .

is driven by the underlying principles of green infrastructure. These principles call for management of water to mimic natural conditions. This essentially means allowing water to move through a city as if the city had never been built. In a pristine forest, up to an inch of rainfall would have been stored in tree canopies. Water that falls from tree canopies would be filtered and absorbed by layers of vegetation before reaching the ground, which would be uncompacted soil, rich in organic matter that absorbs and infiltrates water. Water that isn't absorbed or infiltrated would slowly move over land, be stored in wetlands and lakes, or find its way to small, meandering streams that would flow into larger streams and rivers. The result of this process is clean, cool, slow water with only small amounts leaving forests. Conversely, urban development creates dirty, hot, fast water with large amounts of runoff.

Water management in cities has evolved to come full circle. Early developments used open ditches or swales to move water through a site. These open swales were eventually replaced by sub-surface pipes to quickly remove water along with waste from city streets. In order to mimic natural water movement, cities need to manage water at multiple elevations, increase contact of water with plants and the ground, move water through surface conveyance systems, and store it for use later. These functions play out aesthetically in the form of visible green infrastructure that enriches the public realm.

This aesthetic has been called sustainable stormwater design, green infrastructure, Artful Rainwater Design, along with others. In each of these, the central theme is that water visibly moves through the urban landscape and is celebrated as an amenity while also being managed. Individual examples can be seen throughout the US, but the most extensive examples exist where policies have been adopted to promote green infrastructure, most notably, Portland, Seattle, Chicago, and Philadelphia. More complete urban environments can be seen in recent, large-scale developments designed with water in mind. The South Waterfront District in Portland, Oregon is one such example with bio-retention and conveyance built into the street grid, and parks designed to manage runoff.

Figure A15   A streetscape with integrated water management in Portland.

Source: Cory Gallo

Internationally, Bo01 in Malmö, Sweden exemplifies the multiple scales of water movement and management throughout the entire district. Throughout these examples the aesthetic of water is illustrated in three forms: Conveyance, Management, and Storage.

AW 2.2

Conveyance. . .

or the movement of water creates opportunities to express how water flows down a building, through a site, or across a watershed. Even when dry, these elements give visual clues as to how water moves and enriches the urban landscape. Green infrastructure solutions require much more surface conveyance because management systems are shallow and near the surface. If water is moved in a pipe, it can simply be too deep to

Figure A16   Roman aqueducts in Spain moved fresh water from miles away to city centers.

Source: Cory Gallo

access and manage in open bio-retention systems. Natural forms of conveyance include springs, gullies, streams, and rivers. Man-made forms of conveyance include downspouts, paver-swales, drain inlets, dry-swales, bio-swales, channels, and canals.

Gargoyles or carved downspouts have been used for thousands of years to give character to the movement of water off roofs. Roman aqueducts built over two thousand years ago carried fresh water to cities from miles away. In both these cases, the need to move water drove the form that was embellished through architecture. Today, the movement of water from a roof to the ground can still be an opportunity to express its movement. Collaboration between design disciplines is essential so that water from impervious roofs can be directed to areas of the site where management is possible.

The earliest forms of street conveyance were simply open ditches, which can still be seen today in rural areas. Romans designed crossings at intersections with raised steppingstones so that pedestrians could step across the rainwater and waste that flowed through streets. Cobbled swales can also be seen in medieval cities to direct rainwater to early drainage systems. Today, street curbs have replaced more elegant solutions. They create a functional but uninspiring aesthetic of water movement directed to gutters and pipes. Green streets are sustainable street designs that move water in a pipe-less street solution. These solutions can increase street maintenance, but they also provide a much richer urban environment full of plants and trees that are designed in open swales that visibly move water through the urban street network.

As water collects in greater quantities, larger conveyance systems are required. In most cities, this is accomplished with ever larger sub-surface pipes or unsightly, concrete-lined ditches. Sustainable conveyance systems attempt to design naturalized conveyance systems that provide amenities to the community. This can be executed as a large bio-swale that moves water through a neighborhood or even on larger rivers where riverine species and buffer strips protect water resources, create habitat corridors, and provide linear trails and riverfront parks.

AW2.3

Management. . .

of water describes facilities to temporarily detain or slow rainwater. These facilities are meant to offset the increase of impervious surfaces by creating concentrated areas of absorption, infiltration, and detention. When done poorly, these facilities create some of the worst aesthetics in urban landscapes. On the other hand, when done well, they create compelling and striking visual features. Examples of steep, deep holes in the earth with high barbed wire fences around them were illustrative of early engineered detention basins. Sustainable stormwater design attempts to

Figure A17   An infiltration basin incorporated into a public park in Portland.

Source: Cory Gallo

break large detention basins into small, shallow, vegetated facilities that blend into and enhance the urban landscape. Natural forms of management systems include vegetation, wetlands, and trees—all of which store and filter rainwater. Man-made forms of management include filter strips, urban forests, constructed wetlands, bio-retention facilities, and green roofs.

As more cities adopt green roofs and walls, the image of cities from above is changing to look greener and lusher (see **LF3.3** and **LF3.4**). On individual lots, bio-retention facilities or rain gardens can look like another type of garden to create form and structure to the site. They can also, however, be adapted to planters and be more structured. In parks and open spaces, formal or structured regional detention parks can be focal points for neighborhoods and communities. With careful collaboration between civil engineers and landscape architects, detention facilities can be designed to create multiple flood event levels where the largest but least frequent events can use open space that's typically reserved for active and passive recreation.

AW2.4

Storage. . .

is the collection of water that allows it to be used for some later purpose, either simply to look at or to flush toilets or irrigate landscapes. The facilities that are created to store water can create some iconic elements in the urban landscape. Forms of natural storage include ponds, lakes, and oceans. Forms of man-made storage include retention basins, ponds, and cisterns. Carefully placed, retention ponds can manage runoff while also providing a visual amenity for a community. Cisterns create opportunities for vertical points and towers in the landscape whose form relates directly to their function.

The New York skyline is filled with cisterns to hold water and increase pressure in the buildings below. Many older buildings in cities like New Orleans used cisterns to provide fresh rainwater for occupants due to the limited availability of clean drinking water. Today, cisterns can be used for a range of water needs. Their size and shape, however, has evolved into a unique aesthetic within sustainable landscapes. Much like a tower or structure, cisterns can provide a unique aesthetic aspect to urban landscapes and visually announce the attempt to collect and reuse water.

Further Reading and Resources AW2:

Dreiseitl, H., Grau, D., & Ludwig, K. H. C. (2001). *Waterscapes.* Basel: Birkhäuser.

Dreiseitl, H., & Grau, D. (Eds.). (2012). *New waterscapes: Planning, building and designing with water.* Berlin: Walter de Gruyter.

Echols, S., & Pennypacker, E. (2008). From stormwater management to artful rainwater design. *Landscape Journal, 27*(2), 268–290.

Liptan, T. W. (2017). *Sustainable stormwater management: A landscape-driven approach to planning and design.* Portland, OR: Timber Press.

SCALE **3**

Figure S1 Aerial view of Paris.

Source: Heather Schmitt

DOI: 10.4324/9781003203049-8

Scale Essentials

Sustainability clearly is not one thing to all people. Its definition is ambiguous to say the least. It is discussed as a cluster of related ambitions guiding the daily actions of individuals and small groups. Or it is the altering of design technologies typically implemented one building at a time but occasionally across an entire neighborhood. Or its the imposing of limits on the programs of a sector of the economy and the policies of discrete government bodies. It is time to correct the record. All of the types of action listed previously are useful and even necessary, but they are at the simplicity and scale of tactics, not strategies. As such, they help secure small objectives but will not win any war regardless of how the battleground is defined.

Sustainable strategies are more complex and operate at much larger scales—from addressing worldwide food production and water management, changing the carbon footprint of shelter and mobility systems both in their physical form and patterns of use, to thinking in broad categories like lifecycle, aesthetics, scale, and technology. But even sustainable strategies should not be confused as sustainability itself. Sustainability cannot be parsed into discrete problems and solved effectively one formula and one variable at a time. The choice between purchasing your groceries in recyclable paper bags or reusable plastic ones does not constitute a metaphor that suggests the whole. Instead, sustainability is a measure of the overall stability of a system. And when we talk about sustainable architecture or landscapes or communities or cities, the system under consideration is the ecology of the planet as a whole—the biosphere.

DOI: 10.4324/9781003203049-9

A practical guidebook on sustainable cities is neither the place for a scientific discussion of the biosphere nor a theoretical treatise on the ideal plan to save it.[1] But biosphere science and theory should be there, in the background, guiding strategy. To that end, the three big takeaways of the science are these: the biosphere is a very large, complexly interwoven, but ultimately finite system in which feedback effects from every action are unavoidable; human survival is dependent on the survival of an unimaginably large number of other plant and animal species; and the best way to preserve those species as well as inanimate resources is to use and impact as little of the Earth as possible. These principles are worth rereading and repeating like mantras. And as we emerge from a global pandemic, it is worth noting that the last mantra—use as little of the Earth as possible—is also key to reducing the transmission of future pathogens from animals in the wild. As our footprints spread, contact increases. And with increased contact, the chances of a repeat of COVID-19, and worse, increase.

Of the four basic human needs used to organize this book, water comes closest to representing the biosphere in microcosm. The surface of the planet can be divided into watersheds or drainage basins. Defining watersheds **SW1.1** is straightforward. The big hydrological systems essentially form one closed loop with water from most streams eventually migrating to the ocean(s), only to evaporate and precipitate as rain in the same or another watershed. Unfortunately, human development is always in a watershed or multiple watersheds, whether we acknowledge this or not, and our constructions create impairments **SW1.2** that must be remediated. Stretches of land where the water table remains at or near the surface for significant periods of each year constitute wetlands **SW1.3**. This constant source of water, in addition to other characteristics, supports a high degree of biological diversity. As a result, urban development that negatively impacts wetlands diminishes sustainability, broadly considered. Preserving existing wetlands and implementing constructed wetlands, on the contrary, reduces environmental impacts such as contaminated runoff and increased flooding due the large areas of impervious surfaces in cities.

Cities complicate natural watersheds and wetlands, as suggested earlier, by creating their own city-sheds. Sustainable approaches to water must begin at the scale of the relation between region and city. Again, however, we cannot proceed formula by formula or variable by variable. The relationship between city and region must address two distinct water systems—rainwater **SW2.1** and potable and sanitary **SW2.2**. Moreover, it must address these systems at ever-finer grains of detail. From region to city, sustainable water management design must scale to neighborhood-sheds and into individual sites, or site-sheds, and there again resolve the two fundamental systems—rainwater **SW3.1** and potable and sanitary **SW3.2**.

Mobility is analogous to water in the way its flow scales from big to small, global to local. Its patterns are similar. As with water, connectivity **SM1.1** is key to sustainable approaches to mobility. Cities exist in larger mobility-sheds and create their own city- and neighborhood-sheds that can enhance or impede the connectivity of the region. The difference between mobility systems that merely function and those that help cities LAST is the degree to which the system promotes accessibility **SM1.2**. A well-planned system that utilizes a range of types (pedestrian, cyclist, buses, rail, etc.) across multiple scales (region to city, city to neighbor-hood, etc.) will reduce the growth of urban footprints **SM1.3**. This last point connects directly to preserving the biosphere, particularly the need to use as little of the planet as possible. The flipside of this approach is the urban and regional planning status quo of maximizing the ease of travel by car. Driving lowers density **SM1.4**, spreads the population across greater area, and derails possibilities for sustainable urbanism.

It is not enough to deal with these issues at the intra-city scale. Local streets **SM2.1** are the neighborhood-sheds of mobility. Designers must approach these both functionally and aesthetically to guarantee multi-modal use (see also **AM 2**). Parking **SM2.2**, on the contrary, must be introduced judiciously and, where possible, eliminated to reduce auto dependence. The elimination of parking alone, however, is neither a suffi-cient nor wise means of reducing car use and increasing reliance on other modes of transportation. Cities can levy taxes and restrictions **SM2.3** as forms of deterrents. Designers and planners should advocate diverting funds **SM2.4** traditionally earmarked for construction of new roads, widening of existing roads, and paving of parking lots to building the infrastructure for more sustainable transit.

Motorized transit requires significant investment. Costs, both in terms of infrastructure and operation, are the most commonly cited reasons for cities providing limited public transportation or none at all. Neverthe-less, sustainability requires cities make such investment. To overcome this dilemma, it is critical to understand where, when, and at what population densities each begins to make sense. The most common, least expensive, and fastest to implement are bus and bus rapid transit (BRT) **SM3.1**. These systems are the easiest to modify over time and also work for the

SCALE

widest range of city sizes and population densities. As populations and densities increase, light rail **SM3.2** becomes viable. When both overall populations and population densities or intra-city travel reaches a critical mass, or ideally both, commuter rail and subways **SM3.3** become not only viable but necessary if the ambition is reduction of automobile dependence.

Motorized transport constitutes only a portion of the mobility options sustainable cities require. Again, it is impossible to solve for one variable in isolation and achieve stability in the whole. Motorized and non-motorized transport **SM 4** must be designed comprehensively. Here again, there are three interrelated components to address. As with buses and trains, design of walking and cycling paths begins with understanding the densities required to support each as well as the densities each will support. Density cannot be considered exclusively from the perspective of blocks or five- or ten-minute walking radii. Success of non-motorized transportation is a matter of adjacency, accessibility, and connectivity. Where, in other words, are people leaving from and going to? This question is not merely a matter of functions or needs. Its solution requires designers and planners taking into account the perceptions of the people who actually live, work, and otherwise inhabit the area (see **AM 1** and **AM 3**).

Systems of motorized and non-motorized transportation come together in response to and in support of the design of the built environment. Transit-oriented development (TOD) is **SM5.1** the synergy of these systems with a city's buildings. Its potential for both short-term and long-term success must be weighed against initial investment through careful cost analysis **SM5.2**. Once financial viability is addressed, planners and designers of sustainable cities should turn their attention to issues of service provision **SM5.3** and determining limits of minimum and maximum density **SM5.4** for the TOD to be feasible. Cost analysis, provision of services, and density range decisions made, a TOD can be realized through implementing a mixed-use and form-based code **SM5.5**.

Shelter defined by these codes can be built at varying scales. Dimension, at root, is a contest of competing needs and ambitions. On the one hand, a massive building campaign is needed to house rapidly growing urban populations and do so in buildings that decrease carbonization. On the other hand, this construction needs to occupy as a little land as possible while limiting the resources utilized in fabrication, operation, and maintenance. These contrasting concerns find resolution in five aspects of dimension. First, floor area **SS1.1** must be understood in terms both of need and environmental impact. Second, floor area–to–surface area ratio

SS1.2 places limits on form that factors into environmental performance in multiple ways both internally—such as passive heating, cooling, and day lighting—and externally in reducing heat island effects. Third, height **SS1.3** should be determined according to maximizing population density per area of ground utilized while balancing the embedded carbon required to structure and operate such buildings. Fourth, large buildings require compartmentalization **SS1.4** to operate efficiently. Fifth, settlement **SS1.5** or settlement type selection supersedes thinking about cities at the scale of individual buildings. The overall pattern of development, from the vantage of sustainability, is greater than the sum of its parts.

Shelter defined by mixed-use and form-based codes and designed to a wide range of sizes is also produced in various ways. These range in scale from hand **SS2.1** fabrication of projects custom-built via site assembly **SS2.2** to prefabrication **SS2.3** of significant portions or the whole in factories and transported to site to emerging processes of automation **SS2.4** through which human hands are removed from construction. To be clear, there is no hierarchy in these as means to sustainable construction. Each has its own environmental footprint, its own feedback in the biosphere, and impact on local and national economies that should be taken into account in the planning and design process.

The dimension and patterns of our shelters along with the construction practices listed earlier significantly alter environmental impact and energy use. Energy, however, will have to be produced no matter how efficient buildings and cities become. The most common mistake in energy planning is to begin with system selection. Sustainable energy production, however, has far less to do with system selection than understanding the value of installing power generation systems across a range of scales: from centralized generation **SS3.1** for a city, state, or region, to distributed energy **SS3.2** generation that typically operates at the scale of individual or small clusters of buildings. Regardless of generation method chosen, however, designers need to address energy storage **SS3.3** as critical to system success. Understanding strengths and weaknesses of a variety of systems across a range of scales allows for a more truly sustainable implementation of any, or a combination, of the five major energy technologies: solar, fuels cells, alternative fuels, biomass, and wind.

Incorporating or planning for the incorporation of food production is an important component of the design of sustainable cities, regardless of settlement type. A food bowl **SF1.1** is a region that typically sustains an urban area with its seasonal food. Historically, such settlements were

SCALE

close to water and native food sources that gave humans the resources to form settlements and evolve traditional agricultural practices over time. The total ecological footprint, or food print **SF1.2**, required to provide food to urban areas can be calculated and used for long-term planning, giving planners a tool to help develop land use policy to protect necessary agricultural lands and other sensitive landscapes. This can also be calculated by individuals to determine what kinds of changes they can make to lessen their impact on resources such as water and land. Taking stock of a region's ability to support urban settlements in the twenty-first century is critical as many urban areas are food deserts **SF1.3**, devoid of quality affordable fresh food. The root of this problem is not economic, however, and its solution is not improved transportation or distribution methods. The negative impacts of shipping food can be calculated in food miles **SF1.4**—that is, the distance each food item is transported from harvest to consumption. Mitigating food deserts via shipping only adds to agriculture's already substantial carbon footprint. We must change our thinking.

Our food future **SF1.5** depends on how we deal with the issues of meeting demand while avoiding deforestation, climate change, and economic disparities contributing to poverty. This looks at the "food gap" or the amount of calories we produce now compared to the amount of calories we will require to feed growing urban areas, the amount of land used now to produce those calories versus the amount of land needed to feed future residents, and the added emissions from agriculture as we produce more food on more land. Creating food zones **SF1.6** for producing goods is the first step. These should be mapped—starting at home in the city center and working outward to the peri-urban food bowl, hinterlands, and larger government entities such as a state, country, or region, and finally addressing imports—so that goods are produced according to appropriate land use in terms of infrastructure, soils, and climate as well as in relation to perishability, with lower-perishability goods sourced further from the urban core.

The need for densification requires that land use be carefully considered. The United Nations stresses the careful consideration of peri-urban farms **SF2.1** which compete for land and other resources that could be used in multiple ways to support a city's population. With this in mind, it is important to distinguish the various types of farms and gardens to make the best use of land within cities. Broadly speaking, urban agriculture is divided into two main types: urban farms **SF2.2** and community gardens **SF2.3**. The major difference is the former is intended for commerce or profit instead of personal consumption or sharing. In community gardening, by contrast, there is no commercial motive. Community gardens produce fruits and vegetables on public or private land tended by individuals or groups. Both forms of urban agriculture differ from forest gardens **SF2.4**, one of the earliest and most self-sustaining forms of food production. While most appropriate in woodlands outside the urban core, urban forest gardens may be possible under certain conditions to grow fruits and nuts, herbs, and perennial vegetables in ways that are beneficial both to the city's inhabitants and a micro-woodland ecosystem. Density in the sustainable city is not simply a matter of people per acre or square mile or kilometer. It is about putting the spaces of the city to use—from small forest gardens to agriculture in rights-of-way **SF2.5**.

Sustainability ultimately is a question of protecting the biosphere. As stated at the outset, providing water, mobility, shelter, and food while using the smallest possible amount of land and other resources is key to sustainable urbanism and the future of humanity in general. Urban agriculture can contribute to the biosphere in an additional way: by promoting diversity over monoculture practices. Biodiversity **SF3.1** of the entire agricultural ecosystem and all the components necessary to its health—including plants, animals, and micro-organisms—is the key objective. The greater the degree of biodiversity and the closer its make-up to the naturally evolved ecosystem of a given region, the lower the need for pest management **SF3.2** practices involving pesticides. This is doubly important insofar as pesticide use and lowered biodiversity form a negative feedback loop: low biodiversity leads to greater pesticide use, which lowers biodiversity. Designers and urban policy makers should utilize the concept of plant guilds **SF3.3**—species that work together effectively—to promote diversity. Understanding plant guilds is one in a larger set of design strategies and principles collectively known as permaculture **SF3.4** that should be required at the policy level but should be instituted by designers even in the absence of such policies.

Notes

1   Eminent biologist and Pulitzer Prize–winning author Edward O. Wilson has written both types of books for the general public: *Biophilia* (1984). Cambridge, MA: Harvard University Press, and *Half-earth: Our planet's fight for life* (2016). New York, NY: W.W. Norton and Company, respectively, serve as good starting points.

Scales
The Fine Print

Scales & Food

C. Taze Fulford

SF1   Food Security

SF1.1

Food Bowl. . .

is the footprint from which a community or region gets its food. As suburbs extend from the city's center, prime agricultural lands may be paved over for industry, commerce, or housing, increasing distances to import food. Australia is a world leader on examining the food bowl and the consequences of the loss of prime agricultural lands and the natural resources that sustain urban life. Efforts in cities should be made to ensure that there is a stable supply of garden-fresh foods for the constituency within 1 mile (less than 2 kilometers) in the urban condition and within 10 to 20 miles (16 to 32 km) in rural areas.

DOI: 10.4324/9781003203049-10

SF1.2

Food Print. . .

is the hidden costs incurred from planting seeds to serving meals. When you examine the true cost of having a meal, you discover many factors have been overlooked. From the water used to irrigate fields or for growing animals to the plastic or cardboard packaging, there are streams of resources being utilized by cities to provide food and drink. Not only is food waste a part of the problem, but packaging as well (see also **LS2.4** and **LS 3**). We typically don't think about the dyes that are used to print on the boxes that hold foods, the plastic wrapping, chemicals that are used to give the same taste or smell to a food for familiarity, the fuels used to transport, or the fuel and water needed to clean and cook the goods. What about the costs of farm labor, herbicides, pesticides, machinery, and the land itself? There is also the cost of runoff from farms into waterways, whether it be industrial chemicals, animal waste, or loss of topsoil. Pollution has a cost associated with it that is paid for by the consumer or taxpayer at some point.

SF1.3

SCALE

Food Desert. . .

is a geographic area that does not have adequate access to healthy foods within a small travel distance. According to the Economic Research Service of the US Department of Agriculture, "2.3 million people or 2.2 percent of all U.S. households live more than one mile away from a supermarket and do not own a car" (URBSOC). These types of settings are typically in minority or impoverished areas that have high incidences of obesity, diabetes, high blood pressure, and other ailments that can be tied to poor diet. Cost is also an issue as foods are typically more expensive at corner stores than supermarkets. Foods may appear cheaper but are smaller servings with a higher cost per ounce. Cultural foods are also part of the food desert as they are not usually carried by typical food marts. Communities may use food in these areas to plan for development.

Farmers markets **AF1.3**, Community-Supported Agriculture **AF2.1**, or other targeted programs that deal with planting, harvesting, and preparing foods can also help bring people together to promote a healthier lifestyle.

SF1.4

Food Miles. . .

is simply the distance your food or each food ingredient has traveled from the time it was grown/made until it has been served. Whether the goods were shipped by ship, train, plane, or automobile, there is associated cost with the emissions resulting from that transportation. The reduction of miles traveled is a reduction in carbon put into the atmosphere for each good transported. Organic foods may be better for you, but if your organic grapes have traveled from Chile to the US instead of being locally sourced, you have added unnecessary food mileage. To remedy this, simply find items that are locally seasonal until you can get the goods you want again. Food transported from local farms may also reduce vehicular load on road systems, eliminating the need for more lanes of traffic or wear and tear on road surfaces.

SF1.5

Food Future. . .

is looking ahead and being innovative as a society with how we look at the food supply chain. Is our food's future commodity-driven, large-scale production, or will it be smaller-scale, locally provided goods? The future of food must look at sustainability in terms of land use, water, the health of animals, and use of pesticides and herbicides, but also in the use of technology to make better decisions with remote sensing or smarter use of collected data (i.e., on farm emissions along the food chain or measuring wastewater). Food Future is about being intelligent as we plan land use and how we manage resources so that we can feed our cities in an efficient manner while providing healthy goods. Conservation policies that

SCALE

require development fees to buy and conserve prime agricultural lands equivalent to prime agricultural soils used in new projects may be one intervention that policy makers can use to ensure agricultural lands are saved. Other recommendations are for designers to identify areas located with access to water and roadways so that new resources can be limited in the process of adding new agricultural systems. The future of food will also provide opportunities for collaboration between agriculture and new partners to help with data collection and tracking progress made in the field. See also **TF 1** and **TF 3**.

SF1.6

Food Zone. . .

is the idea that food production be organized by types of production starting at the urban core and radiating out at different scales or rates of production. The concept is that more perishable foods are produced closer to where they will be consumed while less perishable goods can be grown away from the city center and delivered. Small farming of animals may take place in the city to help deal with waste, provide fertilizer, and provide a small percentage of the protein used in the community.

The food chain infrastructure is planned for in all of the zones for packaging of goods, delivery to points of commerce, and gathering resources such as waste so that it can be taken back to different zones to rebuild soils.

SCALE

Further Reading and Resources SF1:

Access to affordable and nutritious food: Measuring and understanding food deserts and their consequences. (2009). www.ers.usda.gov/webdocs/publications/42711/12716_ap036_1_.pdf?v=41055

Food desert locater map. www.ers.usda.gov/data-products/food-access-research-atlas/go-to-the-atlas.aspx

Food empowerment project. https://foodispower.org/access-health/food-deserts/

Food miles. (2017). www.foodmiles.com

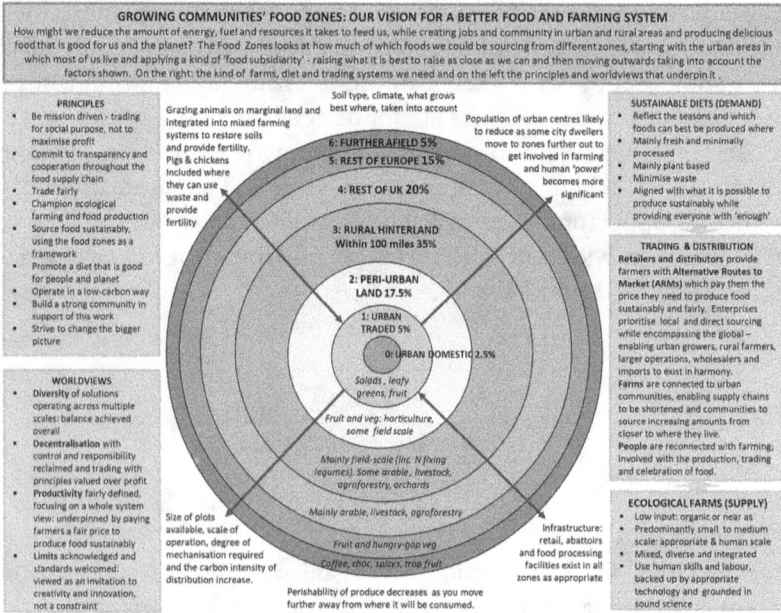

Figure S2 London-based social enterprise Growing Communities created Food Zones as a vision of how cities could feed themselves. Growing Communities aims to put the model into practice through all its activities.

Source: Julie Brown at Growing Communities

Food print. https://foodprint.org

GrowingCommunities.org. www.growingcommunities.org/food-zones

URBSOC. (2018). What is a food desert? https://rampages.us/urbsoc/category/socy327/week8-urban/

SF2 Densification

SF2.1

Peri-Urban Farms. . .

are areas of agriculture that surround our cities and communities. These areas are not considered rural or urban but reside between the two.

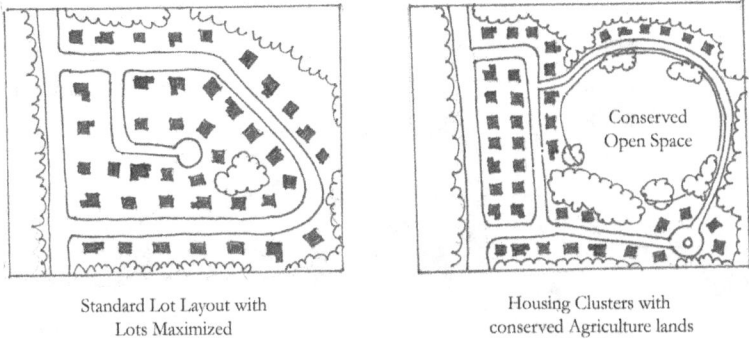

Standard Lot Layout with
Lots Maximized

Housing Clusters with
conserved Agriculture lands

Figure S3   Standard and conservation subdivisions.

Source: C. Taze Fulford III

Suburbanization is a major issue concerning these areas as sprawl—in the form of single-family detached dwellings, roadways, commercial developments, and industry—is a large consumer of prime agricultural lands. Peri-urban farms are located within this suburbanized area, resulting in a reduced cost for shipping goods to the city due to proximity while also providing value in terms of habitat and protection of natural resources. Planners should take note that peri-urban farms help reduce heat island effect in cities while providing place-based local goods, which results in jobs in the community. Conservation subdivisions are a good way for designers to leave prime agricultural soils intact while providing for housing. The typical conservation subdivision doesn't look at maximizing lots across a site but identifying areas good for housing while leaving agricultural areas open. These have a higher density of housing, leaving room for open space.

SF2.2

Urban Farms. . .

produce food within the populated area of a city or community. Unlike community gardens, these are set up as a means of commerce. The urban farm produces goods that are not primarily for personal consumption but are sold to restaurants or other entities. It is a way to produce local food while creating urban jobs. These farms may be developed on brownfields, rooftops, small lots, or even in urban parks. These farms may be owned by non-governmental organizations, private investors, or public-private collaborations. For community planners, this can be a great way to solve food desert issues, remediate soils, help reduce heat island effect, slow water in the urban environment, and begin to develop a closed loop system of food and waste.

SF2.3

Community Gardens. . .

are areas set up for community members to have space for growing food. Some plots within the gardens may be used for commerce, but most are utilized for personal consumption. The gardens are funded through members paying yearly for a plot or multiple plots to plant crops. Funds are used for overall garden upkeep, tools, and potentially water above what is harvested. Community gardens are also useful for cities in terms of providing spaces for people to meet and expand their circle of friends,

Figure S4   Community gardens—Toronto.

Source: Jason Walker

providing opportunities to be outside and exercising, and helping provide healthy fruits and vegetables to members of the community. Skill-building workshops, garden tours, and seed shops can also bring revenue to the community garden, making it more viable for the future. Eyes on the street is another benefit of the gardens for every community. With people in the garden, violence and crime can be reduced.

SF2.4

Forest Gardens. . .

are, according to Dave Jacke, "a perennial polyculture of multipurpose plants." They comprise an "edible ecosystem, consciously designed community of mutually beneficial plants and animals intended for human food production."

But these systems provide more than food. They also provide "fuel, fiber, fodder, fertilizer, 'farmaceuticals', and fun" (Edible Forest Gardens). While humans grow food in clear-cut areas that are typically

Components and Design Strategies

FOOD FOREST
a system which mimics the natural forest ecosystem with food producing species to create a self regulating, ecologically stable, food producing forest
not gardening in the forest, gardening like the forest

1. Canopy - timber, nut, fruit
2. Sub-Canopy - fruit, nut
3. Shrub Layer - fruit, nut, hardy herbs
4. Herbaceous Layer - herbs, vegetables
5. Groundcover/ Creeper Layer - herbs
6. Underground Layer - root crops
7. Vertical/ Climber Layer - fruit
8. Aquatic/ Wetland layer - herbs
9. Mycelial/ Fungal Layer - mushrooms

MIDWESTPERMACULTURE.COM

Figure S5   Components of the edible forest.

Source: Emily Hahn, Midwest Permaculture

SCALE

monocultures **SF 3** or small groupings of plant materials, if we grow our food like a forest, we have fertilizer built into the system in the form of leaves. We can plan for spaces to include habitat for insects to hunt pests in the system, and we can have a harvest of nuts, berries, and mushrooms. The forest naturally builds the soil, sequesters carbon, provides habitat, can provide outdoor spaces of beauty for recreation, and can reduce heat island effect in the city. Planners and local officials can utilize this design concept for multiple benefits to the overall community.

SF2.5

Agriculture in Rights-of-Way

Freeway or motorway rights-of-way can consume 36 acres per mile or 14.5 hectares per 1.6 kilometers, and when borrow pits, interchanges, and overpasses are added, can take up as much as 57 acres a mile (14 hectares per kilometer).

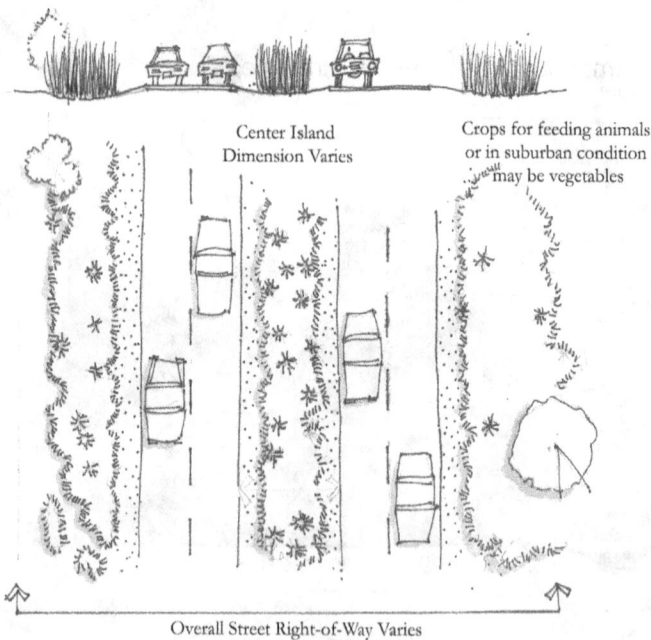

Figure S6 Roadway right-of-way and grasses.

Source: C. Taze Fulford III

This taken land has been predominately farmland or forested land and converted to non-productive use of solely transportation corridors. While food production may not be the best use of these lands, there are opportunities to plant grasses and forbs (herbaceous flowering plants) for habitat and for harvesting biomass. Plant species that will not obstruct vehicular views or are not considered as dangerous in a transportation corridor should be selected.

There is a debate on whether or not food crops, such as corn, should be used in the production of biomass for fuels. As more prime agricultural lands are developed for housing, commercial, and industrial endeavors, and more prime and secondary agricultural lands will be needed to feed a growing population, we must look to other areas to help supply crops for fuels. In terms of sustainability, these rights-of-way not only can help offset fossil fuel usage but can produce forage for animals in the agricultural pipeline, create biodiversity, and help to clean runoff from road surfaces (see also **LW2.3**).

Further Reading and Resources SF2:

Centers for Disease Control and Prevention. (2010). www.cdc.gov/healthyplaces/healthtopics/healthyfood/community.htm

Jacke, D. (2005). *Edible forest gardens, Volume One*, White River Junction, VT: Chelsea Green Publishing, 46–50.

EIP-AGRI: Agriculture & innovation. https://ec.europa.eu/eip/agriculture/en/tags/urban-agriculture

Foley, J. (2017). *Native species for biomass production and roadside habitat in South Dakota*. https://openprairie.sdstate.edu/cgi/viewcontent.cgi?article=2668&context=etd

Greensgrow: Growers of food, flowers, & neighborhoods. www.greensgrow.org

Local Government Commission: Cultivating Community Gardens. www.lgc.org/resource/community-gardens/

Pendleton, W. C., & Vlasin, R. D. (1961). The impact of interstate highways in rural areas. https://docs.lib.purdue.edu/cgi/viewcontent.cgi?referer=www.google.com/&httpsredir=1&article=3057&context=roadschool

Urban Gardening. (2017). www.edu-urban-gardening.eu

SCALE

SF3 Monoculture Versus Diversity

SF3.1

Biodiversity. . .

in agriculture specifically deals with the strength of ecosystems, species, and genetic diversity to provide a resilient system for our food. The system includes more than simply the crops or animals that are harvested but all the organisms that are needed to sustain the system. "Associated biodiversity" is composed of micro-organisms in the soil, pollinators, and wild relatives of domesticated animals, each of which contribute to the agricultural system. While monocultures are the standard way of growing crops in the western world, they are susceptible to attacks by insects or disease which can quickly overtake a system that isn't designed to fight back. Biodiversity means having organisms in place to attack pests, diverse species of plants to help resist being overwhelmed by disease, and integrating the surrounding systems into the agricultural system for redundancy.

SF3.2

Pest Management. . .

may be considered as flora or fauna in agricultural systems. These pests damage crops in the field and must be controlled to prevent loss of product. The Food and Agriculture Organization (FAO) estimates that every year between 20 and 40% of all crops in the developed world (40–50% in the developing world) are lost to pests, with plant diseases costing the global economy US$220 billion (182.5 billion euros), while invasive insects cost around US$70 billion (58 billion euros) in damage. Integrated pest management is the use of multiple pathways to fight pests in the system. Some of these can be utilizing pest/disease-resistant varieties of a species in the system, biological control or control by natural predator or parasite, netting to prevent birds or insects, or targeted chemical controls such as baited boxes or spot spraying. Biodiversity will help prevent population explosion of pest insects and will help slow disease or fungal outbreaks in the system.

SF3.3

Plant Guilds. . .

are a grouping of plant materials (and may include animals) that are mutually beneficial to each other.

These in turn support humans by providing food, medicine, and fibers, or food and shelter to animals in the system. It is a biodiverse, small-scale approach to planting that mimics how nature works. While similar to *companion planting*, which is only concerned with food production, plant guilds provide much more in terms of product. These are like food forests and should include a canopy, an understory, and an herbaceous layer, each adding to biodiversity in the system.

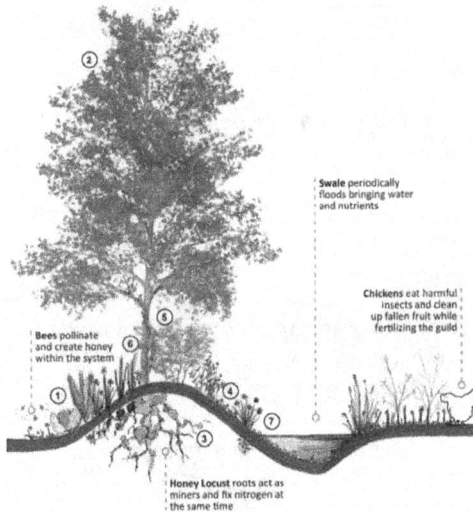

Components and Design Strategies

GUILD
a grouping of plants, animals and insects working together to ensure the survival of the whole system

COMPONENTS OF A GUILD
1. Food for Us
fruits, vegetables, staples, legumes, nuts, fats and animals

2. Food for the Soil
nutrients, nitrogen (legumes), organic matter

3. Diggers and Miners
reach into the soil to pull up minerals (trees, root crops, ants, termites, worms, beetles, mice)

4. Groundcover
plants that keep the soil from drying out and prevent weeds taking over

5. Climbers
maximize vertical space (beans, passion fruit, cucumbers)

6. Supporters
provide a structure for the climbers (trees, shrubs, stalks, houses, walls, fences)

7. Protectors
strong smelling plants to deter insects (onions, chives, spices, lemon grass, pungent flowers) habitat for natural predators such as frogs, birds, and beneficial insects, living fences of thorny and sharp plants

Swale periodically floods bringing water and nutrients

Chickens eat harmful insects and clean up fallen fruit while fertilizing the guild

Bees pollinate and create honey within the system

Honey Locust roots act as miners and fix nitrogen at the same time

MIDWESTPERMACULTURE.COM

Figure S7   Components of plant guilds.

Source: Emily Hahn, Midwest Permaculture

SF3.4

Permaculture. . .

is based on whole-system thinking. Designers utilizing the concept of permaculture are trying to build a system to supply all the needs of the person or group of people living off of the land. The result of an inventory and analysis of the land (or observe and interact) can give rise to a resilient landscape through place-based design. Permaculture is design-intensive, forcing the designer to look at their surroundings and watch how nature works. Diversity is used throughout the system to build redundancy, aggregate and not segregate systems, store energy and water, and eliminate waste. The final design should have the ability to self-regulate and allow the user to become part of the system as a collaborator, not a dominator. Some successful examples of this way of design and living are Findhorn Ecovillage in Scotland, Earth Haven Ecovillage in North Carolina, and Miku Valley Permaculture in Ontario.

Further Reading and Resources SF3:

Bioversity International and (CIAT) International Center for Tropical Agriculture. https://ciat.cgiar.org

Dara, S. K. (2019). The new integrated pest management paradigm for the modern age. *Journal of Integrated Pest Management, 10*(1), 12.

The Food and Agriculture Organization's. The state of the World's Biodiversity for Food and Agriculture. www.fao.org/state-of-biodiversity-for-food-agriculture/en/

Jacke, D. (2005). *Edible forest gardens, Volume One,* White River Junction, VT: Chelsea Green Publishing, 149.

Mollison, B. (1991). *An introduction to permaculture.* Tasmania, Australia: Tagari.

Permaculture association. www.permaculture.org.uk

Permaculture design principles. https://permacultureprinciples.com/principles/

The state of biodiversity in Africa: A mid-term review of progress towards the AICHI biodiversity targets. (2020). https://www.unep.org/pt-br/node/1452

The state of biodiversity in Asia and the Pacific: A mid-term review of progress towards the AICHI biodiversity targets. (2020). https://www.cbd.int/gbo/gbo4/outlook-asiapacific-en.pdf

USDA: National Institute of Food and Agriculture. https://nifa.usda.gov/blog/global-scientists-meet-integrated-pest-management-idea-sharing

Scales & Mobility

Joan Blanton

SM1   Patterns

SM1.1

Connectivity. . .

is a measure of the ease with which one can travel from point A to point B within an urban area. Most often used when describing communication within a network of computers, it has been taken up in the area of urban sustainability to describe the ease or difficulty of traversing the network of walkways, roads, or transit system, within an urban area.

Connectivity is about the structure of the street network. These main streets are almost always connected to each other, thus forming the main streets network. In computing the connectivity of the local streets, one counts the least number of corners a person has to cross to reach the main streets network.

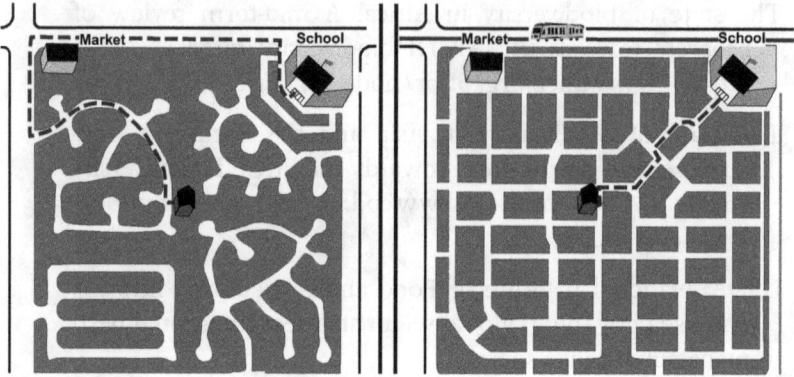

Figure S8   Connectivity available from grid-like road patterns.

Source: Lehigh Valley Planning Commission

SM1.2

Accessibility. . .

is a concern with proximity, i.e., people's ability to reach goods, services, and activities. Accessibility can be evaluated from various perspectives, including a particular group, mode, location, or activity. Factors to be considered include mobility (physical movement), the quality and afford-ability of options, system connectivity, mobility substitutes, and land use patterns.

Increasing accessibility requires shifting the goals of urban planning from favoring automobiles to enacting policies of strategies that locate housing services and activities near one another and enable environ-mentally sustainable modes of transit such as public transit, walking, or biking. Such policies are already a part of the principal policy goals of urban development in many countries, including Sweden, in which the city of Malmö even brands itself as "a city with short distances—an accessible city."

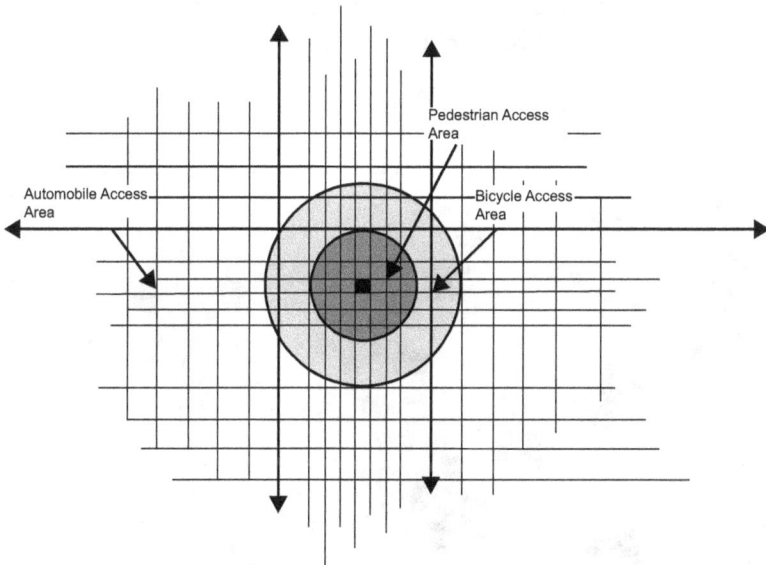

Figure S9   Relative distances from a point available to a pedestrian, bicyclist, and driver.

Source: Todd Alexander Litman

SM1.3

Urban Footprints. . .

is a measurement of the physical extent of a city used in the analysis of its degree of impact on the environment. It can also be used to analyze the spatial distribution of people and services within a city. Generally, a city with a larger footprint and lower density is less efficient and puts more stress on the environment. In Figure S10, it can be seen that the cities of the United States have a much larger footprint for a smaller population than do other world cities.

SM1.4

Driving Lowers Density

Density in the field of transportation is measured by dividing the number of people in a certain area by the square miles or kilometers of that area.

SCALE

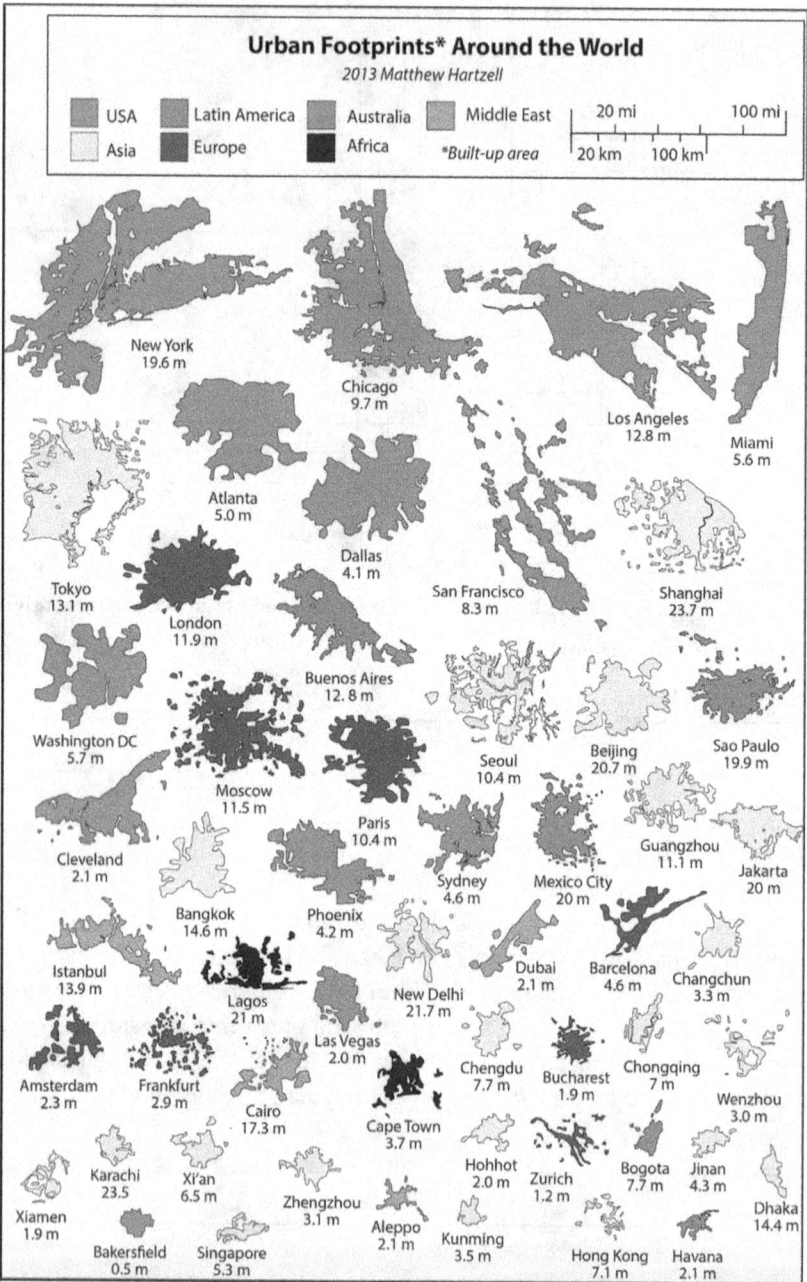

Urban Footprints* Around the World
2013 Matthew Hartzell

USA   Latin America   Australia   Middle East
Asia   Europe   Africa   *Built-up area

20 mi   100 mi
20 km   100 km

New York
19.6 m

Chicago
9.7 m

Los Angeles
12.8 m

Miami
5.6 m

Atlanta
5.0 m

Dallas
4.1 m

Tokyo
13.1 m

London
11.9 m

San Francisco
8.3 m

Shanghai
23.7 m

Buenos Aires
12.8 m

Washington DC
5.7 m

Moscow
11.5 m

Seoul
10.4 m

Beijing
20.7 m

Sao Paulo
19.9 m

Cleveland
2.1 m

Paris
10.4 m

Sydney
4.6 m

Mexico City
20 m

Guangzhou
11.1 m

Jakarta
20 m

Bangkok
14.6 m

Phoenix
4.2 m

Istanbul
13.9 m

Lagos
21 m

New Delhi
21.7 m

Dubai
2.1 m

Barcelona
4.6 m

Changchun
3.3 m

Amsterdam
2.3 m

Frankfurt
2.9 m

Las Vegas
2.0 m

Cairo
17.3 m

Chengdu
7.7 m

Bucharest
1.9 m

Chongqing
7 m

Wenzhou
3.0 m

Karachi
23.5

Xi'an
6.5 m

Zhengzhou
3.1 m

Cape Town
3.7 m

Hohhot
2.0 m

Zurich
1.2 m

Bogota
7.7 m

Jinan
4.3 m

Xiamen
1.9 m

Bakersfield
0.5 m

Singapore
5.3 m

Aleppo
2.1 m

Kunming
3.5 m

Hong Kong
7.1 m

Havana
2.1 m

Dhaka
14.4 m

Figure S10   Urban footprints (or land coverage) of cities around the world, in order of population.

Source: Todd Alexander Litman

In the lower density of suburban areas, Vehicle Miles Traveled (VMT) is significantly higher than in denser city centers. This has been shown to be true even in places with minimal transit service. Along with density, the design of street systems for cars rather than public transit and the dispersion of land uses, e.g., small neighborhood shopping hubs, increases the VMT because of the distances between houses and daily destinations. The increase in VMT is accompanied by an increase in carbon emissions.

Further Reading and Resources SM1:

Comparing urban footprints. (2013). https://geographyeducation. org/articles/comparing-urban-footprints/

Connectivity. (2016). https://medium.com/corridor-urbanism/ connectivity-comes-first-96658b8342ab

Density. (2015). https://grist.org/cities/how-much-does-density- really-cut-down-on-driving/

Esch, T., Heldens, W., Hirner, A., Keil, M., Marconcini, M., Roth, A., Zeidler, J., Dech, S., & Strano, E. (2017). *Breaking new ground in mapping human settlements from space—The global urban footprint.* Cambridge, MA: German Aerospace Center (DLR), German Remote Sensing Data Center (DFD), Massachusetts Institute of Technology (MIT).

Measuring Urban Footprint. (2019). https://medium. com/urbandataanalytics/measuring-urban-footprint-to- understand-city-behavior-42d45384442c

Sola, A., Vilhelmson, B., & Larsson, A. (2018). Understanding sustainable accessibility in urban planning: Themes of consensus, themes of tension. *Journal of Transport Geography, 70,* 1–10.

Transportation Research Board and National Research Council. (2009). *Driving and the built environment: The effects of compact development on motorized travel, energy use, and Co2 emissions* (Special report 298). Washington, DC: National Academies Press.

Victoria Transport Policy. (2021). http://vtpi.org/access.pdf

SM2   Streets and Parking

SM2.1

Streets

Many researchers contend that the sustainability of urban areas can be enhanced simply by changing street design. Most existing roadways were developed with emphasis on vehicle mobility, safety, and minimizing costs. Little attention was given to social aspects or environmental impacts. In most US cities, street rights-of-way comprise 40% of land use. Improving the sustainability of streets would therefore result in large-scale positive impacts on the environment.

Excellent guidelines and examples of street design, both interim and permanent solutions, that would contribute to the sustainability of cities can be found in the National Association of City Transportation Officials' (NACTO) *Urban Streets Design Guide* (see resources later). One such interim solution is "Moving the Curb" (see Figure S11). There

Figure S11   Possible intersection improvements to increase pedestrian safety.

Source: Global Street Design Guide, by NACTO. Copyright © 2016 National Association of City Transportation Officials. Reproduced by permission of Island Press, Washington, DC.

is also a *Global Street Design Guide* (https://globaldesigningcities.org/publication/global-street-design-guide/) that offers new approaches for designing streets for pedestrians, public transit, and cars. These approaches honor the concept that streets are public spaces as well as routes for movement.

SM2.2

Parking

The vast number of automobiles (as of 2018, **838** vehicles per 1,000 in population in the United States (see Figure S12 for comparison to European Union countries)) creates a vast demand for parking, but where and how that parking is provided can affect sustainability and the environment. The attention given to parking is reflected in an article on

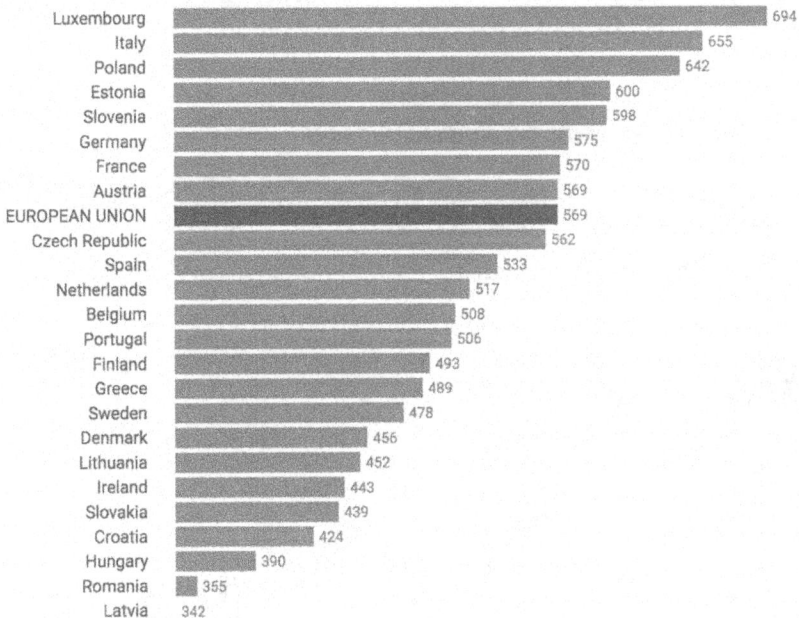

Country	Value
Luxembourg	694
Italy	655
Poland	642
Estonia	600
Slovenia	598
Germany	575
France	570
Austria	569
EUROPEAN UNION	569
Czech Republic	562
Spain	533
Netherlands	517
Belgium	508
Portugal	506
Finland	493
Greece	489
Sweden	478
Denmark	456
Lithuania	452
Ireland	443
Slovakia	439
Croatia	424
Hungary	390
Romania	355
Latvia	342

Figure S12   European Union passenger car, commercial vehicle, and bus counts. Luxembourg has the highest car density in the EU (694 per 1,000 people), and Latvia the lowest (342).

Source: ACEA, www.acea.be/statistics/tag/category/vehicles-per-capita-bycountry/

FastCompany's website entitled "How Much Space U.S. Cities Waste on Parking" as follows:

- Seattle, Washington: 1.6 million parking spaces—more than 5 per household
- Des Moines, Iowa: 1.6 million parking spaces, or 19.4 per household.
- Jackson, Wyoming: 27.1 parking spots per household.

Recent research has found a strong correlation between the amount of available parking and the percentage of commuters that use automobiles (McCahill, et al., 2015). Cheap, excessive parking was also related to increasing traffic congestion, higher rents, and other collective costs of over-reliance on cars for mobility.

Reigning parking expert, planner Dan Shoup, states that urban planners typically set the minimum parking requirements for every land use to satisfy the peak demand for free parking. As a result, parking is free for 99% of automobile trips in the United States. Urban planners typically set minimum parking requirements to meet the peak demand for parking at each land use, without considering either the price motorists pay for parking or the cost of providing the required parking spaces. Shoup gives policy recommendations to reduce the space relegated to parking and increase the quality of design of parking areas. These include:

- Remove off-street parking requirements from city policies,
- Charge the right prices for on-street parking,
- Spend the parking revenue to improve public services on the metered streets.

SM2.3

Taxes and Restrictions

When cities want or need to decrease the volume of traffic or limit the amount of sprawl or dispersion of development, or they want to increase housing affordability, one of the tools available to them is placing taxes and restrictions on parking. These types of taxes increase the cost of commuting and therefore increase the attraction of living closer to the core or commuting by public transit or both. They include 'per-space parking levies,' which apply to parking facilities, 'commercial parking taxes' on parking rental transactions, and 'congestion charges,' which are daily fees for entering the city or specific zones within the city. This approach to decreasing traffic volume has been enacted in several large cities, such as London and Toronto, to some success. Smaller cities, however, may do well to attempt a change in parking and zoning regulations first.

SM2.4

Diverting Funds. . .

is a method of Tax Increment Financing (TIF) which is used as a subsidy for redevelopment or infrastructure improvements in blighted areas of cities and where public and private financing is insufficient to complete a project. Typically, expected future tax revenues are diverted, or reallocated, into funding improvements. Most planners and architects don't have a lot of influence on tax policies but should look for chances to increase the awareness of the possibilities when working with elected officials and other stakeholders.

Further Reading and Resources SM2:

The Atlantic. (2012). www.theatlantic.com/international/archive/2012/08/its-official-western-europeans-have-more-cars-per-person-than-americans/261108/

Bevan, T. A., Sklenar, O., McKenzie, J. A., & Derry, W. E. (2007). Sustainable urban street design and assessment. 3rd Urban Street Symposium, June 24–27, 2007, Seattle, WA.

Bloomberg. (2016). Parking provision and car commuting in 9 U.S. cities, 1960–2000. The cities included were Albany, Arlington (Virginia), Berkeley, Cambridge, Hartford, Lowell, New Haven, Silver Spring, and Somerville. www.bloomberg.com/news/articles/2016-01-12/study-the-strongest-evidence-yet-that-abudant-parking-causes-more-driving.

FastCompany. www.fastcompany.com/90202222/heres-how-much-space-u-s-cities-waste-on-parking. Author: Adele Peters on FastCompany website. Downloaded July 31, 2020.

SCALE

Litman, T. (2013). *Parking taxes: Evaluating options and impacts.* Victoria, BC: Victoria Transport Policy Institute.

McCahill, C. T., Garrick, N., Atkinson-Palombo, C., & Polinski, A. (2015). Effects of parking provision on automobile use in cities: Inferring causality. *Transportation Research Record: Journal of the Transportation Research Board, 2543*(1), 159–165.

National Association of City Transportation Officials (NACTO), Urban Streets Design Guide. https://nacto.org/publication/urban-street-design-guide/

Rubinstein, R. (2016). *Urban Redevelopment Authority of Pittsburgh parking tax diversion guidelines.* Pittsburgh, PA: Urban Redevelopment Authority of Pittsburgh.

Scharnhorst, E. (2018). *Quantified parking: Comprehensive parking inventories for five major U.S. cities.* Research Institute for Housing America Special Report. Washington, DC: Mortgage Bankers Association.

Shoup, D. (2011). *The high cost of free parking.* New York, NY: Routledge.

Shoup, D. (2018). *Parking and the city.* New York, NY: Routledge.

Street Design Guide. https://globaldesigningcities.org/publication/global-street-design-guide/designing-streets-for-great-cities/key-design-principles/

Vehicles Per Capita. (2017). www.energy.gov/eere/vehicles/fact-962-january-30-2017-vehicles-capita-other-regions-countries-compared-united-states

SM3 Motorized Transit

In analyzing an existing or proposed public transit option, the first measurement to obtain or calculate is the number of people per square mile or kilometer of the target area. This measure of density will assist in determining which mode of transit is suitable and where the routes should be placed.

SM3.1

Buses and BRT

Bus rapid transit (BRT) is a bus-based system that is larger than a basic bus service and typically is conducted along dedicated street lanes. It is a much lower-priced system that imitates the high-capacity, high-performance characteristics of urban rail systems. Curitiba, Brazil is acknowledged for pioneering BRT, with segregated rights-of-way, rapid and frequent service, and high customer service. It takes at least a population density of 5,000 per square mile (1,930/square kilometer) to warrant basic frequent bus service and a much larger population, perhaps 10,000/mile (3,860/km), for a BRT.

Figure S13   Bus rapid transit system of Jakarta.

Source: Creative Commons https://creativecommons.org/licenses/by-sa/4.0/legalcode

---

SM3.2

Light Rail Transit (LRT) . . .

combines tram (a rail vehicle that runs on tramway tracks along public urban streets) and metro, or rapid transit, features. It often operates on

Figure S14 One of the light rail cars of the Metro Transit of Minneapolis, Minnesota.

Source: Metro Transit, Minneapolis/St. Paul

its own right-of-way. Research shows that large areas with densities from 10,000 to 19,000 people per square mile (3,860 to 7,336/square kilometer) are needed to sustain LRT.

SM3.3

Commuter Rail and Subways

Commuter rail is a transport service that primarily delivers suburban passengers to downtown locations. They are usually considered 'heavy rail' and are powered generally by electricity or diesel engines. It is not a term used for rapid transit or light rail. Subway is a term for underground rapid transit rail systems. The population and employment density to make these systems sustainable is approximately 30,000 per square mile (11,600 per square kilometer). Heavy rail and subway systems are more than four times as expensive to build as LRT and require relatively stable populations along their service corridors as their routes cannot be altered to follow shifting densities. If there are sufficient numbers of riders, however, commuter rail and subways are less expensive to run.

Further Reading and Resources SM3:

Brock, T. J., & Souleyrette, R. R. (2013). *An overview of U.S. commuter rail.* University of Kentucky, Kentucky Transportation Center Research Report, 316. https://uknowledge.uky.edu/ktc_researchreports/316

SCALE

Cervero, R. (2013). Bus Rapid Transit (BRT): An efficient and competitive mode of public transport. Working Paper, No. 2013–01, University of California, Institute of Urban and Regional Development (IURD), Berkeley, CA.

Dueker, K., & Bianco, M. J. (1999). *Light rail transit impacts in Portland: The first ten years*. Portland, OR: Portland State University.

Light Rail and Street Cars. www.wsp.com/en-GL/sectors/light-rail-and-streetcars

Spieler, C. (2018). *Trains, buses, people: An opinionated atlas of US transit*. Washington, DC: Island Press.

SM4   Non-Motorized Transport

Non-motorized transportation (NMT) or 'human-powered' transportation includes walking, bicycling, small-wheeled transport (cycle rickshaws, skates, skateboards, push scooters, and hand carts), and wheelchair travel. The efficiency and sustainability of these forms of transportation often depends on the attention given to providing available paths, ADA, or other disability accessibility enforcement, and building a culture in which these forms are respected and encouraged. See also **AM 2**.

How a community sees and values the availability of walkability, biking, and other NMT forms will determine the success or failure of such efforts. A cost-benefit analysis done on the local level would yield insight into a community's existing situation and could be the basis of a public education program. Figure S15 shows the benefits and costs of NMT.

	Possible Benefits	Possible Costs
Increased NMT Options	Improved Health	Infrastructure Costs
	Increased Accessibility	Equipment Costs
	Reduced Traffic	Car Speed Reduced
	Energy Conservation	Increased Travel Times
	Increased Community Cohesion	Increased Development Costs

Figure S15   Examples of a cost-benefit analysis for non-motorized transport.

Source: Blanton Design

SM5   Transit-Oriented Development (TOD)

SM5.1

Transit-Oriented Development (TOD) . . .

is a mixed-use area that is densely populated and walkable with integrated transit stations always in close proximity. Mixed use includes commercial, residential, office, and entertainment establishments.

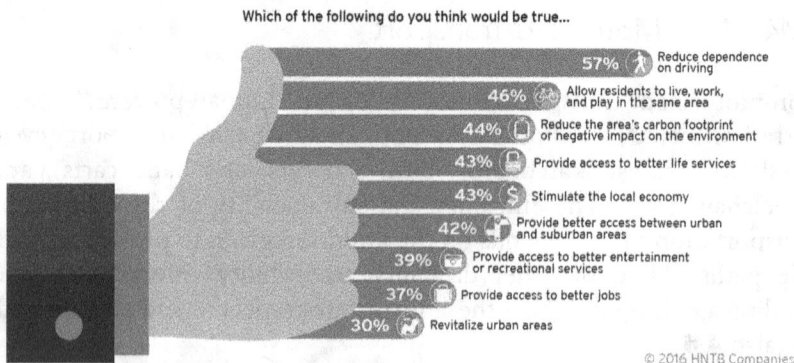

BENEFITS OF TRANSIT ORIENTED DEVELOPMENT
Americans believe transit oriented development provides an array of benefits ranging from lifestyle to environmental to economic.

Which of the following do you think would be true...

57% — Reduce dependence on driving
46% — Allow residents to live, work, and play in the same area
44% — Reduce the area's carbon footprint or negative impact on the environment
43% — Provide access to better life services
43% — Stimulate the local economy
42% — Provide better access between urban and suburban areas
39% — Provide access to better entertainment or recreational services
37% — Provide access to better jobs
30% — Revitalize urban areas

© 2016 HNTB Companies

Figure S16   The benefits of Transit-Oriented Development.
Source: HTNB

SM5.2

Cost Analysis

Analyzing the cost of constructing Transit-Oriented Development areas involves measurements of land value, construction costs, resulting housing costs, and savings in transportation costs for those residing in a TOD and for the city or regulating agency. Recent research has shown that although housing costs are higher in TODs, these costs are more than offset by savings in transportation costs.

SM5.3

Service Provision

Creating a high-density area of mixed uses and accessibility to transit decreases the carbon footprint and the cost of governmental services. TOD walkability is usually achieved through reduced parking area **SM2.2** and the design of smaller block sizes, with a maximum of 3 acres dedicated to residential uses, up to 7 acres for blocks with commuter rail, subway, or LRT stations.

SM5.4

Density. . .

is a measure of humans, housing units, or some other measure per physical space such as square feet, meter, mile, kilometer, or acre (see **SM3.1 SM3.2 SM3.3**). The key to density in TOD is that enough potential users live within a five-to-ten-minute walk to a transit connection. From design and policy perspectives, this density is achieved through increases in floor area ratio (FAR) so that buildings occupy less ground area while providing more square feet or square meters (and thus more people) in a given distance from transit.

SM5.5

Mixed Use and Form-Based Code

Mixed use requires that building and zoning codes allow for residential, retail, recreational, and other uses to be contingent and overlap. Form-based code is a way of designating allowable land uses that stresses the physical form of buildings and streets over function to produce a more 'livable place.' Attention is paid to the mix of uses rather than their separation.

SCALE

Further Reading and Resources SM5:

Cervero, R., Ferrell, C., & Murphy, S. (2002). Transit-oriented development and joint development in the United State: A literature review. TCRP research results digest. http://onlinepubs.trb.org/onlinepubs/tcrp/tcrp_rrd_52.pdf

Cervero, R., Murphy, S., Ferrell, C., Goguts, N., Tsai, Y-H., Arrington, G. B., Boroski, J., Smith-Heimer, J., Golem, R., Peninger, P., Nakajima, E., Chui, E., Dunphy, R., Myers, M., McKay, S., & Witenstein, N. (2004). *TCRP REPORT 102: Transit-oriented development in the United States: Experiences, challenges, and prospects*. Washington, DC: Federal Transit Administration.

Charter for the New Urbanism. (1999). www.cnu.org/who-we-are/charter-new-urbanism downloaded April 15, 2018.

Dillmar, H., & Ohland, G. (2012). *The new transit town: Best practices in transit oriented development*. Washington, DC: Island Press.

Duany, A., Speck, J., & Lydon, M. (2009). *Smart growth manual*. New York: McGraw Hill Education.

Rennea, J. L., Tolfordb, T., Hamidic, S., & Ewing, R. (2016). The cost and affordability paradox of transit-oriented development: A comparison of housing and transportation costs across transit-oriented development, hybrid and transit-adjacent development station typologies. *Housing Policy Debate, 26*(4–5), 819–834.

Suzuki, H., Murakami, J., Hong, Y.-H., & Tamayose, B. (2015). *Financing transit-oriented development with land values: Adapting land value capture in developing countries* (Urban Development Series). Washington, DC: World Bank.

Scales & Shelter

Caleb Crawford

Even as this is being written, debates on issues of scale are shifting. Climate and infectious disease emergencies create competing narratives. Compactness and minimal space are questioned by the need for physical distancing. Those things that are good for energy efficiency and lower embodied carbon may be problematic for the spread of infectious diseases. Tightly packed offices and densely packed public transit may be conducive to the spread of disease.

The other issue of scale in question is the immensity of addressing the climate emergency. The entire building products industry needs to be retooled, and products redesigned. Building trades need to be trained to produce low-energy buildings. In addition to new buildings, tens of millions of shelters worldwide will require a deep energy retrofit over the next ten years. In economics, cost is related to the scale of production. Generally, the larger the scale, the lower the cost per unit. We have a significant challenge to scale up the design and construction of high-performance buildings to achieve these goals.

Dimension, means of production, and source of energy are the three areas affecting sustainable shelter and scale. Dimension affects the embodied carbon and the operating energy use of a shelter. The means of production is how we build, from the oldest and most basic (the scale of the hand) to factory construction and automation. Finally, we will examine scale as it relates to energy production—how we make the energy needed to build and operate our shelters.

SS1 Dimension

Scale is frequently referenced when looking at the dimensions of one kind of shelter compared to another, say an office tower compared to a single-family house or a convenience store relative to a supermarket. We are comparing dimensions: floor area, volume, height, number of stories, exterior surface area, and the number of occupants. Dimensions affect the quantity and quality of materials and equipment, which affects the embodied carbon and can affect the operating energy.

SS1.1

Area. . .

is the most common measurement for dwellings mostly because ceiling heights tend to be within a consistent range. Area per person or area per dwelling unit varies immensely worldwide, from rural to urban, from

SCALE

developing to developed nations. The poorest have on average 10 m² per capita in both developing and developed nations, though typically lower in developing. In most developed nations, the average range is 30–50 m² per occupant, with the most spacious in the US and Canada at over 70 m²/occupant, and in Australia, where it is 89 m²/occupant. In the US, the median size of a new single-family house was 2386 ft² (222 m²) in 2010. There are similar trends in retail, though commercial office space has seen declining floor area per occupant globally.

Floor area should be kept low. Square footage correlates directly to increased embodied carbon and energy use during construction and operation. There are new trends in urban areas for smaller units, micro apartments, and tiny houses, where floor areas max out at 38 m² (400 ft²). Units in new multiple dwellings are typically less than half the size of single-family homes—100 m² (1081 ft²) in the US.

SS1.2

Floor Area–to–Surface Area Ratio

The envelope is the point of interaction between the exterior environment and the interior of a shelter. The exterior envelope is the point of greatest heat loss or gain. It is also a costly assembly, both in terms of dollars and the environmental costs of materials.

If floor area is a standard measure for usable space, we can consider different ways of configuring that floor area. In a typical new, two-story, American single-family house, there is a floor area to surface area of about 1:2. The same floor area, configured as a four-story row house, reduces the ratio to less than 1:1. If we look at the floor area being the footprint of a twelve-story multifamily building, the ratio remains at 1:1 if a tower, but reduces to 1:0.38 if it is on an infill site between similar buildings. Heat loss or gain in a building is a factor of surface area, thermal conductance, and change in temperature. If we reduce one of those variables by a factor of almost six, there is a great deal of energy to be saved. When the size of the dwelling unit is then halved, as is the case for the average multifamily apartment compared to a single-family home, the energy savings is in the order of twelve times.

There is a material efficiency to be had when we build denser and larger. Long, low, narrow structures versus tall, wide structures further

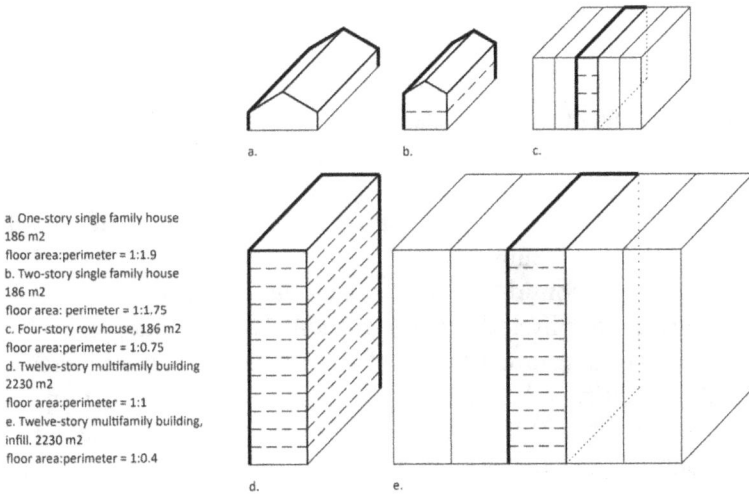

a. One-story single family house
186 m2
floor area:perimeter = 1:1.9
b. Two-story single family house
186 m2
floor area: perimeter = 1:1.75
c. Four-story row house, 186 m2
floor area:perimeter = 1:0.75
d. Twelve-story multifamily building
2230 m2
floor area:perimeter = 1:1
e. Twelve-story multifamily building,
infill. 2230 m2
floor area:perimeter = 1:0.4

Figure S17   Floor area–to–surface area ratios.

Source: Caleb Crawford

confound the ratio. Form factor is another condition. Long, narrow rect-angular shelters will have higher surface-to-volume ratios than those close to being squares. Additional surface area results in additional materials. All materials have embodied energy, which currently means embodied carbon (see **LS2.1**). That said, there are other conditions to consider, like access to daylight and solar gain, which may make a shallower floorplate more desirable for a given site.

SS1.3

Height. . .

can be considered in terms of the raw dimension and in terms of the number of stories in a shelter. Height affects aesthetics but also affects interior cli-mate. Higher ceilings are common strategies in hot humid climates to induce air movement through natural convection. Conversely, in cool tem-perate to cold climates, low compact forms serve to reduce the volume to be heated and to reduce the overall surface area. With the increased use of climate control in all climates, however, the traditional forms that work with natural forces are not necessarily as pertinent as they once were.

SCALE

There is a worn shibboleth that tall, dense cities are inherently more efficient than sprawl. While this is generally true, we must examine the impacts of height and how high to build. Stacking and clustering dwellings have distinct advantages as noted earlier. A four-story row house of the same floor area as a one-story free-standing shelter requires one fourth of the roof area and one fourth of the foundation size, with less wall area. Stacked and clustered spaces also insulate each other. But there are compromises to stacking. Use of stairs becomes increasingly difficult with height and is considered impracticable above six stories. Greater use of stairs promotes physical activity in addition to a reduction of energy used for elevators. Above a height of six stories, it becomes increasingly difficult to identify individuals on the ground, which is a compromise to community. Energy use increases with height. Buildings less than six stories consume half the energy of buildings greater than twenty stories. Above a height of six stories, municipal water supply must be augmented with pumps, pressure tanks, or water towers. Elevator use increases with height, increasing energy use.

At four stories, the building roof area available for renewable energy, photovoltaic panels specifically, reaches the minimum needed to provide electricity for all building energy needs. Depending on the distance between buildings, solar access is reduced or eliminated if taller buildings shade a roof. The distance between buildings in dense urban cores is generally between 60 to 150 feet (18 to 46 meters). Once shelters rise above six stories on a narrow street, access to daylight is significantly reduced on lower floors. The largest cost of height is with embodied carbon. As shelters grow taller, loads increase on the structure, requiring more material than a shorter structure. Shelters more than ten stories generally require significantly more structure. The floor area for vertical circulation increases in area, with a corresponding loss of usable floor area.

SS1.4

Compartmentalization

Larger buildings must be broken down into smaller areas with air sealing between them. This reduces problems that occur in large buildings by reducing the scale to manageable divisions. Compartmentation should occur at the scale of a dwelling unit or a tenant space, and each floor level should be sealed. The benefits are better control over ventilation and temperature, noise reduction, and hygiene issues such as pests and disease transmission. Tall buildings have problems with the stack effect. Unwanted stack effect results in increased air exchange and heat loss through air infiltration (see **TS2.1**), temperature discomfort due to draft, and increased introduction of outdoor pollutants. This is the result of many shafts penetrating from level to level. Air pressure on the building skin increases with height. By isolating floors through careful air sealing—essentially creating a stack of individual buildings—the stack effect pressure is reduced. This is taken further with tall multifamily residential shelters, where each unit must be separated from the adjacent units and the common hallways.

Compartmentalization in this manner requires a rethinking of building services, particularly heating, cooling, and ventilation. Tall buildings historically use central heating and cooling plants (boilers and chillers in cellars, cooling towers on roofs, and equipment rooms at floor level intervals of twenty to thirty stories feeding up and down and building height air supply and exhaust). The stack effect on these buildings is huge. Contemporary solutions see floors treated individually, with heating and cooling equipment, and sometimes more than one equipment room located on each floor.

SS1.5

SCALE

Settlement. . .

is the relationship between shelters in a landscape, the distance between them, the size of those shelters, and the use of individual shelters. What is the 'Goldilocks density' for shelter deployment in an urban area? This city is too spread out. This city is too dense. But this city is just right! It has to be dense enough to make for walkability and bikeability, and easy access to public transit (see **SM 5**) and goods and services. But it shouldn't be so dense as to increase the energy use intensity and embodied carbon. How and what we build determines how we get around. Whether densely urban, suburban, rural, or somewhere in between, every city breaks down into individual neighborhoods, from dwellings to commercial districts, transit hubs, offices, and manufacturing areas. Clustering within easy transit time (on foot or animal) was the origin of cities. When determining where and how big to build, clustered settlement is a priority. Clustering reduces mechanized transport and increases social interaction. Clusters require a diversity of uses: residences, work spaces, cultural, retail, government, educational, and recreational.

SS2   Means of Production

The scale of building shelter varies widely, from a rural shelter built by hand from local materials to entire cities accumulated across vast expanses of time and incorporating a wide variety of technologies. Contemporary construction is a complex orchestration of specialists from many fields, both professionals and workforce. Scale ranges from bespoke to mass production. For the most part, the building industry has not standardized in the same manner as the auto industry, but that is changing. We could refer to prefabrication in the building industry as 'mass customization.'

In any technology when the demand for a product and the cost of production meet, widespread deployment is possible. We call this coming to scale.

SS2.1

Hand

Hannah Arendt describes humans not as homo sapiens but as *homo faber*, man the maker. The hand is, and will remain, the fundamental scale of making. In much of the world, this isn't a choice. Construction systems like mud brick, dry-laid stone, and thatch are still employed. In factory production of buildings, the human is still the critical component of assembly and installation. Even with prefabrication, we will continue to customize and personalize our environments.

SS2.2

Site Assembly

Prefabrication and standardization have been a feature of construction for thousands of years. Contemporary building materials and components (dimensional lumber, concrete masonry units, windows, faucets, air conditioners, etc.) are produced in factories, and there is standardization in the systems of assembly. Site construction involves the assembly of a structure from individual components on the building site. Prefabricated elements such as concrete block, steel or wood columns and beams, windows, and pipes, are cut to size and assembled in place. The drawback is waste, typically about 15% of the materials on a project, and most of this waste doesn't get recovered.

SS2.3

Prefabrication. . .

is a process whereby materials and assemblies are fabricated off-site, under controlled conditions. Construction can be broken down into site constructed and modular.

The benefits of scale and consistent quality of factory production has long been with us. In the early modern period, most building materials (bricks, wood beams, decorative trim, ironwork, etc.) and assemblies (windows, doors, cabinetry, etc.) were standardized and made in specialized factories. The use of prefabrication can reduce costs, increase quality, and reduce the environmental impact of construction. Assembly of components in climate-controlled conditions, with better ergonomic working environments, is better for worker health. Prefabrication can result in less material waste—feed materials can be properly sized, and offcuts can be captured and recycled. Prefabrication can improve the quality, resulting in tighter envelopes.

There are three kinds of prefabrication: materials and components, panelized modular and assemblies, and unit modular. Prefabrication of whole buildings is usually referred to as modular construction. Prefabrication can be of components (windows, cabinets, air conditioners, light fixtures) and have been part of construction for centuries. In recent years, this has extended to rooms such as bathrooms and kitchens. Prefabrication of wall and floor assemblies is known as panelized modular construction. Prefabrication of 3D structural modules—entire rooms, floor, walls, ceiling—is known as stacked modular. Both panelized and stacked modular construction are becoming more common.

SCALE

SS2.4

Automation

The next evolution in prefab is robotic site and factory construction, which is already happening with the manufacture of components. This will allow more rapid construction, high levels of precision, 24-hour-a-day/7-day-per-week work. Eventually this will deploy to the construction site as well. We are already seeing experimental large-scale 3D printing and robotic brick laying. Of course, automation leads to a problem—what do we do with 9 billion people if we eliminate one of the largest employment sectors in the world economy?

SS3 Energy

Operating energy for shelter accounts for approximately one third of worldwide carbon emissions, and when energy for making shelters (materials, assemblies, transportation, etc.) is included (the embodied carbon) energy consumption for the building sector is over half. For energy to be sustainable, it must be renewable, non-polluting, and resilient, and not cause environmental degradation. Fossil fuels are convenient because they pack a high energy density into a small space. However, they don't meet any of the criteria for sustainable energy. Currently electricity is emerging as the dominant energy medium for the future. It already powers most of our lives and has a robust infrastructure. There are two basic kinds of electrical energy generation: centralized and distributed.

SS3.1

Centralized Generation. . .

is the traditional form of power generation that serves a regional grid. Large cities with many tall buildings, such as New York City and Hong Kong, are largely reliant upon centralized generation. This is due to the buildings' lack of surface area relative to their energy consumption to generate sufficient energy on site. Fossil fuel–burning power plants are being replaced by renewable sources. The most common form of centralized renewable energy is hydro followed by wind, both onshore and offshore. Emerging sources are wave, tidal, and geothermal energy for electricity generation. Most centralized renewable sources are inherently distributed—a wind farm is a collection of individual turbines, solar farms a large aggregation of individual panels. Nuclear fission is carbon-free electrical production, but its fuel, uranium, is non-renewable; the disposal of nuclear waste has yet to be safely resolved. Many biofuels don't meet the sustainability criteria because of the environmental degradation associated with their production. Even renewable energy installations are not free of environmental damage. Land-based wind installations require access roads and high-voltage electrical cables to transport the energy. Foundations are required for turbine towers or photovoltaic supports, and all these things can be damaging to untold hectares of wilderness or farmland.

SS3.2

Distributed Energy. . .

is located close to the loads (shelters) that they serve. The two scales are on-site and district generation. On-site energy is generated at the level of the individual shelter. District generation serves a collection of shelters. In terms of strategy for design, a shelter must generate the greatest possible amount of renewable energy on site. Centralized power generation has far more negative impacts than distributed generation because of the amount of infrastructure required. Most distributed electrical systems are connected to the electrical grid to deal with intermittency of generation and to distribute excess production. Because of the density of shelters in urban areas, it is unlikely that urban areas can generate all their energy needs within their borders. Renewable energy for urban areas must come from both distributed and centralized sources.

Photovoltaic panels are the most common distributed electrical generation, with small wind turbines and an even smaller amount of

SCALE

micro-hydro in rural areas. The roof is the most effective location for installation since it ensures the highest annual output for the panels and the least site disturbance. Panels can be mounted vertically on building faces, but typically this lowers the output by at least one third, depending on the area shading. Solar hot water is still popular in regions with little risk of freezing and abundant sunshine, such as the Middle East, North Africa, and parts of Europe and Asia along the Mediterranean. Solar hot water has the advantage of being technically simple and low cost.

SS3.3

Energy Storage. . .

is coupled with energy generation for load equalization due to the intermittent character of most renewable energy sources (the sun doesn't always shine, and the wind doesn't always blow). Intermittency is at odds with the relatively predictable character of energy demand—loads increase as people wake and go to work, then decreases at bedtime. At the distributed scale, storage is generally achieved with chemical batteries, such as lead acid and lithium ion. At grid scale, the solutions are mostly kinetic, like pumping water up and releasing it to power turbines (this is the most common and works much like hydro power), lifting weights, or spinning flywheels.

Further Reading and Resources SS3:

Bergdoll, B., & Christensen, P. (2008). *Home delivery: Fabricating the modern dwelling*. New York: Museum of Modern Art.

C40 cities. www.c40.org/

Owen, D. (2010). *Green metropolis: Why living smaller, living closer, and driving less are keys to sustainability*. New York: Riverhead Books.

SCALE

Scales & Water

Cory Gallo

SW1   Watersheds

SW1.1

Defining Watersheds. . .

is a simple process. The concept of a watershed, however, is not readily understood by the general public. The simplest definition is the area of land that drains to a specified point. The key term here is "specified point." If the point is the mouth of the Mississippi River, then its watershed is the largest in North America, comprising 1 million square miles (2.59 million sq. km) of land that drains into the Gulf of Mexico. On the other hand, if the specified point is the bottom of a children's slide, then the watershed is simply the upper part of the slide that drains onto the ground below. Even a small site can have several watersheds. These are typically defined to manage flow into a basin or swale. These watersheds have practical applications for sizing detention structures and drainage systems in site design.

   In the US, the Environmental Protection Agency (EPA) defines a watershed as "the land that drains to one stream, lake or river" (EPA). For their purposes in the protection of waterways, each specified point relates to a specific waterway. Official US watersheds were defined by the US Geologic Survey. These Hydrologic Units are defined in up to six levels of detail. Level 1 watersheds are defined by Hydrologic Unit Codes with two digits and are thus called HUC 2 watersheds. A HUC 2 might cover one or more states and be associated with a major river or waterbody. Level 6 or HUC 12 watersheds are the smallest officially designated watersheds and might cover several towns and be associated with a small stream or waterbody. Each of these levels allow the EPA and other government agencies to assess and regulate watershed health. Understanding what watershed(s) a city sits within is vital to understanding threats to the water quality of the region.

SCALE

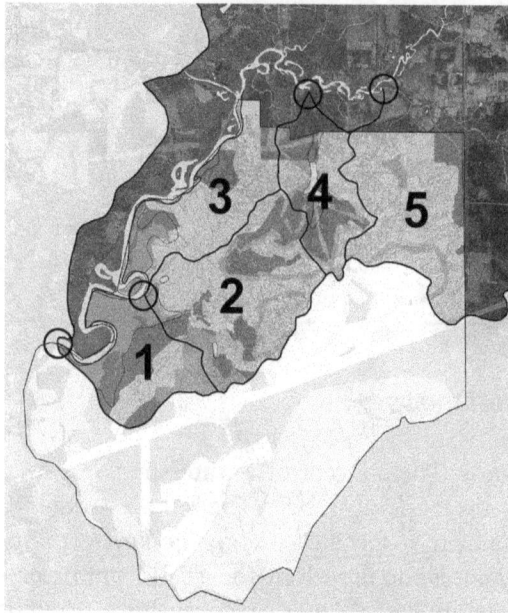

Figure S18   Diagram illustrating the overlap of political boundaries and watershed
boundaries.

Source: Cory Gallo

SW1.2

Impairments. . .

in watersheds are typically tracked by environmental agencies. For
instance, in the US the Environmental Protection Agency, empowered
by the Clean Water Act, assists states in identifying polluted waterways
and creating plans to restore them. Each state is then responsible for identifying Total Maximum Daily Loads or TMDLs for each water. TMDLs
define the maximum level of a pollutant allowed in a waterway. Based
on impairments, states and municipalities can create plans for improving
watershed health through various programs and regulations.

Humans create various forms of pollutants that can be isolated to three
primary sources: urban development, agriculture, and industry. Agriculture, especially industrialized agriculture, can produce vast amounts of
sediment, nutrient, chemical, and bacterial pollutants. Excess nutrient
runoff is a major watershed concern as increase nutrient loads lead to

eutrophication and major loss of aquatic life. Industry can also create a range of pollutants including chemicals and hydrocarbons, most of which can be regulated at a factory or pipe. Leaks and overflows, however, can cause major environmental damage. Focusing on urban development, pollutants can come from a variety of sources:

- Increased flows generated from rainwater moving across smooth impervious surfaces and in pipes are considered a type of pollutant because of the impact they have on streams and waterways. Increased flows create Urban Stream Syndrome, where streams become narrower and deeper, and lose biologic function.
- Increased water temperatures from water coming in contact with hot, impervious surfaces impact aquatic life and reduce water's ability to hold dissolved oxygen.
- Sediment most often originates at construction sites or is a byproduct of downcutting of streams from increased runoff. Sediment increases turbidity, which raises water temperature and decreases oxygen, negatively impacting aquatic life.
- Trash from various sources ends up in waterways, adding plastics and other consumer waste to natural environments downstream.
- Hydrocarbons are commonly generated from asphalt and by car leaks of oil or gasoline. They create toxins and carcinogens harmful to many forms of life.
- Heavy metals, including iron, copper, and magnesium, typically wear off brake pads but might also oxidize from metal roofs and surfaces.
- Nutrients originate from fertilizers on lawns, playfields, and golf courses. Most of these sources can be reduced through proper management.
- Bacteria, specifically fecal chloroform, is a product of pet waste. In urban areas that still have combined sewers, however, increased flows to treatment plants might create an overflow event and release non-treated human waste directly into the watershed.

SCALE

SW1.3

Wetlands. . .

are critical landscapes in watersheds for water quality, water retention, and habitat protection. Because of their immense value, they are

Figure S19   Wetland creation as a natural and recreational resource on a large scale in Harbin, China.

Source: Cory Gallo

typically protected by environmental agencies. Interestingly, a landscape does not have to be wet year-round to classify as a wetland. They are typically identified by the soil type and plant communities in the landscape. Both coastal and inland wetlands are critical to ecosystems, carbon sequestering, and nutrient cycles. They support the creation of organisms that are the bottom of the food chain which supports insects, amphibians, shellfish, fish, birds, and mammals.

Any form of impact to an aquatic system or waterway should be avoided at all costs. Unavoidable impacts will typically require some form of mitigation. This is often accomplished through wetland land banks, which are restored, improved, or created wetlands that provide compensation for the impairment. The use of banks, however, can be a difficult compromise. Questions of overall impact, location within the watershed, and total value to ecosystems can be difficult to quantify. While not always possible, mitigation to a watershed best serves the impairment by making improvements to the same watershed.

Further Reading and Resources SW1:

Environmental Protection Agency (EPA). Healthy watersheds protection. https://www.epa.gov/hwp/basic-information-and-answers-frequent-questions

Juhola, S. (2018). Planning for a green city: The Green Factor tool. *Urban Forestry & Urban Greening, 34,* 254–258.

USDA Natural Resources Conservation Service. (2007). *Watersheds, hydrologic units, hydrologic unit codes, watershed approach, and rapid watershed assessments.* Washington, DC: Author.

SW 2   City-Sheds

SW2.1

Rainwater. . .

management at the scale of the city requires an understanding that a city is not separate from a watershed but an integral part of it. Most cities lie in more than one watershed because they're often built on ridges or higher lands that drain in multiple directions. Each waterway may have individual impairments that impact how development or mitigation or both might occur. Even a mid-sized city can add over 100 acres/200 hectares of impervious surfaces in a single year through new buildings, parking lots, and other development. Additionally, landscapes replaced with turf are not much better at managing rainwater.

Conceptually, from a city-shed perspective, a sustainable rainwater management approach would:

- Preserve riparian stream corridors as natural drainage systems that manage flows, create detention, and provide habitat networks.
- Provide flood protection in multi-functional regional or shared open spaces that are allowed to safely flood during the largest storm events.
- Manage rainwater as close to the source as possible, which means each site would include green infrastructure solutions to mimic native or pre-human settlement conditions.

Beyond direct management, regional development and density of a city have a direct impact on watershed health. Density and concentrating development in isolated areas may degrade one watershed, but it will help to preserve other watersheds from development. Research indicates that as little as 5% of impervious land cover can degrade streams and watersheds. From this perspective, a dense city that creates nearly 100% impervious cover in one watershed is much more sustainable than a sprawling suburban city

SCALE

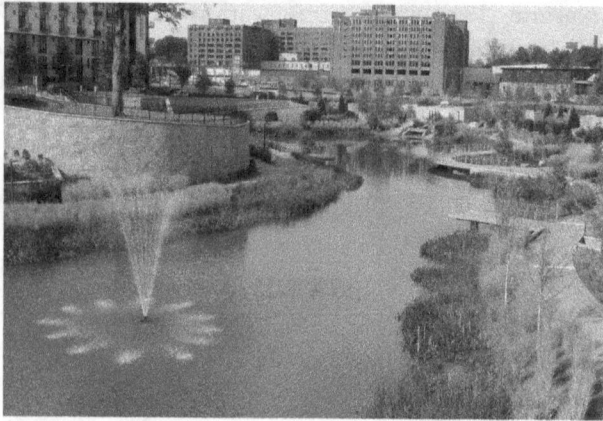

Figure S20   Regional detention park designed to mitigate up to the five-hundred-year event in Atlanta, Georgia.

Source: Cory Gallo

that creates 30% impervious cover over a dozen watersheds. The ideal sustainable approach to development and water management would be to concentrate development, utilize green infrastructure to manage development to mimic native or pre-human settlement conditions, and preserve as many watersheds as possible to a pristine condition.

Effective sustainable management of watersheds from urban development is difficult because of the scale and history of cities. Most cities were built to move water away as fast as possible and are difficult to retrofit once built. Codes and ordinances, however, can help to improve watershed health over time if they are designed to:

- Manage all new impervious surfaces' water quality and quantity to native or pre-human settlement conditions.
- Manage all redeveloped sites to manage all impervious surfaces' water quality and quantity to native or pre-human settlement conditions.
- Require the use of naturalized and open drainage systems wherever possible to mimic natural flows.
- Require the use of green infrastructure facilities that maximize infiltration and retention of rainwater to mimic native or pre-human settlement runoff rates.

Because green infrastructure has multiple benefits including water management, habitat creation, energy savings, and economic value,

Figure S21   The natural state of a site should always be the goal for stormwater mitigation.

Source: Cory Gallo

some cities have created unique codes to encompass all these benefits into a single metric. With variations adopted in Berlin, Seattle, and Helsinki, a green factor code is based on a ratio or percentage system where the total area of the project is defined by a factor of '1' and the combination of each green infrastructure technology counts toward that total in varying degrees depending on its impact. With this system, developers are given maximum flexibility to implement a range of technologies within a simple formula. This approach also reflects a need to simplify the sizing and design of complex systems to increase creativity and maximize implementation.

SCALE

SW2.2

Potable and Sanitary. . .

water systems, like cities, should be thought of as part of the overall hydrologic cycle. As with rainwater, there are inputs and outputs to city water use. Potable water is water that has been treated or accessed from a source that is safe for human consumption. Cities access potable water from various sources depending on availability—such as rivers, lakes, aquifers, and oceans. Each source has potential implications on watersheds in the larger region. All these sources need inputs from rainfall, which means that global warming and climate change are a major concern for future access to potable water.

- Aquifers are generally the preferred water source because water quality is typically quite high. Aquifers, however, may not be a renewable water source if extraction exceeds the rate at which they replenish. Development in the recharge area, which might be over a large area, can reduce infiltration. Additionally, leaks from deep fracking wells pose threats to aquifers as the drilling process can contaminate drinking water with hazardous chemicals, heavy metals, and hydrocarbons.
- Lakes can be a stable water source if the watershed feeding it is properly managed. New York City's water supply comes from lakes that capture water from a watershed 125 miles (201 km) away from the city. Heavy restrictions on development and industry are required to ensure the watershed and the city's primary water source are kept clean.
- Rivers are a common source of potable water since many cities are located along rivers for transportation. Typically, river sources require treatment to ensure water quality before distribution. Drought, pollution, and competing demands all threaten water availability. A city's needs can conflict with protection of habitat that requires a minimum flow level or agriculture which needs vast amounts of water for crop production.
- Oceans are becoming a source of potable water due to population increases, threats on other potential sources, climate change, and development in arid climates. Desalination, however, requires large amounts of energy, which, depending on the energy source, can make the process both economically and environmentally unsustainable.

Graywater is a form of output, but it can also be an input. Any water used in cities that isn't flushed down a toilet is typically considered graywater. This water does not require the same level of treatment as blackwater. Additionally, treating blackwater to a graywater level that's not fit for human consumption but is appropriate for irrigation and other non-human sources requires much less treatment and energy. Therefore, cities, most often in arid climates, have begun to use this water in a separate distribution system. Called Purple Pipe systems due to the purple pipes that distribute the water, cities that have invested in the technology can require the use of recycled graywater for irrigation instead of precious potable water. In this way, water is recycled multiple times through the city, and demands on natural water systems are greatly reduced.

Treatment for sanitary systems is commonly accomplished through energy-intensive physical, chemical, and biological processes in wastewater treatment facilities. These facilities require energy, inputs of chemicals, and constant management. A more sustainable approach that is viable in certain conditions is to use constructed wetlands to treat wastewater. While land-intensive, the process uses less energy and creates valuable habitat and recreational resources.

Further Reading and Resources SW2:

Knight, R. L. (1997). Wildlife habitat and public use benefits of treatment wetlands. *Water Science and Technology, 35(5)*, 35–43.

SW 3   Site-Sheds

SW3.1

Rainwater. . .

management at the site or building level is perhaps the most well known and visible representation of sustainable water management. Protection of the overall watershed depends on every site managing its own runoff, and it's the cumulative management of thousands of individual sites that determine the overall health of a watershed. Green infrastructure strategies on a site level utilize technologies to manage and convey rainwater at multiple levels. When designing on-site systems, water should be considered in flow or management paths, where water that lands on each unique surface is managed and conveyed in the best way possible to mimic native or pre-human settlement runoff rates. Conceptually, the best management approach would manage every impervious surface on that surface or as close as possible. Through each step, options need to be considered based on technological, economical, and physical limitations. Ideally, these steps would consider collection area, conveyance path, storage potential, management technology, and disposal (off-site conveyance) path.

To use this approach on an example site that has a building and a landscape area, a path and management approach should be developed for each zone or sub-watershed. Using hydrologic models, runoff from each area could be calculated in terms of pre-development, development without mitigation, and development with mitigation to ensure that flow rates are mimicking pre-developed conditions. In the example, if rain fell on the building a designer might ask the following series of questions to develop a management approach:

- Is a green roof possible? The answer might depend on cost, value of additional benefits of green roofs, load-bearing ability of the roof, and access for maintenance.
- How is the water conveyed down from the roof? Many larger buildings use internal drainage pipes that push water below grade, making it difficult to access for management in the landscape. Directing water to where it can be managed is a key component to sustainable management.

Figure S22   Rainwater harvesting as visual amenity and street art in Seattle, Washington.

Source: Cory Gallo

- Is there the need and/or potential to store rainwater for site or building use? Irrigation demand, cost of water, cost of cistern, available land area, distribution complexity, elevation change, and building function might all influence the decision to store rainwater.
- Where and how is the water managed on the site? If a green roof is implemented, the management requirement would change. The answer would depend on land availability, soil condition, rainfall characteristics, distance from building, topography, and disposal location.
- Where should water be directed as it leaves the site? Depending on location, this might be to a city storm sewer, swale, drainage way, river, lake, or ocean. Each of these might have unique limitations. However, elevation or grade change from the management location will be most limiting factor.

SW3.2

Potable and Sanitary. . .

water systems for buildings and sites most often rely on municipal systems for management of inputs and outputs. Sustainable regional or city-wide strategies have a distinct advantage over site-level strategies because they isolate management and have the potential to impact many more users. There are, however, numerous strategies for reducing, reusing, and recycling water within a building and site. The USGBC's LEED rating system provides guidance and incentives for implementing the three strategies. A more progressive concept is defined by the Living Building Challenge, which proposes that buildings use only water available through the site's water budget or water that falls on the site as precipitation. This regenerative approach requires collection and storage of rainwater, treatment for various uses, collection from primary uses, and more treatment to attempt to recycle water within an almost-closed system.

Reduction strategies can drastically reduce water demand and can be mandated by building codes and laws. The most common strategies include low-flow fixtures in buildings and efficient landscape irrigation systems. More progressive reduction strategies include composting toilets and xeriscape landscape design. Reuse strategies, or strategies that use one output for another use, require some kind of storage cistern (see also

SCALE

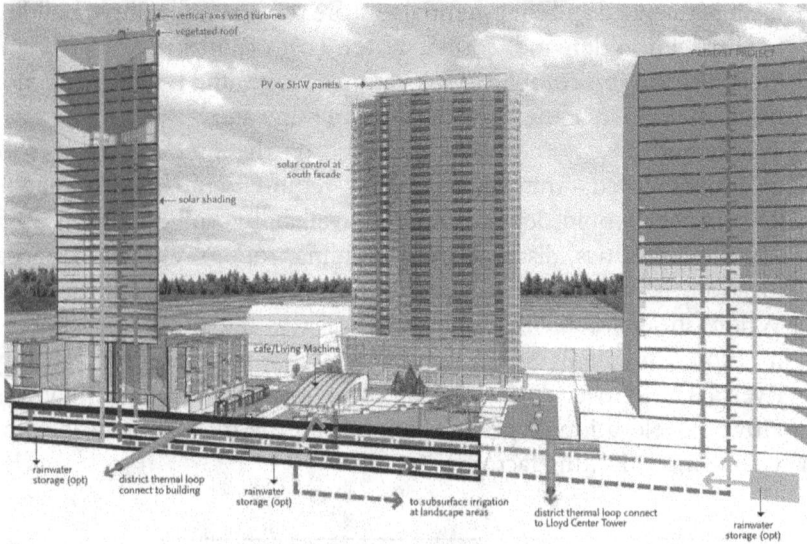

Figure S23   Diagram illustrating the collection and reuse potential of water at the scale of the neighborhood.

Source: Design and image credit: Mithun

AW2.4). The most common approaches collect rainwater for landscape irrigation, fire suppression, and flushing toilets. Comparatively, systems that store rainwater need much larger cisterns than those that collect graywater because rain is not a constant input and the cistern needs to hold enough water to last until the next rain event.

Recycling strategies or approaches that collect water, filter it, and recycle it for the same or similar use require a cistern and filtration system. Graywater harvesting systems collect water from sinks and showers, filter it, and redistribute it for toilet flushing or irrigation. Buildings that collect water from sinks to be used later in toilets require twice the amount of plumbing as a traditional building to move two lines of inputs (potable and graywater) and two lines of outputs (graywater and blackwater) to each lavatory. More advanced ecological sewage treatment systems, such as the living machine, can be implemented at small scales to treat graywater and blackwater to levels appropriate for reuse in toilet flushing or irrigation. These systems act like small-scale wetland treatment systems that use mechanical and biological systems to sustainably treat wastewater.

Further Reading and Resources SW3:

Living Building Challenge 3.1. (2017). *Early Project Guidebook.* International Living Future Institute. https://living-future. org/wp-content/uploads/2017/05/LBC_3.1_Guidance_ Handbook.pdf

Wise, S. (2008). Green infrastructure rising. *Planning,* 74(8), 14–19.

SCALE

TECHNOLOGY 4

Figure T1 Prague Astronomical Clock.

Source: Anne Graveur

DOI: 10.4324/9781003203049-11

Technology Essentials

Treatises on sustainable urbanism, and sustainability in general, often begin where this one ends: the so-called green technologies. For us, the authors of this book, this reversal of convention is not a choice rooted in novelty or the desire to place emphasis on the technologies of sustainability by drawing our argument to a close with them. For us, the order of the terms laid out in these pages parallels importance. Technology comes last, and matters least, in making cities LAST. That is not to suggest that it doesn't matter. It is to state clearly that the myriad available technologies often touted as earth- or environment-friendly by 'green' manufacturers merit consideration only where issues of lifecycle, aesthetics, and scale have been addressed. The addition of such technologies has the effect of enhancing performance in places already made sustainable by careful planning—sometimes to a remarkable degree. To apply the same technologies, however, to poorly designed streets, neighborhoods, and cities in hopes that the result will be sustainable is to fall prey to incremental and compartmentalized, and ultimately self-defeating, thinking. To borrow McDonough and Braungart's oft-quoted phrase: "Being less bad is not being good; it's being bad by definition, just less so."[1] In most cases, relying on technological solutions without getting the other stuff right is worse than being less bad; it squanders resources in a futile attempt to make unsustainable patterns, practices, and things last.

Assuming issues of lifecycle, aesthetics, and scale have been addressed, what then? While most essays and chapters on sustainable technologies privilege those directly related to buildings or transportation, ours begins

DOI: 10.4324/9781003203049-12

with the first and arguably most fundamental to civilization: the cultivation of food. Feeding urban populations while using as little land as
possible is of paramount importance to protecting the biosphere from
us and us from pandemics. Technologically speaking, systems of inventory and analysis are a crucial first step. Four categories of such technologies are particularly important for policy makers and designers to note:
geolocation of resources **TF1.1**, mapping plant type **TF1.2**, crop/plant
analytics **TF1.3**, and post-harvest evaluation **TF1.4**.

It is easy to oversimplify our thinking about food. Food is natural and
organic and best harvested by traditional analog technologies. Agriculture is artificial, chemical, and digital. Such ideas immediately come
to mind when we think of farming, and yet this oversimplification
diminishes our attention to best practices. Modern food production is a
hybrid of the organic and the man-made. These can be thought of as two
forms of nature or two technologies. And either way, farming should be
approached with both analog and digital tools and processes.

Minimizing the footprint of farming, and urban farming in particular,
requires methodologies that not only protect the soil from chemical fertilizer degradation but actually serve to replenish the soil. Understanding
biodynamic farming **TF2.1** is a first step. This entails awareness of natural processes such as the cycles of seasonal production **TF2.2** as well
as the interplay of sun, water, and nutrients **TF2.3**. It requires learning
about pests and biologically based pest management **TF2.4**. Finally, it
demands renewed appreciation for soil under your fingernails **TF2.5**.

The digital and infrastructural aspects of farming are expanding
rapidly. While planners and designers should remain open to advances
and new ideas, the following technologies form a good preliminary list
for inclusion in twenty-first-century sustainable cities: drones **TF3.1**;
Farmbot **TF3.2** or CNC-based robotic farming; harvesters **TF3.3**; the
autonomous farm **TF3.4**; and container farms **TF3.5**.

In order to minimize the footprint of cities, it is necessary to not only
consider architecture as potential armature for food production but to
begin mandating it in certain situations. This will require integrated landscape architecture and building architecture **TF4.1** heretofore unprecedented in the contemporary categorization and separation of professional
duties. This will allow integrated biodynamic systems in support of
building-integrated agriculture **TF4.2**. As urban populations expand,
buildings will grow taller on average. It is therefore useful for planners
and designers to become familiar with the possibilities and limitations
of vertical farming **TF4.3**. And while incorporating such integrated

approaches in new buildings during the design phase is easier, it is important to evaluate existing building stocks as well. In many instances, retrofitted buildings for agriculture **TF4.4** offer social, environmental, and financial benefits that new construction seldom can. Through policy and incentive programs, cities can merge organic and inorganic infrastructure into living machines **TF4.5**. Numerous examples of integrated approaches to sustainable urban food production exist. An overview of five such projects are included in the Fine Print for reference: Environmental Laboratory for Sustainability and Ecological Education (ELSEE) **TF5.1**; O'Hare Rotunda Building—Aeroponic Garden **TF5.2**; Iron Ox **TF5.3**; the Community of Findhorn **TF5.4**; and Serenbe Farms **TF5.5**.

It is now profitable to return to the first principles of shelter with an expanded vision of the role of architecture and its relationship to the environment in mind. To affect the type of change required, everything about the process of how buildings get built needs to be rethought. This begins with the need to fully understand the environment **TS1.1**. Even armed with this knowledge, it is still daunting to determine how the environment will interact with various building forms and how construction technologies will perform over time as the environment changes. It is necessary to model **TS1.2** proposals early. Affecting change also requires coming to grips with the optimum size of the buildings that make up the city—a process called right-sizing **TS1.3**. All of these efforts are aided by developing strong lines of communication **TS1.4** between parties of the design team from the beginning of a project. Such integrated project delivery increasingly relies on building information modeling and artificial intelligence. Design teams, therefore, must begin to embrace integration and automation **TS1.5** as tools of the trade. Finally, even if all of the previous is done, it is incredibly valuable to include third-party verification or commissioning **TS1.6** in the design phase.

Changing the design process is not enough. The building itself—the hardware of shelter—also must change, balancing the need for longevity against carbon produced in manufacturing processes and embodied in the resulting artifact. This begins with the buildings' passive systems **TS2.1**. These include site, structure that utilizes materials that are renewable or of such long lifecycles that carbon expenditure per annum is effectively less than other options, and building envelopes composed of exterior finish, insulation, and assemblies stitched together with thermal bridge-free construction techniques and surfaced with healthy, VOC-free interior finishes. And where door and window penetrations exist, these openings need to perform comparably to the rest of the envelope.

TECHNOLOGY

With the support and skin of shelter rethought, attention must turn to active systems **TS2.2**. As with traditional buildings, sustainable shelters need to provide mechanical heating, cooling, ventilation, and other equipment. One difference between traditional and sustainable buildings is that the latter will increasingly incorporate biological systems. Another difference between traditional and sustainable building hardware lies in the need to radically reduce energy consumption. Some of these savings can be affected via the active systems themselves. It will, however, be necessary for buildings to begin to supply and store their own energy. This requires a move toward regenerative systems **TS2.3**.

Additional gains can be derived from the digital technologies that operate smart buildings. These include both hardware **TS3.1**, in the form of sensors and controls, and software **TS3.2** such as predictive analytics. Policy mandates for the inclusion of such smart technologies in new construction is an important step toward eventual widespread adoption in older existing building stocks. The most important operators **TS3.3**, however, are the people who own and inhabit the buildings. Efforts to improve building performance hinge on the operators' awareness of how and why the systems function as they do.

Sustainable shelters and food production demand an equivalent rethinking of responsible water management, which can be divided into two broad streams—the potable/sanitary system and rainwater—each of which can be subdivided into distinct technologies and best management practices (BMPs). Rainwater collection plays a central role in water conservation and should address two scales of technology: building-integrated BMPs **TW1.1** and site-integrated BMPs **TW1.2**. The former includes the design of green roofs, flow-through planters, and cisterns. The latter pertains to an even wider set of design considerations. Site-integrated BMPs begin with site analysis and design through which opportunities for the incorporation of rain gardens, bio-swales, and pervious pavements as well as urban trees/urban forests are identified.

Similar to rainwater, potable and sanitary water systems are best divided into building-integrated technologies **TW2.1** and site-integrated technologies **TW2.2**. Both should take advantage of recycling and reduction technologies to maximize effectiveness. Water recycling technologies contribute to the concept of a living machine introduced earlier and involve the design of systems for graywater harvesting, blackwater harvesting, and municipal treatment. Reduction technologies, such as irrigation systems and low-flow fixtures, complement recycling by ensuring that potable/sanitary systems are not strained beyond capacity.

Finally, there are the technologies that allow us to move. Two related reasons mobility is included in this book as an essential component of sustainable urbanism are 1) the existing patterns and infrastructure of transportation (primarily highways and cars) are gross contributors to environmental degradation, and 2) small improvements in this sector will pay huge dividends toward healthy cities in the future. As with shelter, the technologies of mobility have to improve in terms of longevity and, simultaneously, reduce carbon outputs in both transit infrastructure and the energy systems that power it. These demands can be summarized as improving energy for mobility **TM1.1** and paying greater attention to surfaces and substrates **TM1.2**. Determining the appropriate power supply for any municipality requires careful study but, in general, it is important to evaluate all the major types, including solar, fuel cells, alternative fuels, biomass, as well as electric and hybrid motors. See also **SS 3**. Decisions regarding the surfaces and substrates of mobility are nearly as important as those related to energy. Nevertheless, choices of surfaces and substrates fall into routines of "we've always done it this way" as often as any other city planning decisions. The roads, pavements, and even rails of sustainable cities are subtly different. Here again, longevity and environmental impacts are crucial.

Significant research is available to guide city planners and urban designers in selecting appropriate mobility options. It is useful to become familiar with the major research centers worldwide **TM2.1**. These include the Transportation Technology Center in Pueblo, Colorado, the Canadian Center for Sustainable Transportation, the MIT Center for Transportation and Logistics, among many others. Most importantly, planners and designers should identify centers whose research focuses on regional concerns including culture, climate, and available resources. Regardless of research resources used, policy makers, and designers need to identify key economic, environmental, and societal sustainability indicators **TM2.2** early in mobility planning. Sustainability indicators provide metrics for pursuing technologies such as automated highway systems **TM2.3** or instituting green supply chain initiatives **TM2.4**, including eco-design, green purchasing, and reverse logistics. The technologies and initiatives almost inevitably will come into conflict with each other or across indicators. Economic sustainability, for instance, is often at odds with environmental concerns. For this reason, planners and designers are encouraged to understand and undertake multiple-criteria decision-making processes—or MCDM **TM2.5**.

TECHNOLOGY

Once the selection of transportation modes has been made, computational approaches to planning their most efficient layout and operations can save the city significant energy and operational costs. Four such technologies, in some combination, are recommended to optimize the sustainable city: vehicle-routing problems and traffic simulations (VRP) **TM3.1**, mobile mapping **TM3.2**, traffic simulation **TM3.3**, and agent and multi-agent systems of modeling **TM3.4**. Deployed in concert with appropriate energy and substrate selections, these technologies are capable of transforming mobility from an ecological problem to a positive contributor in making cities LAST.

Note

1   McDonough, W., & Braungart, M. (2002). *Cradle to cradle: Remaking the way we make things*. New York, NY: North Point Press.

Technologies

The Fine Print

Technologies & Food

C. Taze Fulford

TF1   Inventory and Analysis

TF1.1

Geolocation of Resources

Precision agriculture allows not only farmers to direct and track machinery as it works the land, but also calls for fields or other agricultural lands to be tagged. Utilizing Global Positioning Systems (GPS), Geographic Information Systems (GIS), and remote sensing, 'frameworks' can be used by planners to tag the uses of parcels of land for crop type, animal husbandry, water bodies, and other resources and link these to other data sets with benchmarks. The Food and Agriculture Organization (FAO) of the United Nations is working on precisely this through its World Programme for the Census of Agriculture 2020. By using these types of information, government entities can make informed policy decisions across multiple levels of scale from the site to the region. While the FAO is conducting in-depth studies across countries, Flavio Lupia of the Italian Institute for Agricultural Economics (INEA) in Rome helped develop ways to locate

DOI: 10.4324/9781003203049-13

urban agriculture lands via Google Earth, Google Maps, Microsoft Bing Maps, and ground truthing to verify the findings.

TF1.2

Mapping Plant Type

Along with GIS, GPS, and remote sensing, satellites are used for in-depth monitoring, crop health assessments, yield production, and crop type mapping. Firms that specialize in this technology are using machine learning algorithms that identify crop type and acreage in a satellite image. The use of these types of technologies can lead to better rotation of crops and increase in yield, and even track farm activities daily. Predictions can also be made for crop conditions based on real-time weather conditions as well as make recommendations on amounts of fertilization required and when to sow seeds, leading to more productive fields.

TF1.3

Crop/Plant Analytics

While agricultural spaces can be mapped by satellites and drones, it is sensors that can also help sustainability by giving real-time information concerning irrigation needs, root depth, temperature, lighting, weight and size of the plant material, as well as nutrient amounts in the soil mixture. Urban farming will depend to a great extent on analytics and data sharing for crop health with more and more urban farming taking place inside structures. As population of cities grow, crop yield and health will need to be maximized to feed the people in a healthy and profitable manner. Analytics can help ensure this is the case. Firms across the globe are aiding farmers with sensors for both modern indoor growing environments as well as traditional fields with software, sensors, and training to provide the information to the people that will be feeding urban populations. Groups such as ATLAS (Agricultural Interoperability and Analysis System), which is a consortium of experts from across Europe, can provide single-site data-driven recommendations to regional information to aid in policy making, while Urban Crop Solutions based in Belgium with an office in Miami can give recommendations and provide expertise in the building of indoor growing solutions from LED lighting and irrigation to plant biology and efficiency.

TF1.4

Post-Harvest Evaluation. . .

is needed to ensure that crops meet certain requirements to be safe for consumers. Weight and compaction of harvest materials, contact with insects and rodents as well as exposure to exhaust or smoke, protection from sun or rain, cleaning, storage temperature, and moisture in the plant material all play a role in the evaluation of crop harvests in the traditional farm. In the modern container or autonomous farm, nutrient levels may also be a part of this evaluation. Post-harvest evaluations are important to maintain lower incidences of plant disease, rot, or contamination from humans or other animals. Planners and farmers should work together to apply policies that promote safe cleaning and storage spaces before goods are taken to local restaurants, markets, or straight to the consumer.

Further Reading and Resources TF1:

Algricoltura Urbana. (2014). *Mapping urban agriculture in Rome.* Lupia: Flavio. https://agricolturaurbana.com/2014/12/04/386/

ATLAS (Agricultural Interoperability and Analysis System). (2020). www.atlas-h2020.eu/pilot-studies/

FAO—World programme for the census of agriculture 2020: Volume 2 operational guidelines. (2018). https://unstats.un.org/unsd/statcom/49th-session/documents/BG-Item3j-WCA2020-Volume-2-final-E.pdf

Handbook on sampling frames for agricultural statistics. (2016). http://gsars.org/wp-content/uploads/2016/02/MSF-010216-web.pdf

Urban Crop Solutions. https://urbancropsolutions.com

TF2 Analog

TF2.1

Understanding Biodynamic Farming

Developed by the scientist Rudolf Steiner, biodynamic farming is a "holistic, ecological, and ethical approach to farming, gardening, food, and nutrition" (Biodynamic Association). Treated as a living organism, the farm is a set of interdependent features. These features depend on diversity of plants and animals that work together to make a regenerative system. The farm is rooted in its place and utilizes seeds and technologies appropriate to the location. Biodynamic farms also strive to meet social and economic sustainability and, along with the ecological aspect, express the triple bottom line approach to community.

TF2.2

Seasonal Production. . .

is selecting produce or goods for consumption shortly after harvest. Fresher foods are more nutritious and have not been harvested early and stored for shipping to your local store. The implications for urban sustainability are great as the support of local foods keeps tax money within the community and supports local jobs. Your farmer can tell you how the produce was grown and about different varieties that are available.

TF2.3

Sun, Water, Nutrients

In outdoor farming, sunlight is typically available unless the site is in a shadow of trees or buildings (site selection is important for growing food), rain falls for irrigation but can be supplemented when necessary, and soil either exists or you can build your own to have the nutrients you need through composting. In indoor farming, there is a need to provide lighting for plant growth through grow lamps or LED lighting, access to water is needed for both plant trays with soil or for hydroponic situations, and nutrients can be built into the soil or hydroponic mixtures used for growing (see also **LF1.2**, **LF1.3**, and **LF 2**). Regardless of the urban or peri-urban site, the farm must be able to have access to or manufacture these things for plants to thrive and be a part of the food stream of the city.

TF2.4

Pests and Biologically Based Management. . .

utilizes natural enemies (predators, parasitoids, or pathogens) of insects that destroy crops to help with control of insect outbreak and destruction of yields. This usually takes human intervention and is harder to accomplish when working with larger monocropping techniques. Conservation of existing predators is a good way to maintain a healthy system, which means the farmer must identify and understand the types of insects that will help versus harm crops. In some cases, biological control such as ladybeetles may be purchased and released to control aphid populations. See **SF3.2**.

TF2.5

Soil Under Your Fingernails. . .

indicates that you are out and participating in the growing of food you consume or provide for others. You gain knowledge of the place, the make-up of the soil, how it feels in your hands, how hard it is to dig (compaction), what kinds of insects or worms live there (are there pests?), and what it smells like. It is participation in the cycles of nature from birth to death in seasonal rhythms. The dynamics of food is revealing itself to you—along with its ecological, economic, and social benefits—through

TECHNOLOGY

Figure T2   Children feeling the soil in their hands.

Source: Karen Schauwecker

active participation. It sounds poetic, and it is. Community members are part of the technology of food. Take part in how nature provides you sustenance.

Further Reading and Resources TF2:

Biodynamic Association. www.biodynamics.com

TF3   Digital

TF3.1

Drones. . .

can be utilized in mapping potential urban spaces for optimal agricultural lands, monitoring crop health, identifying weeds and eliminating them, monitoring crop conditions, and even managing livestock. These machines are also used to seed trees, spot spray herbicides, fertilize, or even irrigate fields, reducing the need for larger machines and large amounts of time to do work on the ground. Being able to pinpoint areas in need also saves resources—for example, in the past, an entire field would be sprayed with insecticide or herbicide; now software can identify those areas and limit chemical use. These machines are becoming more affordable, allowing the farmer to have a new tool for creating a sustainable and profitable agricultural endeavor.

TF3.2

FarmBot. . .

is an open-source machine and software that allows you to build and customize your own machine or buy one of the company's products. The application software will provide users a plan of type of plant and where to plant within a planter. FarmBot will seed, irrigate, and weed the planter by moving across the planter area with a gantry attached to a drivetrain and tracks. The machine can be powered by solar and monitors how much irrigation is needed, allowing for reduced water usage. The size of the units is more conducive to small-scale applications, including home use.

Figure T3   FarmBot at Mississippi State University Community Gardens.

Source: C. Taze Fulford III

TF3.3

Harvesters

Fleets of robot drones are able to help farmers in times of labor shortages to pick fruits when they are ripe. Countries such as Israel are using these machines as the fruit-picking labor population has dwindled while fruit consumption has grown. Larger fruits are easier for the most common harvesters to pick and could be utilized in urban edible forests to bring to local markets. More labor-intensive crops such as strawberries are not suitable to be harvested by these as damage can happen to the fruit. Other land drones, however, have been manufactured that are capable of performing these tasks without harming the produce. These drones are able to detect size, color, and ripeness, and then "pick" the fruit and take it to a waiting bin. These drones can also be tasked with pruning trees. Tractors and other farm vehicles may also be fitted with a navigation system and can be remotely driven.

TF3.4

The Autonomous Farm

Drones and robots are part of modern agriculture. Here all machines are autonomous through the use of artificial intelligence, navigation systems, and satellites working together to produce crops without humans on the ground. Artificial intelligence is helping build other components of the autonomous farm to discern viable vegetables and fruits from those that may be considered second-hand in some markets or may need to be discarded all together. The autonomous farm will prepare the field, seed, monitor, weed, irrigate, harvest, and prepare to send to market all with minimal human input on the ground. As the use of these technologies increases and becomes perfected, resource use will be only as needed, reducing water usage and the use of fertilizer and herbicides. Robots have even been built to drive through fields vacuuming bugs from the plants.

TECHNOLOGY

TF3.5

Container Farms. . .

are a good choice for small areas in the urban fabric. There is a large surplus of shipping containers worldwide that can be verified safe to use and retrofitted into vertical farming centers. These small structures can be put together if needed for larger production and can do everything from monitoring soil mixture and nutrients to modifying lighting amounts as needed for perfect growing conditions. The ability exists to produce more per square foot in a container versus traditional farming methods. There may be issues with humidity if not closely monitored, leading to disease, but if staff are trained to monitor and keep conditions optimal the container is able to produce food close to the city center, reducing time to market for fresher organic produce. These are typically hydroponic systems with LED lighting and Smart Climate Control to reduce water usage and increase harvests per year and yield, and are capable of being placed in any climate.

Further Reading and Resources TF3:

Agrobot. (2020). www.agrobot.com

Alesca Life. (2019). www.alescalife.com

FarmBot. https://farm.bot/pages/open-source

Freight Farms. www.freightfarms.com

Houtman, J. (2016). Optimal design and plan of a modified hydroponic shipping container. Major Professor: Robert M. Stwalley III. Open Access Theses. 856. https://docs.lib.purdue.edu/open_access_theses/856

Pure Greens. (2019). https://puregreensaz.com

Twilley, N. (2017). A field farmed only by Drones. *The New Yorker.* www.newyorker.com/tech/annals-of-technology/a-field-farmed-only-by-drones

TECHNOLOGY

TF4　Architecture as Structure

TF4.1

Integrated Landscape Architecture and Building Architecture. . .

is the practice of designing and developing projects that act as whole systems. Architecture and the landscape's architecture are not separate but intertwined to make a resilient system that fits within the place it is designed. Climate, materials, and cultural variables all come together to form spaces for people to be a part of the system. Landscape architects should perform more than simply decorating architecture. Work should be done to develop true social partnerships to study energy flow, waste, water, technology, form, and food, to bring forth not machines for living, but living machines.

TF4.2

Building-Integrated Agriculture. . .

is rapidly happening in many parts of the world as populations rise and land becomes more expensive. Rooftops are being designed to carry structural loads for green roofs on which crops can be grown, and interiors may have vertical green walls that are used for food production and aid in air quality (see also **LF 3**). Composting stations are used to help close the ecological loop so that waste can become food for plant materials. Water collection and cisterns are a part of the design for irrigation and household use. All of these can promote use of local energy, utilize local water, reduce the use of fossil fuels, clean wastes, grow fish, support vermiculture to break down waste, integrate mycology for breaking down paper waste streams, and create a healthy human living or working experience overall.

TECHNOLOGY

TF4.3

Vertical Farming. . .

utilizes a small footprint to grow a larger amount of produce than does trad-itional agriculture. Reduced distance to local markets resulting in fresher foods is a major draw for these businesses. Water is a resource that is used and reused in the system, and rainwater-harvesting methods are typically used (see **SW2.1** and **SW3.1**). The grow systems are limited by access to sun-light (but can be put on rotating frameworks to share access) and ventilation. Systems are more suitable to grow leafy vegetables than grains or other crops that can be produced for low cost in the field. Nutrient cycling **LF2.1** through integrated aquaponics **LF1.3** is another way to close the resource loop. High-rise buildings will become centers of agriculture in the urban fabric.

TF4.4

Retro-Fitted Buildings for Agriculture. . .

provide a long list of benefits for the urban area. These are typically large buildings in warehouse districts that served another purpose in the past but can easily house vertical farms or aquaponics due to their size. Some of the "unseen" economic benefits are keeping the embodied energy of the material used for original construction, reduced carbon footprint, and reduced heating and cooling costs; and social benefits, such as the import-ance of the building itself to the community in terms of landmark or place, are immense. It also creates local jobs and fresh local food. Where gardens are put on rooftops, the repurposed building also increases biodiversity.

TF4.5

Living Machines. . .

were developed conceptually by Dr. John Todd. While the major use of the machines has been to treat sewage, a side benefit has been the ability of these to grow fish as part of the system that can be used for food. Snails and bacteria from the roots of local plant materials seeded into digesters break down sludge and chemicals before passing the water to different tanks with combinations of plants to further clean the water. These systems are located in greenhouse conditions and therefore can grow produce.

Further Reading and Resources TF4:

Beacham, A. M., Vickers, L. H., & Monaghan, J. M. (2019). Vertical farming: A summary of approaches to growing skywards. *The Journal of Horticultural Science and Biotechnology,* 94(3), 277–283.

Despommier, D. (2009). The rise of vertical farms. *Scientific American, 301*(5), 80–87.

Droege, P. (Ed.). (2012). *100% Renewable: Energy Autonomy in Action.* New York: Routledge, pp. 229–241.

EPA. (2002). Wastewater technology fact sheet, the living machine. https://www3.epa.gov/npdes/pubs/living_machine.pdf

Estee, L. Y., & Kishnani, N. T. (2010). Building integrated agriculture: Utilising rooftops for sustainable food crop cultivation in Singapore. *Journal of Green Building, 5*(2), 105–113.

Gould, D., & Caplow, T. (2012) 8—Building-integrated agriculture: A new approach to food production. In F. Zeman (Ed.) *Woodhead Publishing Series in Energy, Metropolitan Sustainability.* Sawston, UK: Woodhead Publishing, pp. 147–170.

John Todd. www.toddecological.com

Skyscraper Farm. https://skyscraper.farm

Specht, K., Siebert, R., Hartmann, I., et al. (2014). Urban agriculture of the future: An overview of sustainability aspects of food production in and on buildings. *Agriculture and Human Values, 31,* 33–51.

Todd, N. J., Todd, J., & Todd, N. J. (1994). *From eco-cities to living machines: Principles of ecological design.* Berkeley, CA: North Atlantic Books.

Van der Ryn, S., & Cowan, S. (2007). *Ecological design* (10th anniversary ed.). Washington, DC: Island Press.

Wilkinson, S., & Torpy, F. (2018). Living green roofs. *Urban Pollution*, 131–145.

Wilkinson, S. J., Ghosh, S., & Page, L. (2007). *Options for green roof retrofit and urban food production in the Sydney CBD*. Sydney: School of Built Environment, University of Technology.

TF5   Sustainable Examples

TF5.1

Environmental Laboratory for Sustainability and Ecological Education (ELSEE) . . .

is a model adopted by schools across the state of California. Ecological systems are used as a framework to develop the land use of schools and, in the curriculum, for teaching. Goals of the lab are to teach preservation, sustainability, urban land use, environmental benefits of gardening using ecological approaches, and methods of growing and preparing both native and conventional food, and to "promote local biodiversity using native plants" (ELSEE).

TF5.2

O'Hare Rotunda Building—Aeroponic Garden. . .

became the first airport in the world to install an aeroponic garden. Twenty-six towers with over 1,100 plants are irrigated in a way that eliminates evaporation. The produce grown is organic, using no chemicals or fertilizers. Year-round cultivation, higher production, and on-site location give restaurants in the airport access to local produce at all times. Nineteen varieties of plants are continually grown, with most of these being herbs, lettuces, peppers, and edible flowers.

TECHNOLOGY

Figure T4 O'Hare Airport Tower Gardens.
Source: Dr. Ellen Vincent

TF5.3

Iron Ox. . .

is an autonomous system for growing produce. Humans and robots work together to reduce resource use in the food production process. The hydroponic systems reduce water usage by 90% over traditional agricultural techniques and can produce 30 times the crops per acre (0.4 hectares) of land. While automation is claiming jobs in some areas, there are areas of the world such as Israel and the southwestern United States that have agricultural worker shortages.

TF5.4

Community of Findhorn. . .

is an intentional community located in Scotland and founded in 1962. Construction of the Ecovillage started in 1982. The Ecovillage is founded on sustainable principles and works to be a model for human settlements. The community has its own ecological wastewater treatment plant, which was the first living machine in Europe (see **TF4.5** Living Machines).

The building methods include strawbale experimental structures and buildings made with natural, local materials. The community uses solar for heating water, wind-generated electricity, and sustainably harvested wood for heating. In the production of food for the settlement, there is a forest garden **SF2.4** and community-supported agriculture **AF2.1**, which is a biodynamic system called EarthShare and covers 25 acres, or roughly 10 hectares.

TF5.5

Serenbe Farms. . .

is an agriculturally based community outside of Atlanta, Georgia in the United States. Based on the historic villages of Europe, the community has multiple centers. Roadways were developed to work with the land to reduce grading of the soil and to create green spaces and save wetlands from destruction. Energy for heating is from geothermal and solar energy, while some homes are Net Zero Energy buildings. The community has its own certified organic farm that sells produce at the local market and to the three farm-to-table **AF1.6** restaurants in the community. Biophilia is also a part of the community, with the foundation of the place rooted in

Figure T5   Serenbe Farms greenhouse with cluster housing in the background.

Source: C. Taze Fulford III

TECHNOLOGY

the language of humans and natural systems having a bond. This bond is realized through nature walks, organic foods, and community.

Further Reading and Resources TF5:

American Society of Landscape Architects: Interview with Steven NyGren, California Native Garden Foundation. https://cngf.org/elsee/

Center for Ecoliteracy. www.ecoliteracy.org/book/ecological-literacy-educating-our-children-sustainable-world

Findhorn Ecovillage. www.ecovillagefindhorn.com

Founder of Serenbe. www.asla.org/ContentDetail.aspx?id=47383

Iron Ox. https://ironox.com

O'Hare International Airport. www.flychicago.com/ohare/ServicesAmenities/amenities/Pages/garden.aspx

Serenbe. https://serenbe.com

USGBC. (2016). https://plus.usgbc.org/middle-grounds/

Vincent, E. Clemson University. (2012). www.clemson.edu/cafls/vincent/garden_profiles/ohare_urban_garden_july_aug_p4-7_2012.pdf

Technologies & Mobility

Joan Blanton

TM1 Infrastructure and Energy

TM1.1

Energy for Mobility

To decrease CO_2 emissions, transportation goals must include renewable energy. For cities to make the large range of transportation systems sustainable and energy-efficient requires pulling together the many available technologies and coordinating them with similar improvements in energy power production. City designers, planners, engineers, and administrators must work together to choose the appropriate tools. Some of the available tools are described next, but the technical nature of these options might require that experts in the field be consulted.

TM1.1.1 Solar: Photovoltaic devices have been used for decades for converting solar energy into residential and commercial electricity. Solar power for transport systems has been a subject of research, but this research has centered on solar-powered cars. Natural gas has been applied in many bus systems and does abate the production of emissions but is not a long-term solution since natural gas is a not a renewable resource. The potential of solar technologies for buses, light rail, and rail transport must be developed, tested, and applied. Designers and planners need to remain cognizant of developments in solar power for future application.

TM1.1.2 Fuels Cells: A fuel cell converts a fuel, usually hydrogen, and an oxidizing agent, oxygen, into water. That reaction produces electricity. The process is very efficient and does not produce toxic emissions. Though quite promising as a sustainable technology, the use of fuel

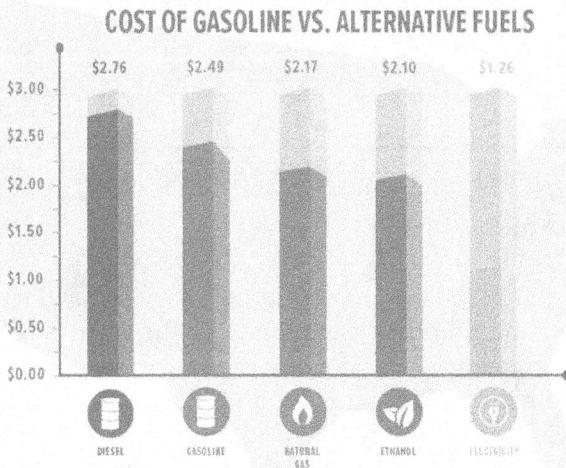

COST OF GASOLINE VS. ALTERNATIVE FUELS

Figure T6   The cost of gasoline versus alternative fuels.

Source: Fuel Freedom

cells in cars is a small and slow-growing market, and their use in buses, to date, is extremely limited.

TM1.1.3 Alternative Fuels: With the inevitable decrease in oil and gas, alternative fuels have been sought to fill the gap for transportation. Those studying existing transportation infrastructure find that liquid alternative fuels would be preferable over electricity and hydrogen, which would not be as efficient or sustainable. Policy makers need to be aware of all the alternative fuels and make more successful long-term decisions.

TM1.1.4 Biomass . . . is a renewable source of energy. It is the organic material of plants and animals that can be converted to energy or fuels such as ethanol. As of 2017, these fuels provided about 5% of the primary energy use in the US.

TM1.1.5 Electric and Hybrid Motors: With the vast number of vehicles and kilometers of transportation infrastructure dedicated to such vehicles, electric and hybrid motors are a sustainable alternative to gas-driven motors. Electric cars are Zero Emission Vehicles (ZEVs), which come in two varieties: battery electric vehicles (BEVs) and fuel-cell electric vehicles (FCEVs). Hybrid cars have both a battery-powered electric motor and a gas or diesel internal combustion engine. Hybrids have the following four classifications: mild hybrid electric vehicle, hybrid electric vehicles (HEVs), plug-in hybrid electric vehicles (PHEVs), and range-extended electric vehicles (REEVs).

TM1.2

Surfaces and Substrates

Road and rail surfaces and the composition of the subsurface, or substrates, can make a difference in the sustainability of these infrastructures and can contribute to easing runoff and other surface problems. For instance, there are many permeable pavements available that allow groundwater to soak through the surface **TW1.2**. This reduces runoff and potentially aids in replenishing aquifers. It is also important to carefully study the topography of proposed road and rail right-of-ways to minimize cut and fill of soil, thereby limiting impairments to watersheds **SW1.2**, destruction of viable agricultural land **SF2.5**, and impacts to movement patterns of other species.

TECHNOLOGY

Further Reading and Resources TM1:

Babu, M. K. G., & Subramanian, K. A. (2013). *Alternative transportation fuels: Utilisation in combustion engines.* Boca Raton, FL: CRC Press.

Blanch, H. W., Adams, P. D., Andrews-Cramer, K., Frommer, M. W. B., Simmons, B. A., & Keasling, J. D. (2008). Addressing the need for alternative transportation fuels: The Joint BioEnergy Institute. Published online January 18, 2008. DOI: 10.1021/cb700267s.

Hall, J. (2015). Hardscaping 101: Eco-friendly paving solutions. www.gardenista.com/posts/eco-friendly-paving-solutions/

Husain, S., Jaffery, I., Khan, M., Ali, L., Abbas Khan, H., Ahmad Mufti, R., . . ., Jaffery, S. M. (2014). The potential of solar powered transportation and the case for solar powered railway in Pakistan. *Renewable and Sustainable Energy Reviews, 39,* 270–276.

Lund, H., & Clark, W. W., II. (2008). Sustainable energy and transportation systems introduction and overview. *Utilities Policy, 16,* 59e62.

Nice, K., & Strickland, J. How fuel cells work: Polymer exchange membrane fuel cells. *How Stuff Works.* https://auto.howstuffworks.com/fuel-efficiency/alternative-fuels/fuel-cell.htm, accessed 5 August 2020.

Riba, J.-R., López-Torres, C., Romeral, L., & Garcia, A. (2016) Rare-earth-free propulsion motors for electric vehicles: A technology review. *Renewable and Sustainable Energy Reviews, 57,* 367–379.

Searcy, E., Flynn, P., Ghafoori, E., & Kumar, A. (2007). *The relative cost of biomass energy transport.* Totowa, NJ: Humana Press Inc.

The ultimate beginner's guide to electric and hybrid cars. www.theaa.com/driving-advice/electric-vehicles/electric-hybrid-car-guide#diff

U.S. Energy Information Administration. (2018). *Biomass— Energy Explained, Your Guide to Understanding Energy.* https://www.eia.gov/energyexplained/

TECHNOLOGY

Zhao, B. (2017). Why will dominant alternative transportation fuels be liquid fuels, not electricity or hydrogen? *Energy Policy, 108*, 712–714.

TM2   Research

TM2.1

Research Centers

There are many transportation research centers that focus on transportation technologies and mobility issues that designers and planners will face. Each center maintains an extensive website that offers general and more detailed information on these issues, and databases that are helpful when studying and analyzing regional and local concerns or problems. Designers and planners facing mobility issues would find it valuable to search for an appropriate research center to aid them in their work.

TM2.1.1 The Transportation Research Center (TRC): This is North America's largest multi-user automotive proving ground. It is operated by TRC Inc. The center is located 40 miles northwest of Columbus, Ohio. Research focuses on advanced energy storage and electric drive systems, including fast-wired and wireless charging; lightweight materials and multi-material structures for harsh environments; advanced combustion engines and alternative biofuels; data science, analysis, and vehicle cybersecurity; vehicle systems integration; and intelligent mobility systems.

TM2.1.2 National Center for Sustainable Transportation (NCST) . . . is one of seven national centers funded by the US Department of Transportation's University Transportation Centers (UTC) Program, and the only national center focused on the Fixing America's Surface Transportation (FAST) Act research priority area of Preserving the Environment.

TM2.1.3 Transportation Technology Center (TTC) . . . in Pueblo, Colorado seeks to be the provider of choice for advancing railway safety and technology. They provide highly effective and efficient railway research, testing, training, and technical support.

TM2.1.4 The Centre for Sustainable Transportation . . . was created by Environment Canada and Transport Canada. Since 1996, the Centre has sponsored two major projects: the Sustainable Transportation

TECHNOLOGY

Performance Indicators (STPI) project, and the University Curriculum project.

TM2.1.5 The Canadian Transportation Agency . . . is an independent, quasi-judicial tribunal and economic regulator. It makes decisions and determinations on a wide range of matters involving air, rail, and marine modes of transportation under the authority of Parliament, as set out in the Canada Transportation Act.

TM2.1.6 The MIT Center for Transportation and Logistics (CTL) . . . is based in the MIT School of Engineering in Cambridge, USA and maintains extensive ties with other MIT schools. Its mission is to expand insight on global supply chains and establish a network of affiliated research centers in Asia, Europe, and South America. The MIT Global Supply Chain and Logistics Excellence (SCALE) Network strives to develop and disseminate supply chain expertise around the world.

TM2.1.7 European Conference of Transport Research Institutes (ECTRI): Founded in 2003, the ECTRI is a European transport association. It is comprised of twenty leading national research organizations and tertiary institutions from seventeen European countries. It is involved in transport research in regional, national, European, and international programs, and its primary focus is surface transport. They signed a Memorandum of Understanding in 2006 with the American Transportation Research Board (TRB).

TM2.1.8 The Transport Research and Innovation Monitoring and Information System (TRIMIS) . . . monitors the implementation and effectiveness of the projects developed by the Strategic Transport Research and Innovation Agenda (STRIA). TRIMIS analyzes technology trends, research and innovation capacities, and developments in the European transport sector, providing open-access information.

TM2.1.9 The Micronesian Center for Sustainable Transport (MCST), Republic of Marshall Islands and the University of the South Pacific . . . is a unique program and approach to addressing the need for Pacific states to transition to low-carbon transport pathways. The MCST Framework sets out a structured fifteen-year program to achieve this by first aiming to achieve such transition in one country, Marshall Islands, and then use this as a catalyst to cascade successful results to neighboring states and outward through the region.

TM2.1.10 National Center for Sustainable Transportation (NCST): The Institute of Transportation Studies at the University of California, Davis (ITS-Davis) leads the NCST in partnership with California State University, Long Beach; the University of California, Riverside; the University

TECHNOLOGY

of Southern California; Georgia Institute of Technology; and the University of Vermont. The National Center for Sustainable Transportation (NCST) works to advance sustainable transportation through research, direct policy engagement, and education.

TM2.2

Sustainability Indicators. . .

are selected variables that can assist in making objectives operational and minimize the complexity of system management and intervention. Creating indicators is a three-step process, as follows: *conceptualization* of what is to be monitored, *operationalization* or the selection of measurable parameters and indicator types, and *utilization*, the ways in which the indicators are used in analysis or policy making.

TM2.3

Automated Highway System (AHS)

The AHS program was established in response to the mandate of the Intermodal Surface Transportation Efficiency Act of 1991 (ISTEA) to "develop an automated highway and vehicle prototype from which future fully automated intelligent vehicle-highway systems can be developed," to provide the vision and technology to make highway driving efficient, safe, and predictable.

TM2.4

Green Supply Chain Initiatives. . .

are interorganizational attempts to improve the environmental performance of an entire supply chain. A green supply chain has been defined as one that minimizes the environmental impacts of a product throughout its lifecycle. See also **LS 3**.

TM2.4.1 EcoDesign: a proactive environmental management approach that integrates environmental issues into the product development and related processes. The process requires looking at the six phases of production and their resulting pollution. Those six phases are: choice of material, manufacturing process, packaging of product, the finished product itself, transportation of the finished product, and waste.

TM2.4.2 Green purchasing: an environmentally conscious purchasing practice that reduces sources of waste and promotes recycling and reclamation of purchased materials without adversely affecting performance requirements of such materials.

TM2.4.3 Reverse Logistics: the handling of products, components, and materials during the recovery process, i.e., after their installation or during and after their use. It includes recycling, reusing, and reducing the amount of materials used. An example of reverse logistics would be the use of reusable shipping containers instead of one-way cartons made of corrugated paper (cardboard). Reverse logistics is often compared with green logistics.

TM2.5

Multiple Criteria Decision Making (MCDM)

With the call for making mobility sustainable and energy-efficient, stakeholders, society, government, and scientists need problem-solving methods that consider multiple criteria of quantifiable performance measures. MCDM is used to choose between alternatives that are tested. It requires, however, advanced statistical models to yield results and statisticians to run them.

Further Reading and Resources TM2:

Canadian Transportation Agency—Canada.ca. www.canada.ca/en/transportation-agency.html

ECTRI—European Conference of Transport Research Institutes. www.dlr.de/vf/en/desktopdefault.aspx/tabid-3520/5463_read-7901/

Eltayeb, T. K., & Zailani, S. (2009). Going green through green supply chain initiatives towards environmental sustainability. *Operations and Supply Chain Management, 2*(2), 93–110.

Eltayeba, T. K., Zailani, S., & Ramayahc, T. (2011) Green supply chain initiatives among certified companies in Malaysia and environmental sustainability: Investigating the outcomes. *Conservation and Recycling, 55*, 495–506.

Gudmundsson, H. (2004). Sustainable transport and performance indicators. *Issues in Environmental Science and Technology*, (20), 35–63.

Micronesian Center for Sustainable Transport. https://mcst-rmiusp.org/

MIT Center for Transportation and Logistics. https://ctl.mit.edu

National Center for Sustainable Transportation. https://ncst.ucdavis.edu

Oak Ridge National Transportation Research Center. www.ornl.gov/facility/ntrc

Papenek, V. (1995). *The green imperative: Ecology and ethics in design and architecture*. London: Thames & Hudson.

Pigosso, D. C. A., Rozenfeld, H., & McAloone, T. C. (2013). Ecodesign maturity model: A management framework to support ecodesign implementation into manufacturing companies. *Journal of Cleaner Production, 59*, 160–173.

Rogers, D. S., & Tibben-Lembke, R. (2001). An examination of reverse logistics practices. *Journal of Business Logistics, 22*(2), 129–148.

Transport Research and Innovation Monitoring and Information System (TRIMIS) of the European Commission. https://trimis.ec.europa.eu/

Transportation Technology Center. www.ttci.tech/

US Federal Highway Administration. The Automated Highway System. (1994). www.fhwa.dot.gov/publications/publicroads/94summer/p94su1.cfm

Zavadskas, E. K., & Turskis, Z. (2011). Multiple criteria decision making (MCDM) methods in economics: An overview. *Technological and Economic Development of Economy, 17*(2), 397–427.

TM3   Computational Approaches

TM3.1

Vehicle-Routing Problems and Traffic Simulations (VRP) . . .

focus on optimal routes for vehicles given constraints like time window, route length, etc. It helps to plan routes that can maximize the efficiency of the vehicles and minimize delivery costs.

TM3.2

Mobile Mapping. . .

is the process of collecting geospatial data from a mobile vehicle, typically fitted with a range of remote sensing systems. Such systems are composed of an integrated array of time-synchronized navigation sensors and imaging sensors mounted on a mobile platform. Mobile mapping systems offer full 3D mapping capabilities. A mobile mapping system consists of three components: data acquisition, information extraction, and information management.

TM3.3

Traffic Simulation. . .

is a technique for analyzing traffic data and arriving at solutions for traffic systems in which computer models of the system are created and in which alternative scenarios can be explored. Usually the purview of traffic engineers, such simulations would be of value to designers and planners in making decisions about the effects on traffic of their projects and resulting connectivity within and beyond the city.

TECHNOLOGY

TM3.4

Agent and Multi-Agent Systems of Modeling. . .

are ways of constructing computer models that can simulate real world systems, such as those in transportation. Agent System Modeling is based on an individual agent's choices while the multi-agent system attempts to incorporate the decisions of a plethora of actors or inputs.

Further Reading and Resources TM3:

Barcelo, J. (2010). *Fundamentals of traffic simulation.* Switzerland: Springer.

Fritzsche, H. T. (1994). A model for traffic simulation. *Traffic Engineering & Control, 35,* 317–321.

Mardani, A., Kazimieras Zavadskas, E., Khalifah, Z., Jusoh, A., & Nor, K. M. D. (2016). Multiple criteria decision-making techniques in transportation systems: A systematic review of the state of the art literature. *Transport, 31(3),* 359–385.

Rogers, K., & Seager, T. P. (2009). Environmental decision-making using life cycle impact assessment and stochastic multiattribute decision analysis: A case study on alternative transportation fuels. *Environmental Science & Technology, 43,* 1718–1723.

Vehicle Routing. (2020). blog.locus.sh/vehicle-routing-problem-decoded. . . https://blog.locus.sh/vehicle-routing-problem-decoded-what-why-and-how/ Ibrahim Ethem Demirci

Vincent Tao, C. *Mobile Mapping Technology for Road Network Data Acquisition.* Calgary, Alberta, Canada: Department of Geomatics Engineering, The University of Calgary.

Technologies & Shelter

Caleb Crawford

Technology is the interaction between tools, materials, and knowledge in things. Since prehistoric times, humans have applied technology to fabricating and conditioning shelter, each culture exhibiting variations. While today technology brings to mind digital hardware and software, shelter itself is a form of technology.

Shelter is affected by technology in three ways: design process, hardware, and operations. 'Design process' **TS 1** refers to conceiving and construction. This process is dependent upon digital technology for data analysis and communication. 'Hardware' **TS 2** refers to shelter as a physical artifact and falls into three categories: passive **TS2.1**, active **TS2.2**, and regenerative **TS2.3**. 'Passive systems' refer to structure, envelope, and site characteristics and are the key technological actor in the way a shelter operates. 'Active systems' refer to equipment: heating, cooling, ventilation, lighting, electrical, etc. 'Regenerative systems' refer to energy generation and storage, such as solar photovoltaic systems. 'Operations' **TS 3** refer to the controls, sensors, software, and people required to operate and optimize shelter. This section assumes a developed world expectation of interior comfort of 20–26° C (68–78° F). Cultural expectations can significantly extend this range (see **AS1.1**).

TS1   Design Process

Design process employs technologies. Design process also is a technology; it is a system of tools, standards, and codes that guide the construction of shelters. The sustainability of a shelter requires attention to how it is made. Goals and direction must be established—and tools of visualization, data analysis, and communication implemented—before construction commences. Environmental understanding and design intent are required before an approach is adopted. Required are data analysis to verify assumptions and use of digital tools to model behavior of a proposed shelter as a technological and natural ecosystem. Technology for communication between team members is key.

TECHNOLOGY

TS1.1

Understand the Environment

The environmental context must be analyzed before design begins. This includes site orientation, average and extreme weather (temperature, humidity, wind speeds, and rainfall), topography, vegetation, adjacent structures, utilities, and solar access to cite just some concerns. Environmental considerations must encompass the urban and cultural context as well: transportation, urban relationship, housing, employment, traditions, manufacturing, and maintenance capabilities.

TS1.2

Model

Advanced analysis software (see resources) is available to analyze loads and evaluate options for structural, envelope, and mechanical systems in relation to environmental conditions. Modeling generates detailed and accurate predictions of how those conditions affect energy use and comfort for occupants. Modeling is dependent upon precise technical standards and uses location-specific climate data sets and precise sun angle data. Modeling gives the design team a clear picture of thermal performance of the envelope, mechanical systems, daylighting, overheating, and other issues. This allows the design team to accurately size things like insulation thickness, depth of window overhangs, heating and cooling equipment capacities, and air flow of ventilation systems, among other factors, avoiding unnecessary costs in money and carbon in both construction and operation.

TS1.3

Right-Sizing

Many designers and builders are tempted to oversize systems— structural, envelope, mechanical, and everything else. The intent of

TECHNOLOGY

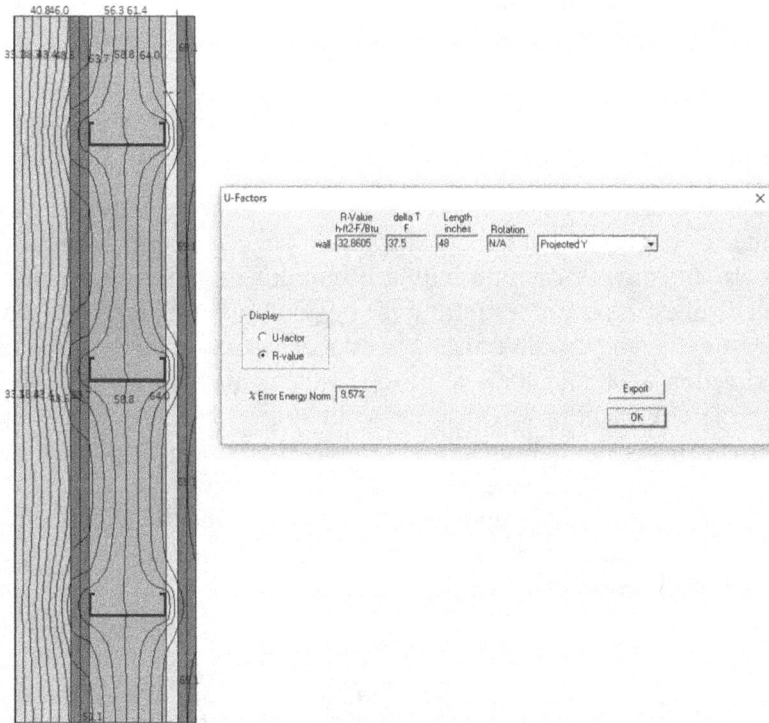

Figure T7　Isotherm diagram to determine thermal bridging modeled in THERM 7.7.10.

Source: Caleb Crawford

modeling **TS1.2** is to be confident that the design will perform as intended. Verify and then trust your modeling. Unless you are designing for emergency facilities, which must operate under potentially extreme conditions, only design for the anticipated loads in average conditions and code-mandated safety factors rather than worst-case scenarios. Oversizing in structural and envelope systems leads to material waste and thus higher embodied carbon. In mechanical systems, it leads to oversized equipment, which adds initial carbon and monetary expenditure and lowered efficiency. Predictions of future climate, however, should be taken into consideration for the sake of longevity and resiliency. Weather data for 2050 and 2080 predictions are currently available (see resources).

TECHNOLOGY

TS1.4

Communication

Early and continuous communication is critical between clients, users, architects, engineers, designers, project managers, contractors, code officials, and any other contributing group. Integrated project delivery (IPD) involves the entire team from the beginning, before even schematic design has begun. The objective is to establish goals, identify issues, and set direction as a collaborative process that is maintained throughout the project. Collaborative software technology can assist in this process by allowing the entire team to see real-time design updates so that the implications can be assessed. Building information modeling (BIM), the concept that every component of a building is identified in a model, allows all users to understand not only design intent but the individual products to be employed.

TS1.5

Integration and Automation

The task of modeling and making even small iterations in design is becoming ever more complex. The use of separate tools and redundant models is time consuming and prone to error. Fortunately, the interoperability of software is becoming more common, as is the development of plugins that mediate between BIM and analysis software, so that a shelter need be modeled only once for both analysis and documentation.

Use of artificial intelligence (AI) in design is growing. AI is useful for applying and analyzing unprecedented amounts of data. AI allows for multiple iterations of form to be considered based on site, building characteristics, weather data, and design parameters. AI optimizes, leading to better and faster decisions, while allowing the team to explore more possibilities early in the process.

TECHNOLOGY

TS1.6

Commissioning. . .

is a final third-party check to make sure that the built shelter conforms with the intent of the design documents, all systems have been correctly installed, controls are properly calibrated, and generally there are no anomalies. While this is the last step in the construction process, bring the commissioning agent in early in the design process. Thanks to building standards such as LEED, this is becoming standard practice internationally and being incorporated into building codes, such as the International Energy Code.

Further Reading and Resources TS1:

American Society of Heating, Refrigeration and Air-Conditioning Engineers (ASHRAE). www.ashrae.org/

Illuminating Engineering Society. www.ies.org/

Integrated Project Delivery: A Guide. (2007). http://info.aia. org/siteobjects/files/ipd_guide_2007.pdf

Next is a list of software options on the market, both free and paid. This is a small sample of available tools:

DesignPH, a graphic user plugin to model building geometry in Sketchup for PHPP analysis.

Energy Plus, a free whole-building energy simulation program. https://energyplus.net/

Flixo, a 2D thermal bridge analysis tool. www.flixo.com/

Future weather file generator: CCWorldWeatherGen https:// energy.soton.ac.uk/climate-change-world-weather-file-generator-for-world-wide-weather-data-ccworld weathergen/

IES VE, an energy modeling software that permits export from BIM for analysis. www.iesve.com/

OpenStudio, a free, open-source graphic user plugin to model building geometry in Sketchup for EnergyPlus analysis. www.openstudio.net/

TECHNOLOGY

PHPP, Passive House Planning Package, a whole-building energy modeling program. https://passivehouse.com/04_phpp/04_phpp.htm

Sketchup, a 3D modeling software that enables plugins like OpenStudio and DesignPH. https://designph.org/?language=en

THERM, a free 2D heat transfer analysis tool used to model thermal bridges and complicated geometry. https://windows.lbl.gov/software/therm

WUFI, for modeling 2D heat and moisture transport in building assemblies. WUFI Passive is used for PHIUS certification. https://wufi.de/en/

TS2   Hardware

Hardware is the fixed assets of shelter—every nut, bolt, and assembly installed. Hardware is divided into three groups: passive, active, and regenerative systems. Passive hardware includes structure and envelope as well as site elements such as landscaping. In sustainable design, these bear the greatest responsibility for maintaining comfort. In conventional buildings, however, all too often little attention is given to passive hardware, and the burden of comfort falls to active hardware (heating, cooling, ventilation, and electric lighting systems). Regenerative systems are rarely considered in conventional buildings. These are site-generated sources of power—solar electricity and wind power being the most prevalent carbon-free examples.

TS2.1

Passive Systems. . .

are the elements of shelter that change least over time, and tend to be relatively static—no motors, pumps, or fans. These include site, structure, and envelope. They are considered passive because they don't require inputs of energy apart from sun, wind, and earth to operate. They manage heat, light, and air through their physicality.

TECHNOLOGY

TS2.1.1 Site . . . is the most permanent asset of shelter and provides enormous possibilities for technological services through its ecosystem services. The soil can manage rainwater and provide heating and cooling passively and in conjunction with active systems. Trees and plants provide shading and filtering of water and air. Carefully choose hardscaping materials (constructed site elements like sidewalks, roads, retaining walls) with high reflectance (to mitigate the heat island effect) and high porosity (to reduce stormwater runoff). These are ecosystem services, but they are technologically structured to enhance the work of the shelter as a part of the ecosystem and reduce the energy input required.

Organization of the shelter in relation to the site has many factors, with the most important being those that affect insolation (sun exposure): solar path, topography, existing trees and plants, water, and adjacent structures. Orientation can promote solar heating where needed, prevent overheating and allow for daylighting of interiors.

TS2.1.2 Structure . . . is the bones of the building: the elements most resistant to change and that carry live and dynamic loads, like people, furniture, wind, and earthquakes. Structure can also have a significant effect on maintaining interior comfort. Lightweight structures tend to fluctuate more in response to exterior climatic conditions. Higher interior mass can reduce extremes of temperature change. On the other hand, structure is the main source of embodied carbon, typically accounting for 80–90% of shelter mass. Avoid excessive oversizing of structural elements while considering future uses. Carefully assess the materials that comprise the structure to evaluate embodied carbon (see **LS2.1**).

TS2.1.3 Envelope . . . is the element that defines the boundary condition between interior and exterior. Also called the skin, it is the key element in the passive systems of a shelter. It consists of the walls, roof, foundation, and openings. The contemporary skin is layered and manages a host environmental conditions: bulk water from rain, wind, temperature differences, air and vapor movement, light, and noise. From the standpoint of sustainability, guided by the Passivhaus standard strategies, the most important components are:

- thermal insulation
- thermal bridge-free construction
- air tightness
- high-quality "super" windows and doors

TECHNOLOGY

Figure T8   30 St. Mary Axe. Diagrid structure uses 20% less material than does a typical trabeated structure.

Source: Photo by Aurelien Guichard

Thermal insulation, in particular continuous insulation, reduces heat transfer to maintain better thermal comfort, but also to reduce and perhaps eliminate energy consumption for heating and cooling. Think of continuous insulation like a sleeping bag around the building.

Thermal bridges happen when materials that are good conductors of heat, like steel and concrete, are continuous from interior to exterior. These bridges can be reduced through reducing the size of the bridge, and the use of lower conducting materials.

Air-tightness is the reduction of infiltration or unwanted air movement through the envelope due to gaps in construction. In conventional buildings, up to half of all heat loss or gain is through infiltration. There are many air-tightness solutions now available on the market. Vapor

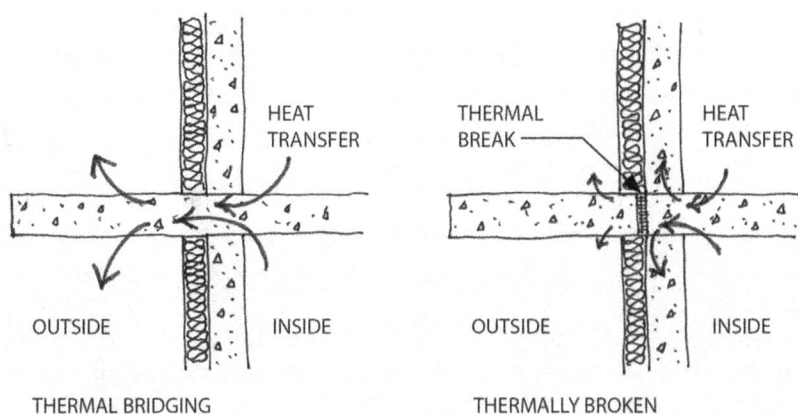

HEAT
TRANSFER

THERMAL
BREAK

HEAT
TRANSFER

OUTSIDE   INSIDE

OUTSIDE   INSIDE

THERMAL BRIDGING

THERMALLY BROKEN

Figure T9   Thermal bridging versus thermally broken.

Source: Caleb Crawford

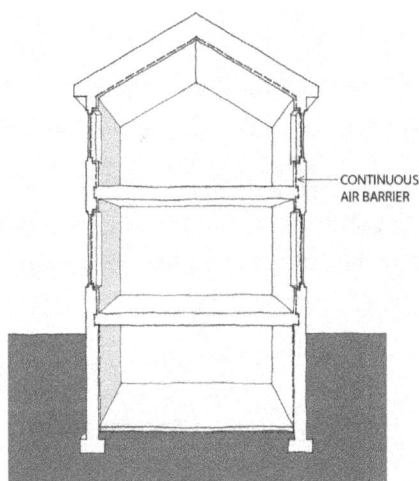

CONTINUOUS
AIR BARRIER

Figure T10   Continuous air barrier construction.

Source: Caleb Crawford

permeability of air barriers must be carefully considered. A lack of permeability can trap water in building assemblies, resulting in mold, corrosion, and degradation of finishes. Careful detailing, meticulous construction, and testing are required.

Super windows, doors, and skylights have exceptionally low air leakage, are typically triple-glazed depending on climate, have coatings to accept or reject solar radiation, and are effectively sealed to the air barrier. Windows require special attention. They tend to have an insulation value about 1/5 or less compared to walls. In the wrong orientation, they may create overheating of spaces, even in winter, and visual glare. East- and west-facing windows require a great deal of consideration because of the low angle of the sun, making it difficult to control sunlight. Conventional windows and doors with high u-values have a risk of condensation on their surfaces, which increases mold and finish degradation risks.

Openings provide multiple functions. Windows, doors, skylights, and vents are selective and operable elements, typically manually, but automation is possible. When closed, these maintain interior conditions. When open, they allow for ventilation, air movement, and cooling. Windows permit daylight to enter, reducing the need for electric lighting. Windows and doors can be fitted with exterior elements such as overhangs, louvres, brise soleil, and shutters, which reduce direct sun at different times of year. They can be fitted with interior or exterior elements like blinds, solar shades, roller shades, shutters, and light shelves, which reduce direct sun or glare, yet still allow for daylighting.

Levels of insulation, the degree of air sealing, the number of layers of glazing, size of overhangs, and many other factors relate directly back to modeling **TS1.2**. Insufficient levels of insulation result in increased energy consumption for heating and cooling. Excessive levels of insulation result in diminishing returns of energy savings, additional construction costs, and higher embodied carbon.

TS2.2

Active Systems

Contemporary shelter relies on a variety of systems to provide for health, safety, and welfare. Those systems that involve life safety are well codified and not covered here. Active systems are those related to thermal comfort and air quality: heating, cooling, ventilation, hot water, and appliances. On the exact kinds of systems to be employed, this article must remain agnostic—technology changes rapidly and an understanding of the implications of particular classes of technology are ever evolving. For example, heat pumps are currently recognized for heating and cooling because they run on electricity, which is potentially renewable. There are still significant problems, however, such as refrigerants being potent greenhouse gases—two thousand times more potent than CO_2. We must allow for current technologies to be displaced by better ones.

TS2.2.1 Heating and cooling . . . are complicated topics. A little over half of the 2018 International Energy Conservation Code section on commercial buildings is devoted to mechanical systems (for comparison, less than 20% is devoted to the envelope). The main challenge is to select systems that do not use fossil fuels. This is relatively easy for small buildings, especially those with efficient envelopes. Decarbonizing tall buildings is more complicated. Large buildings rely on the energy density of fossil fuels for both heating and cooling because they typically have large, centralized boiler and chiller systems. Smaller-scale systems can be employed in big buildings with existing technologies by reducing loads (through efficient envelopes) and compartmentalizing (essentially making each zone a separate building; see **SS1.4**). This brings equipment loads down to a scale manageable by small systems. Heat pump systems are promising, since they have a high efficiency ratio for heating and cooling and rely on electricity for energy.

TS2.2.2 Ventilation: Increased air tightness in building envelopes requires balanced ventilation. Many of our building processes can introduce pollutants, like printers and copiers; carbon monoxide from fossil fuel cooking or heating equipment; particulate matter from fireplaces and tobacco smoke. Avoid fossil fuel combustion equipment in the indoor environment and provide specialized ventilation (see **AS1.2**).

The environment can introduce pollutants from radon in the soil, and from poor outdoor air quality. Keep these pollutants out by adequately sealing the building envelope (see TS2.1.3) and filtering incoming air. Finally, just our human presence in shelters will elevate levels of carbon dioxide and moisture. Carbon dioxide in high-enough levels can impair mental processes. Excessive indoor relative humidity can cause conditions for the growth of mold.

Old-style exhaust-only ventilation relied on a leaky envelope for make-up air—essentially sucking air through cracks in walls and windows. Balanced ventilation requires replacing indoor air (loaded with pollutants and excess water vapor) for filtered outdoor air, free of dust, pollen, and other particulates. 'Balanced' means the supply air equals the amount of exhaust air. Air is exhausted from sources of indoor pollution, such as kitchens, bathrooms, and rooms with heat or equipment fumes. This can also be done for large spaces such as auditoriums.

TECHNOLOGY

Energy recovery ventilation must be used. This is ventilation that uses a heat exchanger to transfer the heat or cool from the exhaust air to the supply air without polluting the incoming air supply. The heat exchanger keeps the air streams separate while exchanging heat energy, capturing 75–95% of the energy that would otherwise be lost. There are two types. The first is simple heat recovery (HRV); the second is known as enthalpy recovery (ERV), where humidity is conserved. The ERV is important in cold climates where the interior air humidity due to heating can be uncomfortably low. Selection must be modeled.

TS2.2.3 Equipment: Shelter in developed nations incorporates many appliances used for both residential and commercial cooking, such as stoves and refrigerators, as well as clothes washers and dryers. These involve heating or cooling. Fossil fuel appliances must be eliminated. Gas-fired cooking introduces water vapor and many toxic gases into the interior, particularly CO_2 and CO. Induction cooktops are more efficient. Electric convection ovens are currently the most efficient. Vents to remove cooking odors must be recirculating or supplied with make-up air. Heat pump clothes dryers are available.

TS2.2.4 Biological systems . . . are integrated increasingly into the envelope and interior of shelters. Site ecosystem services are passive— generally self-sustaining and requiring little maintenance. Building-integrated systems, however, typically require inputs of human attention, water, nutrients, heat, and light to maintain their health, which is why they are included in active systems. These include atrium plantings, green walls both on the exterior and interior, green roofs, and urban agriculture. Biological systems can be integrated with HVAC systems to remove indoor air pollutants. These systems, like site-based biological systems, provide important services. Green roofs **LF3.3**, perhaps the system with the least required maintenance, mitigates the heat island effect, adds insulation to a roof, and reduces stormwater runoff TW 1. Urban agriculture reduces food miles traveled **SF1.4**. Green walls and atria, both indoors and out, help to reduce airborne particulate matter and release oxygen **LF3.4**.

TS2.3

Regenerative Systems

Contemporary shelter requires power to function. There are two main classes of regenerative systems: centralized **SS3.1** and distributed

SS3.2. Power generation can be building-integrated and site-integrated. This section will concern itself with power at the scale of building site.

TS2.3.1 Energy supply: Photovoltaic panels are the most common distributed electrical generation technology and the easiest to integrate into buildings, with some small wind and an even smaller amount of micro-hydro. Site-integrated usually takes the form of solar canopies over parking and other paved areas. Wind turbines are also seen, most often vertical axis turbines. Wind, however, has two issues: it makes noise, and structures can alter wind patterns, thereby decreasing production. The roof is the most effective location for installation of building-integrated photovoltaics (BIPV) since it ensures the highest annual output for the panels and the least site disturbance. Panels can be mounted vertically on building faces, but typically this lowers the output by at least one third because of the angle of sun incidence and shading from surrounding buildings and trees. Solar hot water is still popular in regions such as the Middle East and the Mediterranean where there is little risk of freezing and abundant sunshine, and the installations can be technically simple and low cost.

TS2.3.2 Energy storage: a component of both centralized and distributed systems needed for grid load control (see also **SS3.3**). Storage at the scale of shelter is typically chemical or thermal. Chemical energy is the most common for distributed systems. Lead/acid and lithium-ion batteries are currently the most common, though there are other technologies in development and on the market, such as saltwater batteries and fuel cells. Thermal storage heats or cools mass or fluid for later use, like for domestic hot water or air conditioning. A difficulty with using electricity to heat domestic hot water is the slow recovery rate after use for both heat pumps and simple resistance. Solutions include sizing hot water tanks for peak use times, increasing the temperature in tanks, and using other media for thermal storage, such as phase change materials, which can take advantage of latent energy.

Further Reading and Resources TS2:

Grondzik, W. T., & Kwok, A. G. (2015). *Mechanical and electrical equipment for buildings* (12th ed.). Hoboken, NJ: John Wiley & Sons.

Hopfe, C. J., & McLeod, R. S. (2015). *The passivhaus designer's manual.* New York, NY: Routledge.

Lechner, N. (2015). *Heating, cooling, lighting* (4th ed.). Hoboken, NJ: John Wiley & Sons.

TECHNOLOGY

Passive House Institute US. www.phius.org

The Passivhaus Institute. (2015). https://passivehouse.com, with many publications and resources

TS3 Operations

For optimum performance, shelter must be well maintained and regulated. The envelope must be kept air-tight and water-resistant, and automation of active systems implemented. The internet of things (IOT) is already in all communication equipment, security, fire alarms, and increasingly in other equipment such as HVAC equipment, elevators, appliances, and even individual light fixtures. Wireless technology makes monitoring and control of even private homes very simple. Management tools fall under three categories: hardware, software, and operators.

TS3.1

Hardware. . .

consists of sensors and controls. The first controls were human beings. If it was cold, a fire was made. As buildings have gotten more complex, need for automation has increased. Controls are switches: on, off, or some middle ground between. They control rates of flow and volumes of fluids but also differences (high and low temperatures, mixtures, current). In many instances, sensors and controls combined into a single unit, particularly at the level of home automation (like a Nest thermostat). There is a level of convenience to a home thermostat being both a temperature sensor and the device that controls heating or cooling output.

Sensors monitor flows and quantities—for example, air temperature, light levels, occupancy, whether a particular piece of equipment is on or off—and alert operators to malfunctioning equipment. Sensors provide feedback to systems which activate controls. The greater the feedback, the greater the potential for adjustment to systems. Examples of sensors include air temperature and humidity sensors that give feedback to heating and cooling systems, carbon dioxide sensors that give feedback to ventilation systems, daylight sensors that adjust electric light levels,

TECHNOLOGY

occupancy and vacancy sensors that determine whether there are people present to control lighting, heating, cooling, and ventilation. This feedback allows the system to optimize comfort and to minimize energy use. Contemporary design firms are installing sensors throughout buildings, inside and out, including inside walls, floors, ceilings, windows, and equipment to be able to compare actual to predicted performance, facilitating better design in the future.

TS3.2

Software

Older comfort or lighting systems were either on or off. This was done with a simple switch. System output could not be modulated. Contemporary sensors and controls employ software that monitor sensors and operate controls. A sensor takes some form of physical reaction to an environmental condition—heat, light, humidity, motion—and translates that into a signal indicating quantity. The software reads that input signal and decides to take an action based on a set of parameters. For instance, sensors may indicate outdoor temperatures of 0° C (32° F), indoor temperatures of 18° C (65° F), and a desired temperature of 20° C (68° F). Software will determine optimal temperatures needed to achieve the desired comfort and activate the heating system to provide a fluid at that temperature, perhaps 27° C (80° F), until the desired indoor temperature is reached.

Larger buildings employ building management systems (BMS) that monitor and control thousands of sensors and devices and provide real-time feedback on comfort levels and energy use. BMS systems generally require specialized training to program and operate.

TS3.3

Operators

Better known as people, operators are the most important component of a sustainable shelter. They are responsible for maintaining hardware, software, and the other technology systems. Despite the levels of auto-mation, there need to be operators who understand and program the system, and can respond when there are problems.

Technologies & Water

Cory Gallo

TW1   Rainwater

TW1.1

Building-Integrated Best Management Practices or BMPs. . .

are focused on management of rainwater that comes in contact with a building. Like a tree in a forest, integrating BMPs into a building can manage rainwater at several levels and use it as an amenity. Technologies integrated into a building can be costly. In dense urban areas, however, land value can offset these costs by limiting area on the ground required for landscape management facilities.

Figure T11   A dynamic green roof at the California Academy of Sciences by Renzo Piano.
Source: Cory Gallo

TW1.1.1 Green Roofs . . . are a form of impervious area mitigation where stormwater is managed where it falls. There are two categories of green roofs: intensive and extensive. Intensive systems have up to 3 feet (1 meter) of soil depth, allow for deeper-rooted plants and trees, and require a robust structural support system. Intensive green roofs are commonly found in actively used roof gardens. Extensive systems have up to 6 inches (15 centimeters) of soil depth and are the more common green roof typology because they are relatively lightweight, use drought-tolerant plants, and require less maintenance. Widely implemented throughout the world, green roofs provide multiple benefits including rainwater absorption, heat island effect reduction, habitat creation, extension of roof life, and viewshed improvement. Design considerations include roof weight, roof slope, roof drainage, maintenance, availability of water for periodic irrigation, and use. See also **LF3.3**.

TW1.1.2 Living Walls . . . are a form of green infrastructure that provide some water retention, though much less valuable as a rainwater management technology without additional reservoir or collection systems. Living walls are essentially vertical growing systems that may be a trellis for growing vines or hold soil for growing sedums and other water-tolerant species. Design considerations include wall load, plant needs, aesthetics, and views. See also **LF3.4**.

TW1.1.3 Downspouts . . . are essential for moving water from the roof to a site conveyance or management system. Creative conveyance of water from a roof can reinforce the movement of water, enhance a

Figure T12 Creative convenance of water from the building is key.

Source: Cory Gallo

TECHNOLOGY

building façade, and expand the possibilities of how and where water is managed on the site. Beyond a vertical conveyance system, raised channels can act like aqueducts to transport water into the landscape, emphasize the movement of water, and create points of interest where water falls from above. Design considerations include amount of flow, management location, aesthetics, and climate.

TW1.2

Site-Integrated BMPs. . .

attempt to manage rainwater as close to how a native or un-touched site would have managed it as possible. There are many structural and non-structural forms of BMPs used in cities. Successful sustainable design masterfully uses these technologies in concert to manage rainwater and create an environment that improves the urban landscape. Priority technologies mitigate impervious surfaces by planting trees, using native landscapes, and pervious pavements. After that, site design should attempt to move water at the surface in open-bottomed conveyance systems that allow water to be managed in shallow bio-retention facilities. Beyond site-level strategies, regional strategies help to transport and mitigate large flood events and can be designed as part of the overall open space network of a city.

TW1.2.1 Trees . . . are perhaps the single most beneficial strategy for water management in a city. An urban forest has immense value for water management, but also habitat, aesthetics, energy savings, and property value. Up to 1 inch or 2.5 centimeters of rainfall can be captured in a dense tree canopy, and a single mature tree can transpire up to 40 gallons (151 liters) of water every day. Design considerations include microclimate, species characteristics, orientation to building, solar orientation, soil, access to water, and site needs. See also **SF2.4**.

TW1.2.2 Native Landscapes . . . are both a rainwater and potable water technology. While native landscapes imply using plants that are indigenous to a specific bioregion, adapted species that are not invasive may also be considered because harsh urban contexts are often challenging for native species that are found in pristine landscapes. Plants with deep roots are much better at building topsoil and water retention/infiltration than is turf. These plants also need less or no water for irrigation because

TECHNOLOGY

they have adapted to thrive in their environment. Design considerations include access to sunlight, maintenance, aesthetics, seasonal attributes, soil condition, and access to water for irrigation.

TW1.2.3 Pervious Pavement . . . describes a collection of several paving materials that are used for pedestrian or vehicular traffic and allow water to move vertically into an open-graded sub-base where water can be detained or allowed to infiltrate. Pervious pavement is the highest form of impervious surface mitigation because it spreads water management across the entire site. Types of pervious pavement include porous concrete, porous asphalt, plastic lawn pavers, and porous pavers. The latter is based on a pattern of pavers that allows water to move in between openings in the pavers. Design considerations include soil type, slope, local codes, required storage volume, temperature, base material, area of capture runoff, vehicle weight, aesthetics, and cost.

TW1.2.4 Bio-Retention Facilities . . . are the workhorses of green infrastructure. Often called rain gardens, these facilities are low depressions, often with modified soil mixtures, that detain, absorb, and infiltrate rainwater. Properly designed, they blend into the site and compliment a rich landscape. Facilities should be designed for specific site and climatic conditions to manage specific storm events, filter pollutants for water quality, and ensure water leaves the facility within twenty-four hours or less of a rain event. A more specific naming convention describes a facility in terms of both horizontal and vertical attributes. Vertical variables describe the layers of the facility and have three possibilities: flow-through, partial infiltration, and infiltration. Horizontal variables describe the structure of the facility on the site and have three possibilities: basin, planter, and swale. By the using of these two attributes together, a specific facility type can be described. For instance, an infiltration planter allows for full infiltration and has structured walls at its sides, while a partial infiltration basin requires an underdrain because of very poor native soils and has sloped sides. Design considerations include available land area, required detention volume, soil infiltration rate, utilities, adjacency to buildings, relationship to impervious area managed, aesthetics, and overall site design.

TW1.2.5 Swales and Conveyance Channels . . . are critical for moving water at the surface so that it can be managed in shallow bio-retention facilities. There are many forms of open conveyance systems that can easily be incorporated into urban settings. Swales are flat-bottomed conveyance systems made of soil and plants. Conveyance channels are

TECHNOLOGY

typically concrete or steel channels designed to move water in narrow paths. Sometimes covered to create trench drains, these systems can allow water paths to be revealed even when water is not present. Design considerations include flow amount, pedestrian movement, maintenance, aesthetics, and slope.

TW1.2.6 Streams and Waterways . . . should be preserved whenever possible as riparian corridors. When large drainageways need to be created, replicating or naturalizing drainage ways creates a stable stormwater channel that provides multiple benefits. Properly designed with riparian buffers, these corridors make natural edges to neighborhoods and districts, contribute to the open-space network of a city, create valuable habitat corridors, and help to define the fabric of a city. Design considerations include base flow, flood elevation, management, recreation opportunities, stream crossings, and overall urban fabric.

TW1.2.7 Constructed Stormwater Wetlands . . . are structural facilities that require large watersheds with a constant base flow so that water is continuously moving through the system. In smaller applications, water can be recycled to create a consistent base flow. In these facilities, water moves through several zones including a forebay, high marsh, low marsh, islands, and micro-pool. As water moves laterally through the facility, sediments drop out, and aquatic plant materials filter pollutants. Typically designed as a regional management facility, constructed stormwater wetlands provide sustainable regional stormwater management and a diverse habitat resource. Design considerations include watershed size,

Figure T13   Bio-retention facilities can work seamlessly into the urban fabric.

Source: Cory Gallo

soil type, flood elevations, outfall or discharge point, habitat creation, and management.

TW1.2.8 Regional Detention Facilities . . . create additional detention at the scale of the district or neighborhood to provide additional flood protection above on-site strategies. Sometimes designed as stormwater parks, these facilities can be formal or naturalized multi-functional landscapes designed to flood during major storm events that may only occur every ten years or more. Properly designed, they can serve as iden-tifying landscapes for the neighborhoods and districts they serve. Design considerations include watershed size, soil type, flood elevations, outfall or discharge point, habitat creation, and management.

Further Reading and Resources TW1:

Kraus, H., & Spafford, A. (2013). *Rain gardening in the south: Ecologically designed gardens for drought, deluge, and everything in between.* Hillsborough, NC: Eno Publishers.

Portland, C. O. (2008). *Stormwater management manual.* Portland, OR: City of Portland Bureau of Environmental Services.

TW2   Potable/Sanitary

TW2.1

Building-Integrated Technologies. . .

either reduce or recycle water to offset water use. The largest demand for residential and commercial buildings originates in lavatories. How-ever, water is also used for heating, cooling systems, in kitchens, and for fire suppression. Many governments have actively pursued laws that codify lower water flow rates for fixtures, which can have a dramatic impact on a city's overall water demand. Some technologies are not necessarily viable for use with other solutions. Graywater harvesting, for instance, would not be necessary if composting toilets are used. Therefore, technologies and building water budgets should be thought of as a holistic approach to water management. Water in buildings is also closely tied with energy production for heating water. Therefore,

TECHNOLOGY

water solutions should be considered in concert with energy reduction strategies.

TW2.1.1 Low-flow fixtures . . . are the most widely implemented form of water reduction technologies. Showerheads and faucets are both flow-based fixtures that use aerators and other special fixture designs to replicate the feel of greater flows with much less water. Measured in gallons per minute (gpm), water use in low-flow showerheads and faucets is less than 2.5 gpm. Additionally, fixtures that have time-delayed shut-off valves and infrared sensors achieve even greater water conservation and help improve sanitation by reducing contact with fixtures. Design considerations include water reuse, plumbing, user education, and maintenance.

TW2.1.2 Low-flush urinals and toilets . . . are critical to overall building reduction since these two sources account for one third of residential and commercial water demand. Measured in gallons per flush (gpf), water use in low-flush toilets it less than 1.6 gpf, and water use in urinals is less than 1 gpf. These technologies use special valves, added pressure, and gravity to create greater movement with less water. Additional user choice functions like dual-flush toilets allow even greater water savings. Design considerations include water source, plumbing, user education, and maintenance.

TW2.1.3 Waterless urinals . . . are becoming very popular in institutional settings. They use an oil barrier trap to allow urine to enter the sanitary sewer without allowing sewer gasses to enter the lavatory. These systems have no moving parts, which improves sanitation, but do require periodic maintenance change of the filter trap. Design considerations include perception, education, and maintenance.

TW2.1.4 Composting toilets . . . are a form of waterless system where human waste is collected in a chamber below the toilet. Sawdust is added to the toilet paper and waste to encourage aerobic bacteria to break down waste. Properly designed systems do not create bad odors and are fairly easy to manage. When full, waste can be used for fertilizer on landscapes but not for food crops due to heavy metals and contaminants typically found in human waste. Design considerations include maintenance, education, building design, storage access, and waste distribution.

TW2.1.5 Living machines . . . are types of compact wetland treatment systems that use mechanical and biological systems to treat stormwater. Examples have been implemented both inside buildings and in landscapes and include aquatic plants and even fish to help break down waste. While treatment of graywater is more straightforward, blackwater treatment is possible but requires additional steps and controls. Water cleaned in these systems can be discharged or stored in a cistern for later use as graywater. Design considerations include maintenance, plumbing, collection, storage, temperature, location, and education.

TW2.1.6 Cisterns . . . are chambers for storing water for a later use. An essential component of regenerative systems, cisterns can be below ground, above ground, or on a building. While not required to be attached to a building, they most commonly are because buildings create a natural collection area above the cistern so that water can be gravity-fed into the cistern. Cisterns can be used to capture rainwater and graywater from several sources, including faucets, showers, dishwashers, condensate from air handlers, and treated blackwater from building-level treatment systems. Cisterns for rainwater collection are larger than those for collecting graywater because of the infrequency of rain inputs. Cisterns for graywater harvesting can be fairly small and integrated into a basement or utility room. Depending on the intended use, a cistern may require filtrations systems, a low-level fill valve, pump, depth gauge, access port, and emptying valve. Design considerations can be complex and include water source, plumbing, intended use, distribution system, storage volume need, aesthetics, overflow path, and location on site.

Figure T14   A rainwater-harvesting cistern designed to capture water for landscape irrigation.

Source: Cory Gallo

TECHNOLOGY

TW2.2

Site-Integrated Technologies. . .

for reducing potable water primarily focus on water use reduction. Cisterns (discussed earlier) can be utilized for rainwater harvesting for landscape irrigation or water reuse. Irrigation is a major source of urban water demand. In the US, for instance, landscape irrigation accounts for one third of all residential water use.

TW2.2.1 Efficient Irrigation . . . systems can drastically reduce water demand for ornamental landscapes and urban agriculture. While landscapes that require no irrigation are a better solution, harsh urban landscapes can be challenging for many plant species. Systems that put water directly to the roots of plants reduce overspray and loss. Advanced controllers connected to local weather stations can turn off systems when not needed and adjust water delivery based on specific soil, microclimate, plant needs. Design considerations include landscape area, microclimates, water source, distribution type, and maintenance.

TW2.2.2 Xeriscaping . . . is an approach to planting that eliminates the need for irrigation. The aesthetic of xeriscapes can be challenging for the general public to accept since the landscape is susceptible to periods of drought where plants will brown and die back. A diverse plant palette and

Figure T15   A garden that collects and reuses condensate for irrigation with purple drip irrigation lines.

Source: Cory Gallo

education can help to overcome public perception. By using native and adapted species, these landscapes can be unique and provide high habitat value. Design considerations include landscape function, views, maintenance, and public perception.

Further Reading and Resources TW2:

Kinkade-Levario, H. (2007). *Design for water: Rainwater harvesting, stormwater catchment, and alternate water reuse.* Gabriola, BC: New Society Publishers.

Novotny, V. (2020). *Integrated sustainable urban water, energy, and solids management: Achieving triple net-zero adverse impact goals and resiliency of future communities.* Hoboken, NJ: John Wiley & Sons.

Turner, C., Frankel, M., & Council, U. G. B. (2008). Energy performance of LEED for new construction buildings. *New Buildings Institute, 4*(4), 1–42.

Conclusion
A Matrix for Thinking

Something about the images of sustainable futures in popular media—especially those proposed by architects and futurists and appearing in science fiction—do more harm than good. Instead of inspiring hope, many visions of happy healthy idealized futures inspire the opposite—a sense of hopelessness and dread. These images appear more different to our present-day lives than do cities more than two millennia old (see Figure 5.1). A radical vision I believe in is included in the appendix. That said, most radical visions do real harm because they rely on budgets or technologies, often both, so unattainable that the casual observer can only assume sustainable cities are an impossibility.

This book aims to suggest that flying cars and forests on the tops of two hundred–story skyscrapers or solar arrays orbiting the sun and colonies on Mars are not necessary to build cities that can support billions of humans for the foreseeable future. The answers are nearer to hand. "Cities are almost alright," to paraphrase a famous quip of architect Robert Venturi. And they have been for millennia.

The preceding fifty thousand words are aimed not at images of impossible futures but at providing actionable content for the broad categories laid out in the introduction. Each symbol in the matrix now takes on a wealth of grounded and practical meanings. Readers are encouraged to revisit individual entries and suggested further readings when dealing with particular situations. It is, however, more important to understand the wider implications of the matrix. It is a structure for rethinking

Figure 5.1   Forum Romanum.

Source: Jassen Callender

sustainable cities that takes relationships—not points or products—as central to healthy urban conditions of the future.

The matrix can be read vertically and horizontally. As such, it allows the reader to reconceive relationships quickly. While the preceding pages utilized the matrix to draw out the Lifecycle, Aesthetic, Scale, and Technology implications of the four primary human needs of food, water, shelter, and mobility, it is just as easy and as profitable to shift our reading of the matrix in order to understand how addressing each individual physiological need works to enhance the combined Lifecycle, Aesthetic, Scale, and Technology concerns that make cities LAST.

Given the materials provided in the Essentials and Fine Print portions of this book, a quick rereading of the matrix from the perspective of the four physiological needs might look something like this:

Food

Even in the realm of essentials, food and water stand out as prerequisites for life. Food production policies adopted by municipalities have obvious direct impacts on the long-term success of settlements. Control of both what is planted and where can maximize yield by ecological intensification. Control and careful planning attract pollinators that, in turn, serve the reproduction of plants. Food production policies also impact quality of life and the potential for future life in a given area in multiple ways. Cities, for instance, suffer from degraded soil and air quality. Introducing vermiculture and mycelium and instituting composting programs can produce new soil and rehabilitate soils in brownfields. And the construction of vertical gardens, green roofs, and living walls can greatly enhance air quality and reduce toxicity while also supplementing the food supply.

Food's contribution to quality of life extends beyond nutritional concerns to include quality of place. Farmers markets, the slow food movement, and farm-to-table eateries are all aspects of food that civic entities should not only allow but encourage. Food, in its look and smell and taste, binds humanity. Incorporating the moral uplift of modern-day versions of Victory Gardens—initiatives like Community-Supported Agriculture (CSA), the Edible Schoolyard project, and the Garden to Cafeteria program—is a significant approach to urban resilience.

Resilience, both in terms of attitude and practicality, matters.

Assessing a city's ability to support its population is critical as many urban areas are food deserts, devoid of quality affordable fresh food. Our food future requires us to meet demand while avoiding deforestation, climate change, and economic disparities that contribute to poverty. Establishing food zones—mapped from the city center outward to regional, national, and international imports—is the first step. Densification is the next. These goals require that we distinguish urban farms, community gardens, and forest gardens and that we stop treating them as frills or amenities. Each has its place—in careful coordination with water, shelter, and mobility needs—in order to maximize biodiversity. Understanding plant guilds and permaculture at large is particularly important to this end and serves to provide biologically based pest management. Some technologies, such as chemical pesticides and fertilizers, do more harm than good. Other technologies, such as geolocation of resources, mapping plant types, plant analytics, and post-harvest evaluation, are necessities. Advances such as biodynamic farming support soil replenishment. Other advances, including drones, FarmBot, harvesters, and autonomous and container farms, help minimize the urban footprint of food production, thereby protecting the multitude of wild plants and animals that make the biosphere function.

Architecture and landscape architecture need to find greater synergy through integrated biodynamics systems and building-integrated agriculture. Planners and designers need to embrace vertical farming as new buildings grow taller, and need to seek methods to retrofit existing buildings for agriculture. The overall goal, as stated before, is the merger of organic and inorganic infrastructure into living machines. Although the goal seems daunting, it is achievable in small steps, project by project.

Water

Water is a finite resource. Unwanted abundance in the form of sea-level rise and scarcity in the form of droughts and pollution are significant threats for which opportunities to change both policy and design standards must be sought. All water on the planet can be categorized into cycles: the natural/clean cycle from which we drink and with which we cook; the man-made/dirty cycle which requires systems of mitigation to return it to the environment productively and safely; and a regenerative cycle, which is crucial to the planning of sustainable cities. With the establishment of the latter, hydroponics and aquaponics become feasible and the difficulties of feeding a growing population diminish.

Planners and designers have long appreciated the beauty of water and understood its role in tourism and recreation. People congregate around fountains, riverfronts, and beaches all over the world. And yet, little is made aesthetically of the water collection, conveyance, and storage infrastructures that cities have to build. Across all three forms of infrastructure, there are opportunities for city-, neighborhood-, site-, and building-scaled designs that elicit the passions and concern of citizens and thus help turn the tide against the pervasive build/demolish/rebuild cycle that dooms efforts toward sustainability.

As important as the aesthetic of water can be, the effects of cities on the world's watersheds or drainage basins and wetlands must not be overlooked. These hydrological systems form a closed loop and support biological diversity. While wetlands reduce environmental impacts such as contaminated runoff and increased flooding due the large areas of impervious surfaces in cities, cities complicate natural watersheds and wetlands by creating their own city-sheds. Sustainable solutions must therefore address these problems at the region-to-city, city-to-neighborhood, and individual or site scales across all three types of water systems—potable, sanitary, and rainwater.

Potable and sanitary water systems must take advantage of both recycling and reduction technologies to maximize effectiveness. The former technologies involve the design of systems for graywater harvesting, rainwater harvesting, and municipal treatment. Reduction technologies include irrigation systems and low-flow fixtures. Rainwater collection plays a central role in water conservation and includes building- and site-integrated BMPs. The former includes the design of green roofs, flow-through planters, and cisterns. The latter pertains to site analysis and design through which opportunities for the incorporation of rain gardens, bio-swales, and pervious pavements as well as urban trees/urban forests are identified. Here again, relatively small adjustments in city policy and design thinking offer enormous benefits in managing water abundance and scarcity.

Shelter

Shelter is an essential physiological need, ranking only behind food and water in importance. Shelter here covers the places where we live, work, and play. While food and water are more essential to survival than the extravagance of anything more than a hut or tent, buildings consume so much energy and material resources that careful attention to their lifecycle, aesthetic, and scalar relationships are critical to sustainable urbanism. Decisions of what to build and where, and of what materials, entail environmental and economic costs that must be measured against use or need, adaptability to future need, and resilience after disasters. These issues matter because the first goal of any major construction in sustainable cities is to avoid as much as possible the downcycling, recycling, and demolition paradigms. Upcycling must become the new paradigm.

It is easy to become so enthralled with issues of physical durability and potential reuse that the value of aesthetic durability is overlooked. This is the idea that the, albeit subjective, sensory and sociocultural design considerations for which people come to love buildings often are central motivations for the upkeep and preservation of those buildings. What is loved is more likely to be maintained. Delight, thermal and tactile comforts, acoustics and lighting conditions provide moments of contrast, and their careful design can provide the shock of novel experiences in some instances and the familiar reassurance of tradition in others via style or craft. The key to building such places is engaging the community and learning how much novelty and what degree of familiarity they need or want.

Paying attention to aesthetics does not mean that sustainable shelters require a particular construction technique. Projects can be custom built on site, prefabricated elsewhere and erected on site, or built on site via autonomous systems that remove human hands from the process. Designers need to understand the relative environmental and economic costs of each. Dimension is a more compelling concern that has to balance the competing needs of growing populations, reducing carbon produced or released in construction and embodied in buildings, and using as little land as possible. The solution to these divergent needs lies in building heights, issues of building form and energy performance, and the overall patterns of settlement types. City officials should take more responsibility for formalizing these concerns through mixed-use, form-based codes. Even in the absence of such codes, however, designers need to be proactive in discussions with clients to address these conflicting needs in every building built.

With these issues resolved, changes in the technical aspects of building pay dividends. Integrated project delivery methods, models for understanding a project's technical challenges, and introducing clients to right-sizing processes are important changes to design thinking. The building itself also must change in terms of structure, skins (exterior finishes, insulation, thermal bridge-free construction techniques, and healthy interior finishes), high-performance openings, and high-performance mechanical systems paired with smart hardware and software technologies. Even with these changes, architects and engineers must address sustainable energy production with city-, neighborhood-, and individual building-scale solutions utilizing solar, fuels cells, alternative fuels, biomass, wind, or some combination of these.

Mobility

Food, water, and shelter secured, humans need to move. The cultural experiences that comprise our notions of civilization, and urbanism in particular, are predicated on moving beyond our huts and fields and streams. To be sustainable, the last part of that sentence should read: "predicated on access to inexpensive and efficient mobility beyond . . ." This goal requires planners to deal with three issues: economic constraints that often impede transportation system development before it begins, environmental constraints of potential impacts on the biosphere, and the societal constraints of human values and perceptions of specific modes of transit. Each constraint demands its own form of assessment, such as societal lifecycle cost analysis, lifecycle emissions modeling (LEM), and economic supply chain analyses. Appropriate design rests, ultimately, with effective governance of land use, stable funding, strategic infrastructure investments, and attention to neighborhood design and settlement types.

It is easy, and therefore tempting, to conceive of transit in purely pragmatic terms of connecting place A to place B to place C. Mobility, however, contributes to aesthetic pleasure in multiple significant ways, such as encouraging greater participation in urban life. There is a degree of joy engendered by the vibrancy of the city. People attract people. System affordability, accessibility, and efficiency are keys to ensuring that everyone can enjoy the sustainable city. This does not apply to motorized transit alone. Simply taking a stroll is a meaningful human pastime. Sidewalks, bike trails, and the surrounding landscape benefit all and increase use in such varied ways that careful attention to their design and locations are crucial to a city's evolution.

Understanding the public's needs and desires and the relation of these to the city's larger material and energy flows is key to the sustainability of all systems of mobility. Over the years, a host of tools have been developed to assist planners and designers in understanding the interactions of the complex web of natural, technological, and cultural pressures. These tools, all forms of multi-criteria analysis, reveal potential synergies that subtly open the city to all.

Transportation is a vast and complex system or network of systems that must create equitable access from the local neighborhood level to the global while working to limit footprints of individual cities. Minimizing automobile use is essential to these goals. To achieve this, the design of neighborhoods must be rethought. Local streets need to encourage multi-modal use, parking must be judiciously eliminated, taxes and restrictions imposed to reduce the appeal of private car travel, and funds earmarked for new roads and parking lots should be diverted to purchase right of ways and build sustainable transit including bus and bus rapid transit (BRT) systems, light rail, commuter rail, and in some areas subways.

Non-motorized and motorized transport must be designed comprehensively, with the densities each require being understood. Success of non-motorized transportation is a matter of adjacency, accessibility, and connectivity. Systems of motorized and non-motorized transportation come together in response to and in support of the design of the built environment. The synergy of these systems with the city's stock of shelter is called Transit-Oriented Development (TOD). Cost analysis, provision of services, and density range decisions made, a TOD can be realized through implementing a mixed-use, form-based code.

Nowhere is the status quo more harmful to cities than in decisions related to energy and transit. Determining the appropriate power supply for any transit system requires evaluation of solar, fuel cells, alternative fuels, biomass, as well as electric and hybrid motors. Experts should be consulted early in planning so that the status quo of what already exists doesn't diminish opportunities. Surfaces and substrates are nearly as important. Sustainability indicators provide metrics for pursuing technologies such as automated highway systems or instituting green supply chain initiatives including eco-design, green purchasing, and reverse logistics. The technologies and initiatives often come into conflict with each other. For this reason, planners and designers are encouraged to undertake multiple-criteria design-making processes. Once the selection of transportation modes has been made, computational approaches to planning—such as vehicle-routing problems (VRP), mobile mapping, traffic simulation, and multi-agent systems of modeling—can save a city significant costs and secure a sustainable approach to mobility.

Final Thoughts for a Sustainable Beginning

There is another obstacle to people taking real action toward sustainable urbanism at the opposite end of the spectrum from the flying cars and floating buildings of science fiction and artist-architects looking for press. While those visions make sustainability seem impossible, the simplicity of environmental rating systems make sustainability seem formulaic. Point-based metrics and mandate-based approaches reinforce, and perhaps are responsible for, the perception that sustainability is achievable by simply following rules of maximums and minimums across a set number of variables. Score over 60, and your building is good for the environment. Score over 80, and it's saving the planet. If humanity emits more than one trillion metric tons of CO_2, however, we are all going to die.

The problem is not that these metrics are incorrect, but they operate at extremes that are less than helpful. Most of us have heard of projects that gamed point-based systems—by installing staggering amounts of "green" technology in prefabricated metal buildings that will be obsolete in twenty years or installing bike racks and showers to facilitate biking to work despite the buildings being located on green-field sites dozens of kilometers from where the closest employees live—and were awarded significant status as environmentally friendly. At the other end of the spectrum, while avoiding the one trillion metric ton threshold is necessary, what guidance does that provide to a city in a food desert or in need of new water infrastructure or struggling against a failing transit system or against the inequity of an affordable housing shortage? The metrics encourage us to think either too narrowly or at such global scales that the real problems get missed somewhere in the middle.

The LAST matrix is different but it too can be misused. On one hand, racking up lots of achievements in a few cells, such as those under Technology, does not make up for inadequate attention to the other cells. Success requires balance. On the other hand, simply implementing projects under each individual cell reduces the potential of the matrix to a checklist and, more importantly, doesn't guarantee that the various projects work synergistically to create better cities. To restate a point that has been made multiple times throughout this book, what the matrix provides is an easy way to evaluate the relational aspects of individual decisions. Policy makers, planners, and designers should evaluate proposals across the matrix horizontally and vertically to verify that projects fulfill and balance a host of needs. It is not enough to determine that a new food production initiative fulfills Lifecycle ambitions, for instance, but it should address Aesthetic, Scale, and Technology needs as well (see Figure 5.2). Decision makers then should determine how the initiative could interact with water, shelter, and mobility infrastructures (see Figure 5.3). Thinking every project through the matrix, vertically and horizontally, reduces

Sustainability Measures / *Types of Infrastructure*	LIFECYCLE Durability vs. energy & materials necessary for construction & maintenance	AESTHETICS Place making. The urge to live in & maintain cities for perceived value of (and to) identity	SCALE Building & human density, & green- grey- & brown- field land use for livable cities	TECHNOLOGY A balance of innovations to minimize carbonization & materialization
Food Production & Distribution Systems	**Project:** **Plant urban fruit trees in an underutilized urban park surrounded by weekday uses**	Allied initative: Dedicate an adjacent public-owned lot for a public/private farmers market	Allied initative: Implement pest management practices to support fruit trees & nearby gardens	Allied initative: Require future farmers market to meet Living Machine standards
Mobility Sidewalks, Buses, Light rail, Street Networks, etc	L M	A M	S M	T M
Shelter Housing, Retail, Civic, Industrial, and other buildings	L S	A S	S S	T S
Water Drinking Irrigation, Waste & Runoff	L W	A W	S W	T W

Figure 5.2   LAST matrix—example 1.

Source: Jassen Callender

the likelihood of wasting time and money on futile initiatives—like bike racks in the middle of nowhere.

The examples given here are appropriate to an imaginary place and professionals engaged in city policy and planning. Countless examples could be generated to fit the opportunities of a particular place and account for the perspectives of various professionals. The matrix, however, is not a blueprint for sustainable urbanism. There is no blueprint—no formula. Sustainable cities do not result from checklists or mandates but by every individual project serving its citizens, present and future, in multiple, interactive, synergistic ways. When used to guide decision making in support of these broader relationships, the matrix inevitably

Sustainability Measures / Types of Infrastructure	LIFECYCLE — Durability vs. energy & materials necessary for construction & maintenance	AESTHETICS — Place making. The urge to live in & maintain cities for perceived value of (and to) identity	SCALE — Building & human density, & green-grey- & brown-field land use for livable cities	TECHNOLOGY — A balance of innovations to minimize carbonization & materialization
Food Production & Distribution Systems	**Project:** **Plant urban fruit trees in an underutilized urban park surrounded by weekday uses**	Allied initative: Dedicate an adjacent public-owned lot for a public/private farmers market	Allied initative: Implement pest management practices to support fruit trees & nearby gardens	Allied initative: Require future farmers market to meet Living Machine standards
Mobility Sidewalks, Buses, Light rail, Street Networks, etc	Allied project: Improve sidewalk design and enhance connectivity by bike and bus	**A M**	**S M**	**T M**
Shelter Housing, Retail, Civic, Industrial, and other buildings	Allied project: Revise zoning near park to increase density and encourage housing/off-hour business use	**A S**	**S S**	**T S**
Water Drinking Irrigation, Waste & Runoff	Allied project: Install site integrated technologies for regenerative water cycle	**A W**	**S W**	**T W**

Figure 5.3   LAST matrix—example 2.

Source: Jassen Callender

addresses both local and global concerns—here a farmers market, there a bus stop; here a solar panel, there a cistern; everywhere a reduction in land use, car miles traveled, non-renewable energy used, and water wasted; everywhere a reduction in CO_2. The matrix aims to do these things in ways that amplify the impacts of each individual act so that our cities are truly built to LAST.

Appendix
At the Limits of Practicality

In 2008, the Jackson Community Design Center of Mississippi State University's School of Architecture tackled the problem of evolving one mid-size American city, Jackson, Mississippi, toward a sustainable future. The work led to a design we named Continu(C)ity. This think piece eventually grew to recognize the broad interrelationships that contribute to and limit ambitions for sustainable urbanism. As a result, the final 2009 version presented here proposed a global vision and pondered its implications over the next half millennia. While neither I nor the project team of Nick Hester, Bryan Norwood, and Whitney Grant Swanson believed the project to be fully realizable, its principles are applicable to the realities of cities everywhere. More than any other project, it was Continu(C)ity that drove the development of LAST and the matrix to which this book is dedicated.

MAKING THE AMERICAN CITY A BODY WITHOUT ORGANS It is not the organs that are the enemy. "The enemy is the organism"—the heirachized, dominated, formed, bonded, transcended.[1] It is the organization of the organs.

Although most of America's 50 largest MSAs (above one million people) have existing, dense urban environments whose infrastructure needs to be reimagined with "surgical integration," many of the 288 mid-size metropolises (100,000 - one million people), which hold 47 percent of the the North American urbanized population, suffer from a lack of viable urban place in which to integrate new infrastructure. Sprawling (even the Dallas-Fort Worth MSA, one of the largest and most sprawling in the US, has a higher density than most of these mid-size MSAs) and generic (interstate culture abounds in these nonplaces) these mid-size cities are of utmost importance to the future of urbanism in America.

Interstate culture dominates regions like the southern US where these mid-size metros are littered across a rural landscape, and public transit is largely inviable within a spread out, auto dependent culture. Overburdened lines of movement that only serve to territorialize metropolitan areas pretend to unite cities that are actually singular into a multiplicity. With the exception of some of the top 15 metropolises where continuous cities have formed (particularly the northeast coast corridor and the greater Los Angeles area), the organization of these bodies into lines and points distinct from one another is unsustainable and, even worse, anti-life.

Deleuze and Guattari's Body without Organs (BwO), more aptly named the non-organismic body, is a deterritorialized plane of consistency (immanence) in which new, novel connections can be made.[2] The city conceived as such is never-ending, non-heirarchical, and composed of continuous identity: Continu(C)ity. The Continu(C)ity is a continuous plateau with no external interruption and no climatic moments—no limits.

In this project, we take the I-55 corridor running north through Jackson, Mississippi as a case study for mid-size urban infrastructure and propose a new concept for development pattern: Continu(C)ity. Continu(C)ity is based on two core principles:

Density is the most important question of lively urbanism and sustainability. With the metro population of roughly 531,869 and population density of 187 people per square mile, Jackson is sprawling, invading fragile ecosystems, and turning diversity into a single element—capital.

Congruity is the one-to-one relationship of transit corridors and city. Transit Oriented Development (TOD) has, in recent years, seen more and more interest from metropolitan areas taxed with overburdened roads and bad land use. TOD may be useful for metro-areas, but it focuses on the organs rather than the real enemy—the organism—the very idea of city itself. Congruity has to be applied on a continental, and global, scale in which transit and the city take on the same identity.

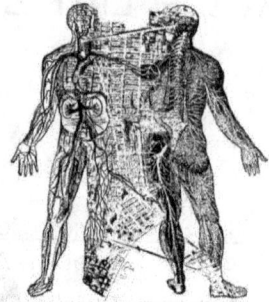

fig. 1 making the American city a body without organs

1 Gilles Deleuze and Felix Guattari, A Thousand Plateaus: Capitalism and Schizophrenia, trans. Brian Massumi (Minneapolis: University of Minnesota Press, 1987), 158-59.

2 Leonard Lawlor, "A New Possibility of Life: The Experience of Powerlessness as a Solution to the Problem of the Worst," unpublished.

3 Mark Bonta and John Protevi, Deleuze and Geophilosophy: A Guide and Glossary (Edinburgh: Edinburgh University Press, 2004), 62-64.

a recent history of nowhere   Louisiana purchase   internal combustion engine
1799   1803   1806

Figure 6.1   Continu(C)ity—Overview.

Source: Jackson Community Design Center (JCDC)

THE CRISIS The evolutionary biologist E. O. Wilson proposed in *The Future of Life* that the US become 50 percent natural and 50 percent developed for maximum biodiversity. Combine this call with the argument that people shouldn't be living in places that can't sustain them, the threat of 6.5 ft. or more of sea level rise, a still expanding population expected to reach 571 million in the US and 9 billion in the world by the end of the 21st century, an economic crisis, and the pressures of the generic city; and a new paradigm for the American city is born.

US population projection 2000-2100[1]

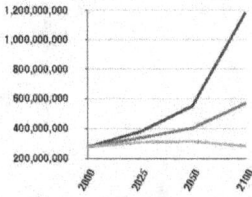

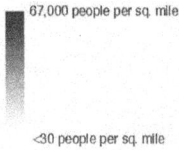

2000 population density

2100 lowest series (282 million people)

2100 middle series (571 million people)

67,000 people per sq. mile

<30 people per sq. mile

2100 highest series (1.2 billion people)

1 US Census Bureau, "Methodology and Assumptions for the Population Projections of the United States: 1999 to 2100," Population Division Working Paper 38, January 13, 2000.

manifest destiny

1820   1839

Figure 6.2   Continu(C)ity—the Crisis.

Source: JCDC

PRINCIPLE ONE

DENSITY The critical mass for intense use of public transit is somewhere around 10,000 people/miles², but to truly go carless, a city probably needs a density closer to 30,000 people/miles². Ten to fifteen story buildings make this density possible. To create Continu(C)ity, what we don't have to do is change the paradigm for the relationship of city streets and buildings. The city is almost alright. It is not the organs that are the problem, it is their relationship.

The southern region, the second fastest growing region of the US, in particular has some of the lowest density in urbanized areas as well as large gaps of rural space between urbanized areas. The three heavily urbanized areas of Memphis, Jackson, and New Orleans are each roughly 200 miles apart (existing interstate and rail lines indicated).

Reconfigured in a zone one mile wide and built to a density of 30,000 people per square mile, the entire population of Mississippi (roughly 3 million) would fit in 100 miles of Continu(C)ity, or roughly half of the distance between Jackson and Memphis.

Ridgeland, MS (a typical Jackson suburb) :: 1,300 people per square mile

Monterey Bay, CA :: 7,800 people per square mile

Rogers Park, Chicago, IL :: 34,000 people per square mile

Manhattan, New York, NY :: 70,000 people per square mile

1841   gold rush
                1849

Figure 6.3   Continu(C)ity—Principle One.

Source: JCDC

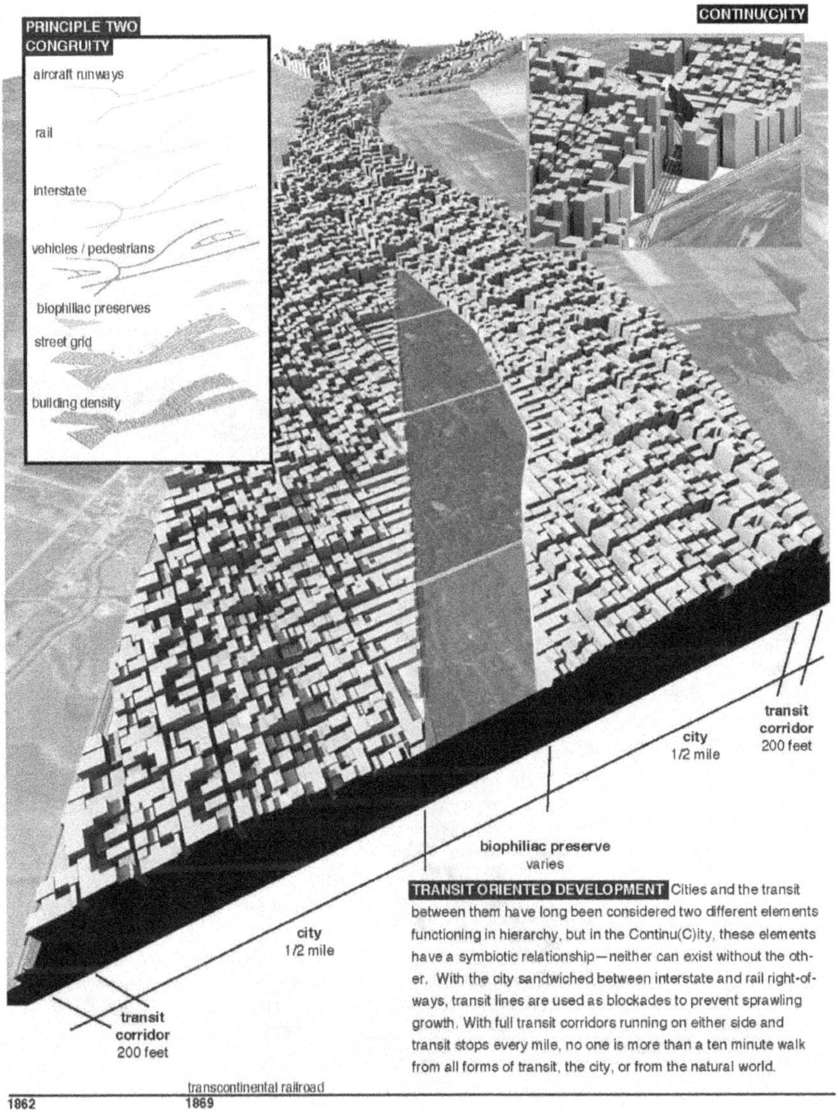
PRINCIPLE TWO
CONGRUITY
aircraft runways
rail
interstate
vehicles / pedestrians
biophiliac preserves
street grid
building density
CONTINU(C)ITY
transit corridor 200 feet
city 1/2 mile
biophiliac preserve varies
city 1/2 mile
transit corridor 200 feet
TRANSIT ORIENTED DEVELOPMENT Cities and the transit between them have long been considered two different elements functioning in hierarchy, but in the Continu(C)ity, these elements have a symbiotic relationship—neither can exist without the other. With the city sandwiched between interstate and rail right-of-ways, transit lines are used as blockades to prevent sprawling growth. With full transit corridors running on either side and transit stops every mile, no one is more than a ten minute walk from all forms of transit, the city, or from the natural world.
1862
transcontinental railroad
1869

Figure 6.4 Continu(C)ity—Principle Two.

Source: JCDC

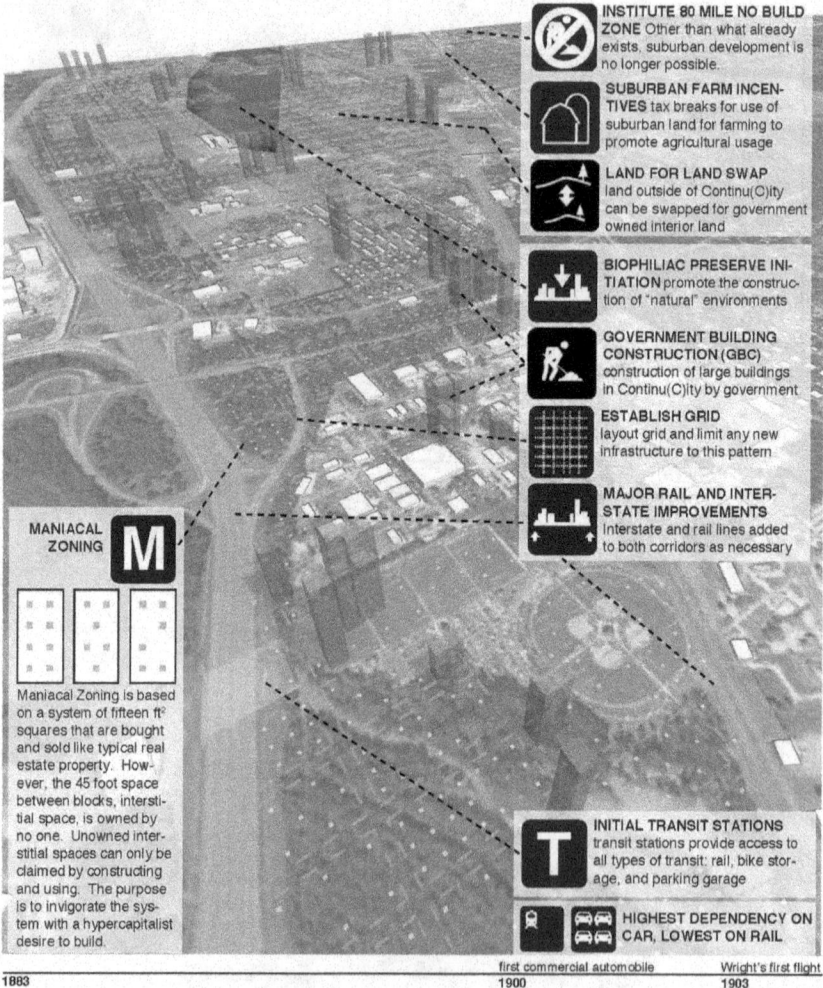

YEAR 00: INITIATE HYPERCAPITALISM

An environment that encourages urban growth and discourages unsustainable suburban and exurban construction. This is accomplished not by dictation but by hypercapitalism—using the market to encourage development. By constructing along major transit routes, the viability of Continu(C)ity is gauranteed.

INSTITUTE 80 MILE NO BUILD ZONE Other than what already exists, suburban development is no longer possible.

SUBURBAN FARM INCENTIVES tax breaks for use of suburban land for farming to promote agricultural usage

LAND FOR LAND SWAP land outside of Continu(C)ity can be swapped for government owned interior land

BIOPHILIAC PRESERVE INITIATION promote the construction of "natural" environments

GOVERNMENT BUILDING CONSTRUCTION (GBC) construction of large buildings in Continu(C)ity by government

ESTABLISH GRID layout grid and limit any new infrastructure to this pattern

MAJOR RAIL AND INTERSTATE IMPROVEMENTS Interstate and rail lines added to both corridors as necessary

MANIACAL ZONING M

Maniacal Zoning is based on a system of fifteen ft² squares that are bought and sold like typical real estate property. However, the 45 foot space between blocks, interstitial space, is owned by no one. Unowned interstitial spaces can only be claimed by constructing and using. The purpose is to invigorate the system with a hypercapitalist desire to build.

INITIAL TRANSIT STATIONS T transit stations provide access to all types of transit: rail, bike storage, and parking garage

HIGHEST DEPENDENCY ON CAR, LOWEST ON RAIL

| 1883 | first commercial automobile 1900 | Wright's first flight 1903 |

Figure 6.5 Continu(C)ity—Year 00.

Source: JCDC

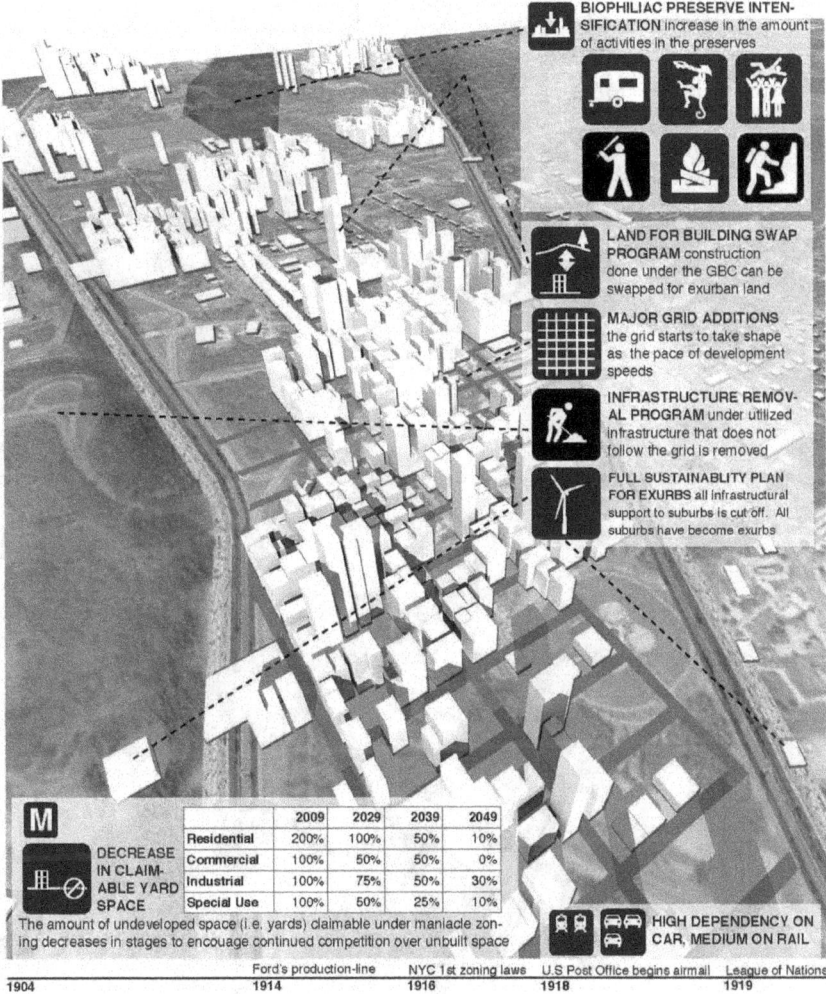

CONTINU(C)ITY

YEAR 33: INITIATE HYPERDENSIFICATION
As construction done under the GBC wraps up, a swap of land exterior to Continu(C)ity for buildings within begins. With the goal of creating a rush towards densification, the grid is rapidly expanded and all infrastructural support to the suburbs is ended.

BIOPHILIAC PRESERVE INTENSIFICATION increase in the amount of activities in the preserves

LAND FOR BUILDING SWAP PROGRAM construction done under the GBC can be swapped for exurban land

MAJOR GRID ADDITIONS the grid starts to take shape as the pace of development speeds

INFRASTRUCTURE REMOVAL PROGRAM under utilized infrastructure that does not follow the grid is removed

FULL SUSTAINABILITY PLAN FOR EXURBS all infrastructural support to suburbs is cut off. All suburbs have become exurbs

DECREASE IN CLAIMABLE YARD SPACE

	2009	2029	2039	2049
Residential	200%	100%	50%	10%
Commercial	100%	50%	50%	0%
Industrial	100%	75%	50%	30%
Special Use	100%	50%	25%	10%

The amount of undeveloped space (i.e. yards) claimable under maniacle zoning decreases in stages to encouage continued competition over unbuilt space

HIGH DEPENDENCY ON CAR, MEDIUM ON RAIL

1904	Ford's production-line 1914	NYC 1st zoning laws 1916	U.S Post Office begins airmail 1918	League of Nations 1919

Figure 6.6 Continu(C)ity—Year 33.

Source: JCDC

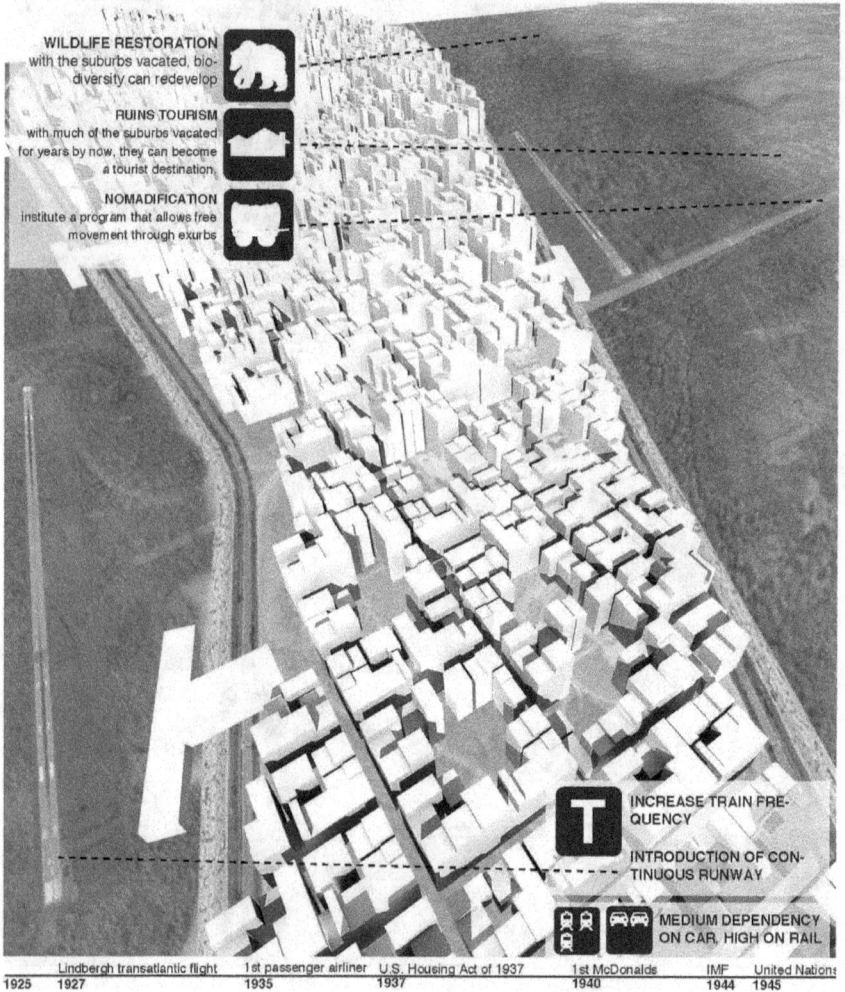

Figure 6.7 Continu(C)ity—Year 66.

Source: JCDC

CONTINU(C)ITY

YEAR 99: FUTUREFORM

With global population peaking, Continu(C)ity's density levels off at 30,000 people per square mile. With a new emphasis on the integration of global transit and the city, Continu(C)ity continues to expand along major transit routes, both towards Jackson close by and towards distant places.

M MANIACAL ZONING

To continue the invigoration of the urban environment by hypercapitalism, new developmental points are strategically located by inserting new competitive groups of ownership points.

T TRANSIT LINES ADDED AS NECESSARY Because transit corridors act as barriers to the urban environment, lines can be freely added on the exurban side as necessary. Stations can also expand indefinitely outward.

LOWEST DEPENDENCY ON CAR, HIGHEST ON RAIL

Levittown	interstate / Pruitt-Igoe built	1st self service gas station	Licklider's "Galactic Network" / 1st Walmart	500th McDonalds	HUD
1946 1947	1956	1958	1962	1963	1965

Figure 6.8 Continu(C)ity—Year 99.

Source: JCDC

YEAR 159: INTER-STATE CONTINU(C)ITY

CONTINU(C)ITY

EXURBANITY The paradigm shift towards sustainability in America is no doubt a good thing, but serious danger exists in faux-sustainability, particularly in suburban and exurban development. In Continu(C)ity urban and exurban development are all that are left and their difference is heightened. If someone wants to live in exurbanity, they have to truly live that lifestyle and provide for all their own needs.

exurban   80 mile no build zone   Memphis, TN

BIOPHILIAC PRESERVES Biophilia, the love of life, is a concept popularized by E. O. Wilson that is meant to capture the uniqueness of humanities ability to understand and know other organisms in the biosphere. Where the distance between the existing right-of-ways is further than one mile, biophiliac preserves—manufactured nature— are created with each side of the city being one-half of a mile deep.

SUSTAINABLE LIVING
Construction is possible here with approval, but no infrastructure is provided. Sustain yourself.

SEPARATISTS
For those resistant to the community, there is plenty of new frontier.

WILDLIFE
unfenced, untagged, sometimes dangerous, and free to roam

NOMADS
Also unfenced, untagged, unplugged and free to roam.

RELICS / RUINS
Visit the remnants of suburbs to see how the American landscape was almost lost.

ROUGHING IT
The exurban world offers the chance to return to nature. Truly live like an exurbanite.

FARMING
Farming is permitted almost everywhere outside Continu(C)ity.

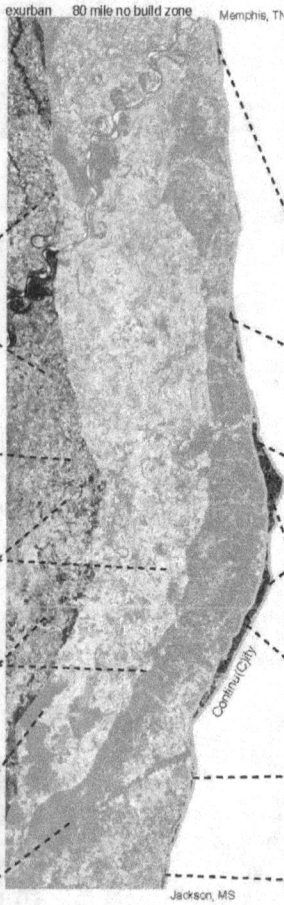

Continu(C)ity

Jackson, MS

RV PARKS
Get away from the stress of city life without getting too far away.

ZOOS
See wildlife without fear of being bitten . . . or worse.

CONCERTS
Short of the freedom of exurbia, this is the place to let your hair down.

SPORTING FIELDS
pristine, beautiful, and green nature . . . a place for organized exercise.

CONTROLLED SPECTACLES
a good explosion, or at least a good campfire

POLITICAL RALLIES
Like motorsports, these have to happen somewhere.

"NATURE"
Experience the thrills of "roughing it" minutes from work, home, or the hospital.

Walmart expands	Apollo 11	Pruitt-Igoe demolished / oil crisis	first meeting of G6	Habitat for Humanity	The Cable Act / Seaside FL
1967 1968	1969 1972-3		1975	1976	1984

Figure 6.9   Continu(C)ity—Year 159.

Source: JCDC

CONTINU(C)ITY

YEAR 259: CONTINENTAL CONTINU(C)ITY

a generic desert forever? In the 1980's Jean Baudrillard visited America and discovered an anti-utopian space of meaninglessness—a desert. American cities differentiate themselves from the space around them, but because of globalization (made possible by technologiza- tion) and sprawl the identity of each of these cities looks very similar. Most cities differentiate themselves from non-city, but this is almost al- ways done in very similar ways. The Continu(C) ity, however, creates one identity, one city from which all differentiation happens. Instead of a series of points, the Continu(C)ity is a series of merging and splitting paths that are never more than 1 mile wide. It is the plane of consistency from which all individual identities have to differentiate. Continu(C)ity is a dream to end genericness by overcoming it with continuity. All production is essentially local and global.

existing population density and transit routes

67,000 people per sq. mile

30,000 people per sq. mile
Continu(C)ity target density

<30 people per sq. mile

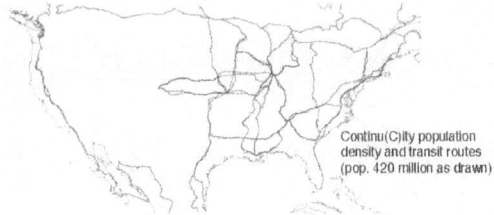

Continu(C)ity population density and transit routes (pop. 420 million as drawn)

YEAR 559: GLOBAL CONTINU(C)ITY

One of the first consequences of the Continu(C)ity is the merging of Canadian, American, and Mexican space— NAFTA on steroids. Country boundaries lose importance when the transit of products becomes congruous with the city. A new (post)critical regionalism develops (after all, what is regional is not humanity).

The landbridge between Asia and North America is reformed by the first oceanic city, which becomes a major hub for the fishing and crab- bing industry, as well as the biggest tourist destination in the world.

With what was once the discrete cities of Jerusalem and Tehran connected by the Continu(C)ity, the dynamics of the relationship are forced to change as people and goods flow between locations. Terrorism and hatred do not end, and the people who allowed Continu(C)ity to form between these places suf- fer from a guilty conscious as lives are lost, but the deterritorialization of the relationship between these two places slowly forms new bonds of community.

NAFTA CERN publicizes World Wide Web WTO / GPS / eBay Google launched Euro circulates internet social networking explodes **generic city**

| 1988 | 1991 | 1995 | 1998 | 2002 | 2003-2006 | 2009 |

Figure 6.10   Continu(C)ity—Year 259–559.

Source: JCDC

Index

Page numbers in italics indicate a figure on the corresponding page. Page numbers followed by "n" indicate a note.

For Product Safety Concerns and Information please contact our EU
representative GPSR@taylorandfrancis.com
Taylor & Francis Verlag GmbH, Kaufingerstraße 24, 80331 München, Germany

www.ingramcontent.com/pod-product-compliance
Lightning Source LLC
Chambersburg PA
CBHW050341270326
41926CB00016B/3562